The Science Fiction
of Phyllis Gotlieb

The Science Fiction of Phyllis Gotlieb
A Critical Reading

Dominick Grace

McFarland & Company, Inc., Publishers
Jefferson, North Carolina

LIBRARY OF CONGRESS CATALOGUING-IN-PUBLICATION DATA

Grace, Dominick, 1963–
　　The science fiction of Phyllis Gotlieb : a critical reading / Dominick Grace.
　　　　p.　　cm.
　　Includes bibliographical references and index.

　　ISBN 978-0-7864-7082-2 (softcover : acid free paper) ∞
　　ISBN 978-1-4766-1508-0 (ebook)

　　1. Gotlieb, Phyllis, 1926–2009—Criticism and interpretation. 2. Science fiction, Canadian—History and criticism.　I. Title.
PR9199.3.G64Z65　2015
813'.54—dc23　　　　　　　　　　　　　　　　　2014041826

BRITISH LIBRARY CATALOGUING DATA ARE AVAILABLE

© 2015 Dominick Grace. All rights reserved

No part of this book may be reproduced or transmitted in any form or by any means, electronic or mechanical, including photocopying or recording, or by any information storage and retrieval system, without permission in writing from the publisher.

Front cover images © Hemera/Thinkstock and iStockphoto/Thinkstock

Printed in the United States of America

McFarland & Company, Inc., Publishers
　Box 611, Jefferson, North Carolina 28640
　　www.mcfarlandpub.com

For my father, John Grace, who turned me on to
science fiction in the first place

Table of Contents

Acknowledgments	ix
Introduction	1
ONE—Early Short Fiction	11
TWO—*Sunburst*	41
THREE—The Dahlgren Diptych	63
FOUR—Mid-Period Short Fiction	99
FIVE—The Ungrukh Chronicles	127
SIX—The Lyhhrt Trilogy	150
SEVEN—Science Fiction and Phyllis Gotlieb's Poetry	171
EIGHT—Final Fictions	187
Conclusion	201
Chapter Notes	205
Works Cited	216
Index	223

Acknowledgments

I am grateful to the editors and publishers of the following articles for their receptivity to my work and for their permission to revisit it here, in greatly expanded, updated and revised form:

"GalFed: The Canadian Galactic 'Empire.'" *Further Perspectives on the Canadian Fantastic: Proceedings of the 2003 Academic Conference on Canadian Science Fiction and Fantasy.* Ed. Allan Weiss. Toronto: ACCSFF, 2005. 55–66.

"Valorizing the 'Normal': Phyllis Gotlieb's *Sunburst.*" *Perspectives on the Canadian Fantastic: Proceedings of the 1997 Academic Conference on Canadian Science Fiction and Fantasy.* Ed. Allan Weiss. Toronto: ACCSFF, 1998. 59–68.

Portions of Chapters Two and Five, adapted from "Animal Planet: Phyllis Gotlieb's Bestiary." *Revista Atenea* 28.2 (2008): 23–36.

"Frankenstein, Motherhood, and Phyllis Gotlieb's *O Master Caliban!*" *Extrapolation* 46.1 (2005): 90–102, and "Gotlieb Upon Caliban." *Extrapolation* 52.2 (2011): 192–203.

"Mind Matters: Intellect and Identity in the Works of Phyllis Gotlieb." *Worlds of Wonder: Readings in Canadian Science Fiction and Fantasy*. Reappraisals: Canadian Writers 26. Eds. Jean-François Leroux and Camille R. La Bossière. Ottawa: University of Ottawa Press, 2004. 105–17.

"'Geffen and Ravna': A SF Sestina." *SOL Rising* (July 2011): 17–19. http://www.thefriendsofthemerril.org/2011_summer.pdf.

In addition, I thank the organizers and paper referees of the following conferences, at which embryonic versions of these papers and other portions of this book have been presented over the years: the Academic Conference on Canadian Science Fiction and Fantasy; the ACCUTE sessions at the Congress of Social Sciences and Humanities; "The Animals in This Country: A Canadian Literature Symposium" and the Canadian Science Fiction and Fantasy Symposium (both at the University of Ottawa); the International Conference for the Fantastic in the Arts; the Popular Culture Association/American Culture Association conference; the Popular Culture Association of Canada conference; the Science Fiction Research Association conference; "Science Fiction: The Interdisciplinary Genre" (McMaster University); and the World Science Fiction Convention, academic track.

More specific thanks are due to Allan Weiss, who strongly encouraged me to tackle this project, and especially to my wife, Lisa Macklem, who not only urged me to write this book but also provided considerable editorial assistance with the manuscript. Thanks as well to the staff of the Beryl Ivey Library at Brescia University College and to the staff of the Merril Collection of Science Fiction, Speculation and Fantasy at the Toronto Public Library for their assistance in tracking down materials, and to Eric Hoffman for manuscript proofing. I gratefully acknowledge the support of Brescia University College for generous research and travel funding and for the sabbatical during which the bulk of work on this project was completed. Finally, I am most grateful to Calvin Gotlieb for his support of this project.

Introduction

Phyllis Gotlieb has been largely overlooked in studies of science fiction (SF). She is rarely mentioned in such studies, even ones focusing on the contributions of women to the genre—even, in fact, in works such as Lisa Yaszek's *Galactic Suburbia* (2008), a book that set out specifically to reclaim post–World War II "woman SF authors [who] were relegated to the margins of literary and cultural history" (4) with the emergence of a feminist-inflected approach to SF as spearheaded by Joanna Russ. Even studies of Canadian SF, of which there have been few, have little to say about Gotlieb. David Ketterer's *Canadian Science Fiction and Fantasy* (1992) is to date the only monograph study surveying the genre, though there have been books with a more narrow focus, such as Amy J. Ransom's *Science Fiction from Québec: A Postcolonial Study* (2009), or that take a biographical or bibliographical approach, such as John Bell's *The Far North and Beyond: An Index to Canadian Science Fiction and Fantasy in English-Language Genre Magazines and Other Selected Periodicals of the Pulp Era, 1896–1955* (1998), or the Douglas J. Ivison–edited Dictionary of Literary Biography volume *Canadian Science Fiction and Fantasy Writers* (2002), as well as essay collections such as Andrea Paradis's *Out of This World: Canadian Science Fiction and Fantasy* (1995) or Allan Weiss's *Perspectives on the Canadian Fantastic: Proceedings of the 1997 Conference on Canadian Science Fiction and Fantasy* (1998) and *Further Perspectives on the Canadian Fantastic: Proceedings of the 2003 Conference on Canadian Science Fiction and Fantasy* (2005), and the Jenifer Burwell and Nancy Johnston–edited special issue of *Foundation* on Canadian SF (issue 81, 2001).

Ketterer's study does accord Gotlieb's work serious, albeit brief, attention. Other well-known scholars of the Canadian fantastic have little to say about her. John Clute, for instance, mentions her only in passing in "Fables of Transcendence: The Challenge of Canadian Science Fiction" (in the Paradis collection), and his *Science Fiction: The Illustrated Encyclopedia* (1995) simply mentions the debut of *Sunburst* in 1964 (and misspells her name in the index). Clute's entry on her in the Peter Nicholls and John Clute-edited *Encyclopedia of Science Fiction* is brief and not entirely accurate in its description of *Sunburst*; its reference to the "gestalt concord the telepaths arrive at, and of their coming to (a somewhat overplotted) accord with the surrounding world" is considerably more positive than the novel's actual conclusion. John Robert Colombo—who published her first poetry collection, *Who Knows One,* in 1960—briefly acknowledges the power of her writing in his essay in Paradis's collection but notes, "she has more successes than readers" because her characters and plots are too complex for the average SF reader (37), adding, "regular readers of science fiction are somewhat resistant to the complex characters and complicated situations found in Gotlieb's GalFed novels, the Starcats series, and the books set in Dhalgren's [*sic*] world" (37), an opinion he rephrases somewhat in the "Canada" entry in *The Encyclopedia of Science Fiction*, where he states that her being largely unknown may result in part from the fact that "her prose is demanding, intricate and psychologically probing." Christine Kulyk, writing of SF and Fantasy by Canadian women, accords Gotlieb only a paragraph, after treatments of Margaret Atwood and P. K. Page, neither of whom has written as much SF and fantasy as Gotlieb, and makes no comment on Gotlieb's status as trailblazer or on her unique strengths. Élisabeth Vonarburg, writing generally of women in SF, ignores Gotlieb, focusing instead on American women. With the exception of Ketterer's *Canadian Science Fiction and Fantasy*, none of the general studies of SF and few of the reference works I have consulted so much as mention Gotlieb (even Neil Baron's very thorough *Anatomy of Wonder* [1987] does not include her, though an insightful entry by Douglas Barbour appears in Ivison's Dictionary of Literary Biography volume), and only a handful of academic articles have been published on Gotlieb's work.

Nevertheless, no critic (Ketterer included) or writer surveyed for *Science-Fiction Studies*'s "Unjustly Neglected Works of Science Fiction: A Survey" mentions Gotlieb, though van Vogt comes up four times, and Élisabeth Vonarburg and "Canadian SF generally" (426) are each cited once as well. Studies of women in SF, of which several have appeared in recent years, also rarely mention her, let alone discuss her work. Gotlieb's concerns are not overtly feminist, so it is perhaps not surprising that studies such as Barr's *Feminist Fabulations* (1992) or *Lost in Space* (1993), Lefanus's *Feminism and Science Fiction* (1989), Rosinsky's *Feminist Futures* (1984), or Wolmark's *Aliens and Others: Science Fiction, Feminism, and Postmodernism* (1993) do not mention her. More surprising is that she is also overlooked in more general studies of women in SF, even ones which explore SF in which Gotlieb's characteristic themes appear. Without being exhaustive, these would include collections and studies such as Armitt's *Where No Man Has Gone Before* (1991), Donawerth and Kolmerten's *Utopian and Science Fiction by Women* (1994), Shaw's *Women, Science and Fiction* (2000), or Shinn's *Worlds Within Women* (1986). She is equally overlooked in studies of Canadian poetry. In her review of *Red Blood, Black Ink, White Paper* (Gotlieb's final poetry collection of new and selected work, which appeared in 2002), Susan Briscoe notes,

> The literary community is often uncomfortable with the crossing of genres, and writers who are successful in one are rarely so well-received by the critics of another. This has certainly been the case for Phyllis Gotlieb who, favoured with lasting popularity as a science fiction novelist, has received little attention for her poetry. In fact, since her previous collection was published a quarter-century ago, she has been virtually forgotten as a poet ["Not Lost in Space: Phyllis Gotlieb"].

As for the fiction itself, Gotlieb's work is occasionally anthologized, but no story by her appears in either volume of Pamela Sargent's expansive *Women of Wonder* set (1995) (though she is listed in the bibliography), not to mention other anthologies of SF by women.

There may be many reasons for this. Though Gotlieb emerged relatively early as a woman author of SF, she was preceded in the field by many other writers, so she lacks the pioneer status of, say, Andre Norton, Leigh Brackett or C. L. Moore. During the 1960s and 1970s, when the field was opening up significantly to female authors, Gotlieb was not as visible as many other writers; through those two decades, she published only two SF novels (*Sunburst* in 1964 and *O Master Caliban!* in 1976),[1] and a baker's dozen of short stories from 1959 to 1977. Over roughly the same period, by contrast, Ursula K. Le Guin (whose first story appeared two years after Gotlieb's) published a half-dozen novels in the Hainish Cycle alone and over forty shorter works, and Le Guin is hardly prolific by SF standards. By the time Le Guin and Gotlieb began publishing, for instance, Andre Norton had already published over twenty novels (not all SF); Norton published more SF novels in the 1960s alone than Gotlieb published in her entire career. Consequently, Gotlieb was largely invisible during the years when women made significant inroads into the genre and began to receive serious commercial success and critical attention. Even when her output increased, she was not prolific. In her most productive decade, the 1980s, she published four novels and a short story collection, as well as a handful of short stories not collected until the 1990s. While this represents a respectable output, it was not enough to keep her constantly before readers' eyes. But her relatively modest output is only one factor, and one that cannot fully explain why she has been generally overlooked.

Gotlieb occupies an odd in-between space in literature, between genre and mainstream literature, and between Canadian and American literature. Her primary output has been SF, but SF of such density and complexity that "regular readers of science fiction are somewhat resistant" to her work (Columbo 37). She is also a "literary" writer; she is well-regarded as a poet in Canada, having been short-listed for a Governor General's Literary Award[2] in 1969 for her book of poetry *Ordinary, Moving*, but Gotlieb herself believed her SF output negatively affected her reputation as a poet: "There was always in my audience a bit of reluctance to take my work seriously because I wrote science fiction, which has never been greatly respected as a form of art in Canada even to this day" (Gotlieb, "All the Blue Apes"). As she noted in another interview, "The fact that I wrote SF put people off, because it's not Canadian. People would ask me, 'What do you think about landscape, as a Canadian writer?' I said, 'I don't think about landscape.' I didn't quite get the same respect that, say Margaret Atwood did" ("Interview"). Gotlieb saw the split between her poetry and her SF—her "literary" and her "commercial" output—as central to her career "as a Canadian poet and an American Science Fiction writer" (qtd. in Ketterer, 1). This bifurcation is as much a function of economics as anything—the English Canadian market offering little to the writer of SF, at least when Gotlieb's career began in the late 1950s (and throughout her active career; most of her SF saw its first publication in the United States), though the current importance of many Canadian writers of the fantastic (Nalo Hopkinson, Guy Gavriel Kay, Robert J. Sawyer, Karl Schroeder, Peter Watts, and Robert Charles Wilson, to name a few) suggests that things have changed somewhat on that front. It also reflects, humorously, the profound concern with the natures of identity and of literary genre that pervades Gotlieb's work. Nevertheless, though Gotlieb has stated, "Je n'écris pas du point de vue d'une Canadienne" ["I do not write from the point of view of a Canadian"] ("Entrevue" 17), and though figures such as A. E. van Vogt or Gordon W. Dickson precede her, Phyllis Gotlieb is often thought of as the first significant Canadian presence in SF; the "About the Author" note in her final novel, *Birthstones* (2007), asserts that "at its founding in 1965, she was the only Canadian member of the Science Fiction Writers of America" (224). Robert J. Sawyer, one of the most prominent Canadian SF writers today, has called her "the mother of Canadian science fiction" ("Phyllis Gotlieb and Kelly Gotlieb"),[3] while, in the academic world, David Ketterer has argued that "from the sixties to the early eighties Phyllis Gotlieb *was* Canadian SF" and "she may still be" (67), even now (Ketterer made his observation in 1992). He sees Gotlieb as typifying a Canadian aesthetic in *Sunburst* that can be contrasted with the Americanism of van Vogt's *Slan* (serialized in *Astounding* in 1940; published in hardback 1946). Ketterer locates Gotlieb's Canadianness in her "compromise" between "British pessimism [...] and the American-style power fantasy of van Vogt's *Slan*" (70).[4]

Gotlieb's melding of the "high" culture elements of poetry and the "low" culture elements of genre fiction is one of the bases for her importance. Arguably, so is her Canadianness, despite her own reluctance to make such a connection (this will become especially evident when we consider the politics of her Galactic Federation stories), as are her gender and her religious roots.

Gotlieb was born Phyllis Fay Bloom in 1926 in Toronto, a Jewish Canadian who grew to adulthood through World War II. Though her family was not devout, the Holocaust unsurprisingly had a profound impact on her development and on her writing. While the Jewish experience in the twentieth century is rarely an explicit element of her SF, it frequently informs her poetry, is key to her mainstream novel *Why Should I Have All the Grief?* and to her one academic article ("Hasidic Influences on the Work of A. M. Klein," 1974), and may, as Douglas Barbour suggests, "underlie the ethical approach to the alien in her science fiction" ("Phyllis Gotlieb" 109). It also resonates in her SF, most notably in one of her best, and best-known, stories, "Tauf Aleph," which explores of the fate of the last Jew in the universe. Religious elements are present in her work from her earliest stories and poems to her final novel, *Birthstones*, in which the Jewish experience lurks beneath a narrative in which an alien culture is threatened with genocide. In fact, most of Gotlieb's characteristic interests coalesce in this final work, despite its brevity.

Her career unfolded in tandem with domestic life; she met her husband-to-be, Calvin Gotlieb, while she was studying English at the University of Toronto and he was studying math and computation. He eventually "became director of the Institute of Computer Science at the University of Toronto" (Barbour, "Phyllis Gotlieb" 109). They married in 1949, and she gave birth to their first child in 1950, the year she completed her MA in English. She balanced writing and family, as well as literary and genre writing. Indeed, she turned to writing SF on the suggestion of her husband when she suffered from writer's block with her poetry, though she worked for some time before finally achieving success publishing her SF (for instance, her first novel, *Sunburst*, had its roots in a short story she first conceived close to a decade before its publication date). She had an affinity for popular and genre work anyway, since her parents owned and ran a movie theatre. "If you see a lot of movies, you're going to have popular tastes," she observed ("Interview"). She loved the classic SF film *Forbidden Planet* (1956), for instance. *Forbidden Planet* is famously a SF take on Shakespeare's *Tempest*, a work that lies beneath Gotlieb's *O Master Caliban!* (1976), as its title suggests. She produced both SF and poetry through the sixties, though she was not prolific.

Family and reproduction are central themes for Gotlieb. Her first published story, "A Grain of Manhood" (*Fantastic*, 1959), deals with a woman impregnated by an alien and with the ramifications of that procreative act. Though her first sale was in fact "Phantom Foot" (*Amazing*, 1959), "A Grain of Manhood" is especially appropriate as Gotlieb's first publication, as it is also the first story to manifest one of Gotlieb's primary thematic interests. Issues of procreation, ranging from the "natural" process of sexual reproduction to various alternative procreative modes, such as the creation of artificial intelligences (notably the ergs and Mod Dahlgren in *O Master Caliban!* and *Heart of Red Iron* [1989], or the robot O/G in "Tauf Aleph," or, more recently, Spartakos in Gotlieb's Lyhhrt trilogy—or, conversely, the crisis caused by the breakdown of reproduction in *Birthstones*) or the construction of new species through genetic manipulation are central to Gotlieb's canon. Genetically modified characters figure prominently in all of Gotlieb's SF novels but *Sunburst*, and even that book explores the effects of mutation caused by radioactivity on children. In addition to such literal invocations of procreation, procreative or generative metaphors frequently serve as the heart of Gotlieb's novels and stories. Significantly, these metaphors involve not only human (or biological) creators but also the synthetic creations themselves coming to terms with reproductive function. The robot O/G in "Tauf Aleph," for instance, "mothers" both the human protagonist and his alien converts to Judaism, and Spartakos in *Violent Stars* (1999) has a Lyhhrt embryo—egg-like in a "small globe" (234)—inserted in his metallic body. He serves thereby as an even more overtly maternal robot than O/G, by taking the embryo into his metaphoric womb—while nevertheless being gendered male, as my pronoun use here indicates. By contrast, the erg leader ("erg" is the term Gotlieb used for robots with artificial intelligence in *O Master Caliban!*) is a robotic "queen" and "hive mother" which (or perhaps who) functions in grotesquely maternal terms, though we are told that "her ambience was not female: only her shape suggested gender" (209), an important qualification. Indeed, however optimistic are the implications of biological mothering in Gotlieb, from "A Grain of Manhood" forward, mothering becomes a Frankensteinian and therefore complex metaphor in many of her works.

Gotlieb further explored questions of family and community in her sophisticated treatment of the alien. Gotlieb was one of the most adept SF creators of genuinely *alien* aliens, but the common SF motif of contrasting the human self with the alien other is repeatedly complex in Gotlieb's work. Though she often based her aliens on animals native to Earth (notably, the Ungrukh, the feline aliens central to the Ungrukh Chronicles, *A Judgment of Dragons* [1980], *Emperor, Swords, Pentacles* [1982], and *The Kingdom of the Cats* [1985], are revealed to be transplanted and modified panthers from Earth),[5] she used the animal/alien/human continuum in ways that force her readers to question easy categorization. In a telling statement about why she saw SF as a worthwhile literary pursuit, she asserted that SF is valuable because "people need to spread their imagination with visions, chimeras, speculations" ("Interview"). Gotlieb's reference to a chimera here associates SF's value with the invocation of imaginary animals and not merely imaginary animals, but an imaginary animal that hybridizes various animal forms into one being. Gotlieb's characters frequently bridge the human/animal gap in arresting and insightful ways. The most productive use of animals in her work interrogates the concept of the human by juxtaposing it with variations and iterations on animality in ways that require her readers to break down the conventional binary opposition between the two. Gotlieb's SF—and even her poetry—is heavily populated by various "animals" (human and otherwise) engaged in a complex symbiotic relationship, though even David Ketterer allows anthropocentrism to override this fact when he presents a human, Duncan Kinnear (who has little to do in the series, overall), rather than the telepathic cats (the Ungrukh) as the hero of the Ungrukh Chronicles (see Ketterer 70). A complex and encompassing view of the "human" (or sentient) as extending well beyond the parameters of human flesh is central to Gotlieb's work, from her first novel (in which animal imagery is used relatively conventionally to depict those who fail as human) to her mature work, in which the concept of the human is almost entirely superseded in a universe in which even being sure what *is* an animal is problematic. Via the tropes of SF, Gotlieb literalizes the moral and ethical problems inherent in being a thinking animal.

She makes use of another standard SF device, the Galactic Empire, as a backdrop for most of her novels—though it might be more accurate to call her Galactic Federation, or GalFed, a series of tenuously linked communities rather than an "Empire," as Gotlieb's approach to the tropes usually associated with such an organization is as unconventional as her other strategies. GalFed is present, at least implicitly, from the beginning of her career, as the first story she sold, "Phantom Foot," is set in that universe; the Qumedni, an important alien species in the series, first appear in this story. Many of her short stories and all her SF novels except *Sunburst* are set in the GalFed universe. Its basic parameters are developed in her early short stories, some of which have never been collected, though GalFed did not emerge as central to her novels until the publication of *O Master Caliban!*

Despite their variety, most galactic empires share several traits, though in more recent work (e.g., Iain Banks's novels about the Culture, which subvert many Galactic Empire tropes) greater diversity is becoming evident. The traditional galactic empire may include alien races, for instance, but stories set therein are all too likely to be anthropocentric, focusing on human characters, institutions, and governing models (indeed, often American models). Though more recent writers are catching up with her, Phyllis Gotlieb was on the cutting edge in the creation of the multispecies galactic organization, in GalFed. GalFed's multiculturalism, and other of its features, invite a reading of GalFed as the Canadian galactic empire. GalFed is a very Canadian version of what a galactic "empire" might be. It is also, as such, a rarity; as Robert Runté and Christine Kulyk note, "Canadians tend not to write about vast interstellar empires" (45). The one exception, other than Gotlieb, is Gordon R. Dickson, in his Dorsai series, but only in Gotlieb do we find what is perhaps, in Douglas Barbour's words, "a distinctly Canadian version of the Galactic Empire" ("Phyllis Gotlieb" 113). This is most evident in the cultural mosaic that defines it (the protagonists of several novels and some stories in the series are not human—or, in some cases, even biological), but GalFed reflects Canadian models and precepts in other respects, as well. John Clute, for instance, argues that Canadian SF can be contrasted with American SF in the following terms:

> It is not community based; it is not about the penetration of frontiers; it ignores the culture heroes who marshall the folk or who save the world; and it ignores the details of the science and technology which are used by culture heroes to weld the community together and to arm it for conquest. Canadian SF—if A. E. Van Vogt is one of its central founders—can therefore be defined as a genre which translates the fable of survival so central to the Canadian psyche into a fable of lonely transcendence [26].

While not everything Clute argues here might apply to Gotlieb (community is very important in Gotlieb, for instance, though perhaps not quite in the way Clute suggests it is in American SF), much of what Gotlieb does in the GalFed stories reflects Clute's notions here of central elements of Canadian SF.

As for GalFed's status as an empire, or "empire," providing galaxy-spanning government in any event, John Robert Colombo's amusing description of what *Star Trek* might have been like had it been Canadian is instructive:

Exploration would not be the starship's mission; it would be peacekeeping in Deep Space. Entire episodes would be related from the point of view of an endangered species. The administration of the ship would be military, with Captain Kirk's rank that of Lieutenant-Governor or Governor General. The operation would be a joint undertaking of private enterprise and public regulation—in other words, a Crown Corporation. Continuing concerns would be wrangles over whether the specific interventions were a federal or a provincial responsibility. Compromise rather than coercion would inform the decision-making process, with the occasional royal Commission to justify delayed action. To respect the national commitment to bilingualism and multiculturalism, officers and crew members would be selected from qualified members of minority groups [...]. In each episode the Québeckers on board would threaten to "go it alone." Half the episodes, or half of each episode, would be produced in French, with English subs or dubs [40].

Again, much of what Colombo suggests here as typically Canadian has its analog in Gotlieb. Exceptions (other than the humorous digs at Quebec) would include the military model (which seems a dubiously Canadian trait in any event); while the military and war have their places in the GalFed series, GalFed protagonists are not generally military officers. Indeed, militarism is generally presented as a last alternative. For instance, the 1973 story "Mother Lode" (*Magazine of Fantasy and Science Fiction*), provides the following information about how GalFed diplomat Elena Cortez tries to deal with colonial problems:

> When a new colony was seriously disturbing the ecology of the native civilization of a planet, no matter how perfect it might be from the point of view of its settlers, she had GalFed authority to ask it to shift, remove, or disperse itself. She had no power to shift or remove it herself, or threaten to do so. [...] She warned gently, listened to impassioned arguments calmly, and almost always succeeded at the unpleasant work. When she did not succeed, she accepted refusals gently. The colony, if endangered, was left to itself; if it was a danger, it was left to legal, political, or military authorities [61].

The syntax suggests, without stressing, that military intervention is the last option, and the passive voice even leaves open to question who, exactly, exercises the legal, political, or military authority. Significantly, one of Gotlieb's few stories to deal directly with militarism, the non–GalFed "The Military Hospital" (*Fourteen Stories High*, 1971), focuses, as its title indicates, on the medical care given to a wounded combatant, rather than on the war itself.

In short, Phyllis Gotlieb's SF is in some ways squarely located within the conventions of the genre. However, it is also unique or unconventional in several important ways, rooted in her experience as a woman, a Jew, and a Canadian, as well as in the ways she straddles generic and national lines—as a

Canadian literary writer and an American genre writer. The following chapters will explore in further detail Gotlieb's SF output, focusing primarily on her fiction but also demonstrating the importance of SF to her career as a Canadian poet as well as her career as an American writer of SF. The discussion will be roughly chronological, tracking Gotlieb's development across her career. Chapter One will explore her early shorter fiction, much of which has been collected in *Son of the Morning* (1983) and *Blue Apes* (1995), but some of which remains available only in the original magazines in which it was published. Chapter Two will focus on *Sunburst*, her first and arguably most significant novel. Chapter Three will explore *O Master Caliban!* and *Heart of Red Iron*, its sequel published thirteen years later. Chapter Four will deal with her mid-period shorter fiction. Chapter Five will explore the Ungrukh Chronicles, *A Judgment of Dragons*; *Emperor, Swords, Pentacles*; and *The Kingdom of the Cats*. Chapter Six will explore the Lyhhrt trilogy, consisting of *Flesh and Gold* (1998), *Violent Stars* (1999), and *Mindworlds* (2002). Chapter Seven will examine Gotlieb's SF poetry. Chapter Eight will return to Gotlieb's shorter fiction, dealing with her later short stories, and will also discuss Gotlieb's final novel, *Birthstones*.

One

Early Short Fiction

Though never prolific, Gotlieb saw her most productive period in the short form in the first several years of her career, publishing ten of her twenty-five short stories and novellas from 1959 to 1969, with fewer than five such works per decade through the 1990s and one final short piece in 2007 (the same year her final novel was published). These stories, several uncollected in either of her story collections and some never reprinted since their initial appearance,[1] offer valuable insights into the genesis of her work, in stand-alone stories as well as in ones that laid the groundwork for the far-future universe in which most of her novels are set. Though *Sunburst* is a standalone near-future post-disaster novel, all her other SF novels are set in the far-future universe of the Galactic Federation, or GalFed. GalFed has its genesis in some of these early stories, though it did not appear in novels until *O Master Caliban!* Consequently, these early GalFed stories lay the groundwork for the bulk of Gotlieb's work at the novel length. The early stories also introduce, in concentrated and distilled form, many of Gotlieb's characteristic themes and stylistic practices. Furthermore, the coherent universe of GalFed, while diverse and flexible, also in some respects contains or limits Gotlieb's range. Her short fiction, therefore, often stands not only as examples of the essential traits of her work as a whole but also as a space in which she could experiment with types of stories that don't fit into the GalFed frame. This is especially true when one factors in the unreprinted stories.

GalFed is not fully formed from the beginning, though it is at least implied from the first story Gotlieb sold, and at least some of the other early stories might be containable within its parameters. Consequently, they need to be considered on their own terms as well as in terms of their contribution to the construction of Gotlieb's universe. This chapter will explore Gotlieb's early short fiction, tracing the development of GalFed as well as following the byways and side channels Gotlieb explored in these early works. However, even her first story shows that Gotlieb's key thematic interests were in place from the beginning of her career.

"A Grain of Manhood" was Gotlieb's second sale but her first published story. It appeared in *Fantastic* in September 1959, was reprinted in the collection *Great Stories from Fantastic* in 1966, and appears in Gotlieb's first story collection, *Son of the Morning*. It is one of her most significant stories, not merely because it is her first publication but also because it showed, immediately, the complexity and allusiveness which is a hallmark of her best work. Its title offers the first of several intertextual elements, as it is a quotation from Milton's dramatic poem *Samson Agonistes*. That is, from the moment of her emergence as a writer, Gotlieb's work announces its literary antecedents. Though not all of her work so overtly invokes other literary texts, this story is in some ways paradigmatic of her work in how it evokes and transmutes literary (and Biblical) tradition.

Nor is this its only significance. The story also introduces other recurring Gotlieb themes and motifs. For instance, telepathy is a major theme in Gotlieb's work, occurring in all of her novels and many of her short stories, to complex effect. It is present primarily as a plot convenience in this story—to allow quick and easy communication between human and alien—but its metaphoric value as an exemplar of how to bridge apparently uncrossable chasms in some of Gotlieb's later work underlies its use here. Gotlieb's characters are frequently damaged, both physically and psychologically, and telepathy is one of the devices she uses to address this element of her work. Indeed, both physical and emotional damage are important elements in this story, notably James's sterility on the physical front and each character's sense of alienation from the other on the psychological front.

The matter of James's sterility touches on the most significant of Gotlieb's recurring thematic concerns, though: reproduction. Among the many things the "grain" of the title might refer to, it surely stands for the seed implanted in Lela; this is a story in which pregnancy is a central issue. Incidences of pregnancy, or of metaphorized acts of reproduction, recur frequently in Gotlieb's work, sometimes as little more than background elements, but other times as central elements, so it is perhaps inevitable that they are central to her first published story, as well. Even in her final novel, *Birthstones*, reproduction is the central concern; it spans Gotlieb's career from alpha to omega or, perhaps more appropriately, aleph to tauf. Linked to this concern is Gotlieb's more general interest in the materiality of the body and of how one's physical nature informs one's moral and psychological nature. Lela is to a considerable extent defined in this story by her biology. This idea at times manifests itself in Gotlieb's work in stereotypical ways (e.g., the occasions on which Gotlieb draws an equation between a character's physical and moral repellence; physiognomy is an old method of characterization, and one that Gotlieb is not above employing from time to time). Complicating this "biology is destiny" thesis, however, is the countervailing trend in Gotlieb's work, also evident here, to focus on psychologically complex characters, even ones who fall far short of the ideals often attached to protagonists in fiction, especially genre fiction. James and Lela are far from perfect people, and the story complicates what might seem simple questions of blame and responsibility in what is, after all, a story published in 1959 about a woman impregnated by someone other than her husband.

The story is in some respects a simple quest narrative. Lela leaves a marriage that is sterile, both biologically and emotionally. However, she ends up in a crash that brings her spacecraft down on an unknown alien planet, enters the world of the aliens for a while and becomes pregnant before leaving the alien world and returning to her husband. Her story therefore parallels the hero's quest into the underworld/otherworld/fairyland and acquisition of a significant talisman to bring back: in this case, the seed that fertilizes her body, ending the biological sterility of her relationship and thereby restoring the wasteland, in a manner of speaking, as well as apparently healing the emotional rift as well. The narrative structure is not linear, however, in contrast to the majority of quest narratives, which track the questor's movement from home into the unfamiliar world and back again in a circular narrative.[2] Instead, the story begins after Lela has returned to her husband, pregnant by another; Gotlieb embeds the primary narrative in the frame narrative of recrimination (but ultimately reconciliation) over the pregnancy and then the birth of the child. As a result of this structural feature, the reader's expectations of the narrative are shaped by knowing that Lela returns from her adventure, and does so pregnant by someone other than her husband. This eliminates suspense as a major narrative element, suggesting a focus not on what will happen but on how what has already happened has affected Lela's life.

The story borrows from narratives of the quest to the underworld or otherworld, in this instance represented by the alien planet. As Corinne Saunders notes, the otherworld is "shifting and vaguely defined, not always explicitly as faery, not always given boundaries" (179); she continues to note, "This is a landscape that can shift from threatening to delightful and back again, and its inhabitants are often distinguished by similarly shifting qualities: the recurrent motif of shape-shifting rewrites classical metamorphosis" (180). This association of the otherworld with physical plasticity is especially germane in Gotlieb's story, both literally, and in how the story transmutes Samson's story, though plasticity is given a thematic weight that moves away from the ambivalence and threat often associated with formlessness or transformation in myth and romance. Instead, and in contrast to the characters in many such narratives, Lela is not only positively transformed by her experience (itself by no means a guarantee for the questing hero), she is also made pregnant. Though the number of stories of otherworldly lovers (either male or female) is enormous, ranging back to myth and recurring frequently in romance and other fiction of the uncanny, stories of humans led into the otherworld in pursuit of an object of desire rarely end well and rarely bear fruit (e.g., Orpheus and Eurydice). Stories of otherworldly lovers pursuing humans in this world also frequently do not end well—for the human, at least—but are more likely to be generative, as any review of the plethora of children spawned on humans by the classical gods will attest. Most faery sexual relationships are at best sterile and are often malign. While they often involve seduction, they rarely involve fruition.

Faery or supernatural seducers often use music as their means of drawing humans, often to destruction. One need think only of the sirens, in a classical context, or the association of music with Satanic temptation in medieval Christian culture (see for instance Kathy Meyer-Baer 284ff), or the pied piper of Hamelin, in a modern secularized folk context, to recognize the potential dangers of following magical music.[3] Music is frequently used to call people to cross the line between the known and unknown world by music, and it is so with Lela. She hears "the trill of a pipe so faint and uncertain it might have been the singing of blood in her brain. But it grew and paced her as she stumbled on; it traced the whorl of her ear" (151). Interesting here is not merely the sensuousness of the image—sound becomes almost tangible, tracing its way into Lela as if on a journey of its own, a sort of answering quester itself—but also the faint echo of the apocryphal myth of Mary's impregnation via the word of God entering her ear. The story invites this connection by having Lela say to James of her impregnation by an alien, "A virgin birth would have seemed more reasonable to you" (149). Though one is of course free to imagine the alien impregnating Lela via more conventional means (and one must imagine it, as anything like explicit sex is rare in SF of this vintage, and is absent from this story except implicitly), this passage represents the initial contact between Lela and the alien, and it does so in ways that not only physicalize it but also associate the external stimulus with her own internal landscape: the "singing of blood in her brain" responds to the pipe.

The most extensive invocation of a specific antecedent, though, is of Milton's *Samson Agonistes* (1671), his closet tragedy telling the story of the end of the Biblical Samson's life. Gotlieb's title quotes the poem, from a passage in which Samson laments his weakness in succumbing to Delilah's blandishments and revealing to her the secret of his strength:

> I yielded, and unlocked her all my heart,
> Who with a grain of manhood well resolved
> Might easily have shook off all her snares:
> But foul effeminacy held me yoked
> Her bond-slave... [407–11].

In this context, the grain of manhood refers to conventional or stereotypical masculine virtues; Samson laments that he lacked even the tiniest particle of manhood, for if he had such a grain in him, he should have been able to resist Delilah's wiles.

Delilah is often conceived of as the stereotypical sexually betraying woman; in his edition of the poem, for instance, Michael Davis associates Delilah with dangerous tempter/transformer figures such as Circe and the Sirens of classical myth. Defenses of her are few. William Empson's "A Defense of Delilah" is one of the exceptions, arguing that Delilah legitimately loves Samson and that her betrayals, if such they are, can be justified with the same arguments Samson uses to justify his own acts. Empson defends her but nevertheless must acknowledge Milton's "Dislike for Delihah" (240). Even more recent studies that attempt to problematize her nevertheless generally concede that she is presented in the poem as "a morally corrupt (evil, perhaps) woman" (Shawcross 79). Gotlieb's Lela, by contrast, might derive her name from Delilah—Lela being a possible abbreviation of Delilah—and she might seem like a sexual betrayer, but Gotlieb inverts and destabilizes key elements of the Biblical and Miltonic story. She reassigns the meaning of the grain of manhood from the power to resist female blandishments to, instead, the source of union and reconciliation through fertility (the Biblical Samson is a miracle baby, like Christ, born of a sterile mother). The figure with transformative power is the male alien, but unlike sexual tempters in myth and folk traditions, the plasticity of the alien becomes the source for renewal. Samson's story ends in destruction; Lela's in birth.

An important element in the story of Samson is the story of his birth: Samson is a type of Christ, in that he is miraculously born of a barren mother after angelic intervention. Described in Judges as "barren" (13.2), Manoah's wife receives an angelic visitor, stating, "Behold now, thou art barren, and bearest not; but thou shalt conceive, and bear a son...; and no razor shall come on his head: for the child shall be a Nazarite unto God from the womb: and he shall begin to deliver Israel out of the hands of the Philistines" (13.3–13.5). Though the precise agency whereby Samson is conceived is unspecified, the angelic intervention is clearly key, just as it is in the birth of Christ. Christian discomfort with sex, especially when it comes to divine reproduction, led to the emergence in the third century of the Christian myth that "Mary was impregnated by the words of the angel. Within a century, the visual image of the angel talking into her ear had become the conceptual image of the angel impregnating her through the ear" (Hazleton 214). Whether Manoah is Samson's biological father is ambiguous; that Joseph was not Christ's is a basic Christian tenet. Nevertheless, in both cases, the child is special because of the divine role in the pregnancy, and the parallels are clear enough, so much so that medieval Biblical allegoresis took Samson to be a type of Christ.

Milton's poem is set at the end of Samson's life, but Milton nevertheless makes a point of reminding his readers of Samson's miraculous birth and ordained role as savior. Lamenting his current status as blinded slave, Samson asks, "Wherefore was my birth from heav'n foretold / Twice by an angel" (23–24), notes that he was "designed for great exploits" (32), and that the "divine prediction" (44) "was that I / Should Israel from Philistian yoke deliver" (38–39). Despite his physical strength—the material manifestation of his importance—his "impotence of mind" (52) led to his downfall when he succumbed to Delilah. Note the sexual metaphor: Delilah's seduction is sterile. The trajectory of the poem carries Samson from his current state of sterility—indeed, of quasi-death, as he describes himself as living

> a life half dead, a living death,
> And buried; but O yet more miserable!
> Myself, my sepulchre, a moving grave,
> Buried, yet not exempt
> By privilege of death and burial
> From worst of other evils... [100–105].

He images his body as his tomb; he is buried in his own flesh, a perverse reversal of pregnancy.

The issue of sterility is also important in Gotlieb's story, but in a reverse of the situation in Samson's story, in that the sterility lies within the paternal as opposed to the maternal figure. Whereas Samson's mother is sterile, Lela is not. Furthermore, James is the initial betrayer. He has married her under false pretenses, knowing of his sterility before marrying her and taking her across space to an alien planet. He is, in a way, a reverse figure to the piping alien Lela encounters. He misleads her to take her from the familiar world to an otherworld, promising her love but in fact denying her "the woman's right she had wanted so deeply" (159) (i.e., a child), whereas the alien leads her to safety and provides the child denied by her husband. James, therefore, also plays the role played by Delilah in scripture and in Milton's version, of the deceiving, sterile seducer. Though Milton does have Samson repeatedly blame his own weakness and effeminacy, as previously discussed, he also clearly images Delilah as a deceiving seducer who led Samson to his downfall.

However much the poem depends on Samson's acceptance of responsibility for his fate, it also repeatedly stresses Delilah's culpability. We might be inclined to take Samson's repeated assertions that she is a "deceitful woman" (202) or "specious monster" (230) with a grain of salt, but the Chorus—generally a fairly reliable source, albeit neither omniscient nor neutral—affirms Samson's judgement: "wisest men / Have erred, and by bad women been deceived" (210–11). Indeed, the theme of female betrayal runs through the poem; Samson is betrayed not only by Delilah but also by his first wife. Furthermore, though Delilah's betrayal is not sexual but rather a betrayal of trust, the poem images her deceit in reproductive terms; due to the offer of gold, we are told, she "conceived / Her spurious first-born: treason against me!" (390–91). Milton therefore sexualizes the transgression, even though Delilah has apparently been sexually faithful to Samson. Milton further colors Delilah by comparing her to a "sorceress" (819) who does not merely ensnare Samson but does so with methods tinged with magical association; he metaphorizes her deceptive strategies as "Thy fair enchanted cup and warbling charms" (934). Michael Davis's note offers this interpretation of the line: "Milton suggests the Homeric legends of Circe, the enchantress whose magic drink transformed humans to brutes, and of the Sirens, whose singing lured sailors onto the rocks" (p. 92). Earlier in the poem, indeed, Samson has imaged himself as "a foolish pilot" who has "shipwrecked / My vessel" (198–99), and the poem reiterates numerous times how he has been transformed, not literally to a beast, but certainly metaphorically: he has been "Put to the labour of a beast, debased / Lower than bond-slave!" (37–38), for instance, and Samson himself and other characters comment repeatedly on his degradation—his loss of his former self.

This question of form comes up repeatedly, with Samson imagined as having undergone a sort of diminishment or dissolution. When the Chorus first enter, they say, "See how he lies at random, carelessly diffused" (118). This is, literally, merely an image of Samson sprawled on the ground lamenting, but the words "random" and "diffused" suggest a figure in the process of disintegration, one who has lost his sense of self and therefore to some extent his physical coherence, his form. However, Samson's climactic accomplishment depends on his reclamation of his original physical strength and the use of it to bring down the palace. Interestingly, though, the account of his triumph metaphorizes him in protean terms—as flame emerging from beneath the ashes, as a dragon attacking farmyard fowl, as an eagle, and finally as the Phoenix:

> That self-begotten bird
> In the Arabian woods embost,
> That no second knows nor third,
> And lay erewhile a holocaust,
> From out her ashy womb now teemed
> Revives, reflourishes, then vigorous most
> When most unactive deemed [1699–1705].

Samson goes metaphorically from the inchoate formlessness of ash to a rebirth as the Phoenix, itself an allegorical representation of Christ in Christian tradition. The image of the Phoenix as "self-begotten" also returns to play on the motif of reproduction. It's a gestative image, and an image of form emerging from formlessness, as well as life emerging from death, all of which resonates in Gotlieb's story.

Gotlieb's narrative differs substantially from Milton's, but these elements play roles in her tale. One might even suggest a structural similarity in that Milton's poem follows the classical convention of episodes followed by choruses, reflected in Gotlieb's alternation between scenes set in the "present" and the "past," with the past scenes informing the present scenes as the choral passages comment on the episodes. Nevertheless, Gotlieb's use of the poem, even in how her story echoes its minor elements, is transformative rather than imitative. For instance, Samson images himself as a ship's pilot, wrecked on the rocks. Lela's adventure depends on her survival of a shipwreck on another planet. However, Samson's image makes him the culpable party; he pilots his own ship to destruction. Lela, by contrast, has no control over the ship but is on it as a passenger attempting to get away from the betrayal of her husband. Gotlieb shifts the focus from a male to a female protagonist, making her version of Delilah the hero.

To do so, Gotlieb needs to be careful in how she deals with Lela's pregnancy. It is a challenge, especially in 1959, to depict a woman pregnant by someone other than her husband in sympathetic terms, to make the husband rather than the wife the culpable betrayer. Gotlieb's typescript of the story reflects her efforts. Lela's first words in the second section of the story as it appears in typescript are, "I was never untrue to you," which is stricken out by hand. The draft also shows her trying phraseology such as "'It's almost impossible to explain' she said, 'I know it's the old song—'" with *"Faithful in My Fashion"* added by hand in the margin (as a note to indicate the song referenced or as an intended addition to Lela's speech, having her quote the song, is not clear). In the published version, this becomes, "'What's there to explain? The old story...'" (149). This version removes the denial of untruth—perhaps because that too overtly suggests sexual fidelity and therefore the idea of the child as the product of miracle—and also removes the song reference, which would seem to make light of the situation. Instead, we get the ambiguous "same old story" reference, allowing for sexual infidelity but removing any hint of light-heartedness from it.

Instead of focusing on Lela as betrayer, Gotlieb focuses on Lela as denied identity and as trapped. The opening sentence tells us, "She was lying formless; the contour of her body was lost except for the white ring of pain that worked its way downward every so often like a wedding ring over a swollen knuckle" (148). This sense of formlessness is key to the story. Here it speaks to Lela's loss of identity in marriage. The simile for labor pains, a wedding ring sliding over a swollen knuckle, suggests that her marriage is painful and confining, something that constricts her, forcing her into a pattern, like the knuckle must be forced through the ring. She is not a literal prisoner, as is Samson, but as a woman stuck in an unhappy marriage and taken to a distant planet far from home, her situation is analogous to Samson's as a prisoner among a different people as a result of the betrayal of his wife. Though Samson is not formless, he has lost his identity, and the text of the poem imagines the Chorus, when they first see him, as describing him as lying "at random, carelessly diffused" (118). He is literally in chains; Lela is metaphorically trapped in her marriage, as the image of the constrictive wedding ring suggests. The initial image associates her formlessness and her entrapment with her pregnant body.

As *Samson Agonistes* is ultimately about Samson's reclamation of identity, so is "A Grain of Manhood" a story about Lela's, albeit in fundamentally different terms. The "grain" image is especially instructive on this front. Gotlieb expands on the meaning of the term in its Miltonic context, where it refers merely to the core element or component of masculinity Samson images himself as lacking when he succumbs to Dalila [*sic*], to bring into play other associations attached to the grain or seed. That Gotlieb is deliberately working with the grain as symbol is evident in the occasionally strained ways she works the idea into the story. The image of Lela's husband James desiring anonymity—"all he had ever wanted was to dissolve among them [the people of his new community on the alien planet] like a grain of salt without much more color or savor" (149)—is an effective invocation of the key term in a way that plays against its predominant meaning in this story, though it resonates with its use in Milton: it is associated with a loss or lack of self. The Old Testament links salt with sacrifice, especially with grain sacrifice: "And every offering of your grain offering you shall season with salt; you shall not allow the salt of the covenant of your God to be lacking from your grain offering. With all your offerings you shall offer salt" (Leviticus 2.13). The image associated with James, however, is not of salt as adding flavor but losing it; the New Testament uses the idea of the loss of flavor in salt as rendering it worthless: "Ye are the salt of the earth: but if the salt have lost his savour, wherewith shall it be salted? it is thenceforth good for nothing, but to be cast out, and to be trodden under foot of men" (Matthew 5:13).[4] The grain idea here, therefore, is used effectively as a negative way of imaging James's sense of identity and indeed of his worth. By contrast, when Lela tries to explain her flight from the planet as linked with her discovery that she and James could not have a family and to the fact that she had not seen her own family in three years, the narrator describes this rationalization as "the time-told tale of alien grain" (150), tying into Lela's earlier description of what has happened as "the old story" (149), but in a way that makes the metaphor creak.

For the most part, however, the image of the grain is associated in the story with fertility—not with the core element of the self, basically, but with what can be implanted. The association of grain with the giving of life is invoked by the aliens who rescue Lela, for instance, when they cull the idea of bread from her mind and make some for her: "'We don't make this kind of thing with our grain, but we baked it when it became evident that you would be with us'" (152). When Lela's alien lover (for want of a better term) eats fruit, he "spat out four green pips into the palm of his hand, and cast them to the winds" (153), explicitly associating this act with reproduction: "'four more zimb trees,' he said" (154). The story twice invokes pearls, once in association with Kollandro's fingernail as he peels the aforementioned fruit, and once with the sky; while these are not obviously reproductive images, the great medieval poem *The Pearl* complexly invokes the image of the Pearl, partly derived from its Biblical associations with wisdom, purity, and the soul, partly as a seed image, when the Pearl poet images the pearl as lost in a garden, buried in the earth:

> That spot of spyses mot nedes sprede
> Ther such ryches to rot is runne:
> Blomes blayke and blwe and rede
> Ther schyne ful schyr agayn the sunne.
> Flor and fryte may not be fede

> Ther hit doun drof in moldes dunne;
> For uch gresse mot grow of graynes dede,
> No whete were elles to wones wonne [25–32].⁵

The pearl here explicitly becomes a grain, or seed, and it becomes clear in the poem that the Pearl is the narrator's child (among other things). And the grain in Gotlieb's story ultimately comes to refer to the child Lela carries. Samson's grain of manhood is translated from his (absent) mark of masculinity to a present mark of reconciliation and restoration between estranged lovers.

Gotlieb invents a unique alien biology to support the point. The story begins with formlessness, linked with a lack of identity. The alien Nevids are creatures for whom form is highly plastic. When Lela first encounters them, she sees that "they were humanoid, but flat-nosed and narrow-jawed; it was hard to find the form beneath the skin" (151–52). Rather than having fixed, uniform features, they display a riot of different ones; as Lela observes, "All you people [...] have the same form basically—I think—but no two of you are alike on the surface. That seems impossible" (154). Kollandro explains that their "germ plasm is almost infinitely tractable," so "we can take in any form of intelligent life. The children become pure Nevids within three generations" (154). This would explain how interspecies breeding—a common SF sin—would be possible, hence explaining how Lela could be impregnated by an alien (assuming that the tractability is transferrable into an alien host's ovum, which is evidently the case). More importantly, the concept converts the grain, or seed—or germ—from something that dissolves and vanishes into something that transforms.

Though Samson's location in Milton's poem is a pleasant place where he can feel "the breath of heav'n fresh blowing, pure and sweet, / With day-spring born" (10–11), he is nevertheless in a metaphoric wasteland, represented by the darkness of his blindness (light as literal and metaphorical source of life is a repeated point in the poem) and the sepulchre of his body. Lela has a similar experience, arguably; she comes to the fecund and beautiful otherworld of the aliens an empty vessel, not literally sterile of course, though she might as well be, given her marriage. She is restored. The quest hero often must return to restore order and health to his or her community—often a literal or metaphorical wasteland that must be restored. Instead, Lela herself is restored, converted from waste to fertility, as Samson is resurrected phoenix-like.

But Lela's restoration is explicitly regenerative and life-affirming, whereas Samson's—however much it might represent a moral victory over his failings and a literal victory over the Philistines—is nevertheless ultimately life-ending. Lela's adventures could of course be destructive; after all, a wife pregnant by someone other than her husband would seem unlikely to be able to use that pregnancy in a restorative way. Indeed, the tension early in the story suggests the destructive potential. How can a relationship survive this? Even the fact that the child in the womb is referred to consistently (and by both Lela and James) as "it" hints at destructive, even monstrous possibility (the monstrous potential of human/alien interbreeding is of course a common SF trope, and one that Gotlieb herself invokes in "Sunday's Child"). On the literal level, the infinite tractability of the Nevid germ plasm contributes to the solution by allowing the form of the child to be itself fluid; when the child emerges "gleaming with the detritus of amniotic fluid [...] he was a complete and perfect replica of James, down to the last neat lock of hair on his forehead" (159). The child *is*, in effect, James's, though he is not the biological father (again, one might think of the father-status of Manoah, or Joseph, for that matter). But if James's form has been imposed on the baby, it can have been only by Lela, the simultaneously unconscious and material manifestation of her attachment to James despite their differences.

The baby's family resemblance is incomprehensible to James—"I can't understand it," he says (159)—but its apparently miraculous nature leads him to confess, finally, his own complicity and deception: that he knew of his sterility before their marriage. They are left at the end of the story, not with a new, ideal relationship—Gotlieb is never that sentimental, even in her earliest work—but with a new potential. James may have lacked the grain of manhood, but the seed grew anyway. The paradoxical sense of formlessness and containment that opened the story is echoed in its final sentence: "She moved her clean drained body under the sheets, grateful enough to have her breasts ripening with milk, the baby in her arm, and James beside her with the faint pulsing of hope between them" (159). She is still under the sheet, but with a more defined form, specifically associated with the materiality of lactation—the nourishment for her seed—and rather than a painful and constricting relationship, one touched by hope. The story promises nothing—it's a "faint pulsing" of hope—but it offers potential. Gotlieb's work frequently offers a balance between hard realities and positive possibilities.

"A Grain of Manhood" has received considerable attention here as Gotlieb's first story, to demonstrate the complexity of even her early work, and to demonstrate key elements of her work that have been present from the beginning. Her other early fiction will not be discussed in such detail, though many of these stories would benefit from extended close analysis. However, many of Gotlieb's techniques and strategies in "A Grain of Manhood" recur in subsequent stories, so they can be dealt with more summarily.

Another of her early stories, for instance, "Gingerbread Boy," echoes many aspects of "a Grain of Manhood," though in a far more ambivalent narrative. Like "A Grain of Manhood," the story has literary antecedents, albeit ones not as elevated as Milton. The title derives from the late–nineteenth-century verse fairy tale "The Gingerbread Man." Like the childless woman in the tale, who bakes a gingerbread man as a sort of surrogate child, only to have him reject her and run away, "Gingerbread Boy" deals with androids created by colonists on Skander V. Unlike the gingerbread man, however, these androids are not fantasy creatures made of dough but genetically engineered from the DNA of colonists: Benno "had been grown from a piece of Peretto's flesh, so the features were Peretto's, but Peretto was a man, and Benno a secondhand copy pretending to be his child" (81). These androids are only partial creatures, not fully formed: "pseudomale and sterile, hairless except for the strong dark line of brow and the close-cropped head of hair so dark and wiry it looked artificial" (81). They were created out of the colonists' desperate desire for some form of progeny at a time when they feared they would be unable to reproduce, as they fled from a radioactive Earth (what disaster, exactly, has befallen Earth remains unelaborated, but it leaves the colonists fearing they will be sterile permanently).

As in "Grain," then, the impetus is the desperate desire to procreate. Unlike that story, however, this one considers the possible complications when one creates offspring that are not really human. Some humans fear the androids—especially since they have learned that their ability to procreate naturally has survived, so they can have genuine children, not merely android substitutes—and the androids generally resent their precarious social position and their own abortive physical natures. The lack of sexual maturity is a key feature here, Gotlieb returning throughout her career to the centrality of reproduction to the self-conception of human and alien alike. The tensions between human-grown and vat-grown creatures threaten to explode. Gotlieb makes the instigator an android named Dickon. The name is a diminutive form of "Richard," a name that means "brave power." This meaning might be appropriate enough given Dickon's bravado and desire to rebel against and wipe out the humans, but Gotlieb perhaps also has in mind the character Dickon from the play "Gammer Gurton's Needle," in which Dickon is the trouble-maker, an almost devilish instigator of community strife.[6] Regardless, Gotlieb here locates the genesis of antagonism within one of the created creatures, thereby rendering one of the physically anomalous creatures also morally problematic, a propensity that will recur in her work; Gotlieb, especially in her earlier work, tends to associate internal and external deformity. Dickon becomes a grotesque, animalistic figure; at the climax of the story, he looks "as if he had evolved from a feral animal, and were now reverting to it" (93). He leads the androids in their abortive rebellion, with Benno the one figure who resists his suasion. Gotlieb here anticipates a key element in *Sunburst*, when the mutant children in that book turn on their progenitors and are imaged as a feral pack.

However, Gotlieb does not take the easy out of simply rendering the scientifically created imperfect creatures monstrous, as is so often done in SF. Instead, she makes and indeed reiterates the point that these creations are images of their creators; if they have the capacity for monstrosity, they come by it honestly. When Dickon is shot by Wenslow (who is the source of the DNA from which Dickon was grown), Benno "looked up at Wenslow's savage face, Dickon's counterpart" (93). The androids have monstrousness projected onto them by the humans who fear and do not understand them. The catalyst for the action in fact is an absurd accusation of pedophiliac rape directed against Benno; as a physically sterile creature, he is literally incapable of such an act, so that a human sees it in him is a reflection of the dark soul of the human, not of the android. The story ends, in typical Gotlieb fashion, with a provisional peace, Benno still in a liminal space, neither fully in nor fully alienated from the human community (he has packed a bag to run away, which he keeps packed even when he decides to stay for now). There is no easy resolution. The androids can never be fully human; "you can only be a man between the ears" (94), Peretto tells Benno.

Important as such a story is to Gotlieb's growth, key to her developing fiction is her Galactic "Empire," the Galactic Federation, or GalFed. Though GalFed is not referred to by name prior to the 1960 story "A Bone to Pick" (*Fantastic*), published a year later, the first GalFed story was also Gotlieb's first sale, "Phantom Foot" (*Amazing*, 1959). GalFed has therefore been a part of Gotlieb's SF since the beginning, though its importance was not immediately apparent; several of Gotlieb's early stories are clearly not set in the GalFed universe (though some, such as "Gingerbread Boy," could be, lacking specific reference to GalFed but including nothing inconsistent with it), and her first novel, *Sunburst*, is a near-future revisionist reading of the superman trope. However, all nine of Gotlieb's SF novels subsequent to *Sunburst*, as well as several short stories, are set in this galactic "empire."

Even in that first story, there is little sense of the galactic organization possessing the characteristic traits of galactic empires, though admittedly there is also little information about the organization at all, except by inference. The protagonists are a multicultural (though entirely human) crew of flawed and complex men, rather than the Heinleinesque omnicompetents one expects to find in such SF of the period. Indeed, the story gently and unobtrusively pokes some fun at such SF. Though his children can watch "*Jett Winslow of the Solar Patrol* [...] fighting ten-legged Vegans" (133) on Tri-V, for Captain Towers of the spaceship *Cayley and Sylvester*, the reality of captaining a space mission combines the tedium of travel over vast distances and of waiting for things to happen with the terror of encounters not with (presumably) easily dispatched Vegans but instead with the ineffable and almost omnipotent Qumedni, whose nature is largely unknown but who can manipulate matter, space, and time at will. Gotlieb makes little of Jett Winslow, referring to him only twice (albeit in a short story, so the references carry more weight than they would in a novel), but the contrast between the sort of space opera suggested by his name and his antagonists and the reality of interaction with the alien within the story is clear.

Indeed, Gotlieb's manuscript for the story shows evidence that she reconsidered the nature of the Qumedni during the revision process, opting to make them less conventional antagonistic aliens, à la *Jett Winslow*. One minor revision—the clause "they've all been held at arms' length, as we are now" (manuscript 5) becomes "they've all been pushed off..." (135), a subtle removal of the human metaphor for the description of the Qumedni. The manuscript also includes this passage:

> Phelps shook his head. "From what we've been able to gather they've got the arrangement usual in intelligent forms of a head with senses, and prehensile limbs. They live in an oxygen atmosphere so they probably don't look like octopuses, but whether they've got six legs andfur [*sic*] like a bear, or warts like a toad we don't know. But they are telepathic—and they have other psi powers." He paused and his face became drawn. "Their whole world—they have a kind of corporate awareness, each person a member cell. They have, also, a cruel humour" [5].

In the published story, this has become "Phelps shrugged. 'Nobody's ever seen one. We suspect they're energy-forms of some kind. We know they can communicate when they want to, they're telepathic—and they have other psi powers.' He paused, and his face became drawn. 'They also have a cruel humor'" (135–36). Again, though even the original is provisional, it suggests a physicality for the Qumedni that Gotlieb discards. A final manuscript passage, offering further hints of the Qumedni as stereotypical aliens, describes a telepathic "final manifestation" in which "a red and purple *something* appeared, writhing its tentacles" (14) was also cut from the published version. Gotlieb consistently removed all such elements of the story that concretized the Qumedni, leaving them in the published version entirely absent except insofar as manifested by their telepathic powers.

If the Qumedni are unusual aliens, Gotlieb's space-faring humans are also unlikely candidates for a serious interspecies contact mission. Towers's crew consists not of a cadre of trained and skilled specialists but rather of a good pilot who "the world [...] had never treated [...] kindly" (137), two "roisterers with thick wits and superb reflexes" (137) good for such a suicide mission but "worthless anywhere else" (133), and the sole survivor of the previous attempt to contact the Qumedni, "a conscript [...] sunk in apathy and self-pity" (133). GalFed evidently has difficulty getting good help. This idea recurs frequently in GalFed stories; while there are many noble and competent figures, the bureaucracy and limited resources of GalFed all too often permit negligence and incompetence.

Such a crew cannot of course prevail in any conflict with such a superior antagonist as the Qumedni, and indeed only one crew member from all previous attempts to initiate contact with them has survived the experience. Military prowess will not win the day (though conflict of various kinds is important in many of the GalFed stories, it rarely is central). GalFed is not defined by imperial power. Instead, this first story suggests strongly not the determination of intrepid heroes against impossible odds but rather dogged adherence to duty required by distant politicians, and the folly, or at least the debatable value, of those requirements as the defining trait of GalFed heroes. Towers has not even been able to choose his own crew, who have been kept in ignorance of the true nature of their challenge until they have already reached the planet Qumedon. The question of why this apparently hostile species ought to be contacted, at the cost of however many crews it takes to establish contact, is almost pro forma: the Qumedni have amazingly advanced technology for which humans would like to trade. Trade, clearly, is central to the future world Gotlieb imagines, as the story refers to the standard contract arrangements with other worlds. However, Gotlieb acknowledges the absurdity of this proposition in this case by having the characters note more than once that humans can have little to offer to energy beings with telepathy and psi powers; indeed, Phelps answers the question of what the humans have to offer with the mordant "beads, maybe" (145). Here in deep space, the humans are clearly not analogous to the Europeans arriving in North America with meretricious baubles with which they can make highly advantageous purchases but are instead themselves in the precarious position of attempting to enter into trade with a vastly superior power. Phelps notes, after the humans do in fact manage to negotiate with the Qumedni, "'We surprised them a little, caught their respect somehow, and they want to know why. Now we've really got to be careful. As soon as they know—' he drew a finger across his throat" (145). Earlier, Towers reflects that "he had seen enough of Earth's meddling with planetary peoples to stuff his craw" (135), hardly an endorsement of galactic colonialism, and the end of the story suggests, as "the first fine warp thread between Earth and Qumedon" (147) is spun, that this time the meddling might bring more cost than profits.

The first GalFed story, then, presents a rather bumbling and inefficient organization forming an uneasy economic alliance with a vastly more powerful neighboring alien species. The protagonists succeed, after a fashion, but there is little sense that success in this case is much better than failure; there is a sense, instead, that humanity's fate is now tied to a much greater power, much the way, we might argue, that Canada's is tied to the United States. The danger and the cost, rather than the profit, of pursuing an accommodation with the Qumedni emerges as the story's concern. Though the Qumedni do feature in several other GalFed stories, notably the Ungrukh Chronicles, Gotlieb does not pursue the implications of this initial story in as pessimistic a direction as I suggest here. GalFed developed quickly in subsequent stories, even before the first GalFed novel, and came to manifest other Canadian traits besides this manifest discomfort with colonization.

"A Bone to Pick" (not included in either of Gotlieb's short story collections) is the first of Gotlieb's published stories to refer explicitly to GalFed, and the nature of the galactic organization is important to the development of the story.[7] Once again, we find flawed and limited protagonists on a virtually hopeless mission with inadequate resources or guidance. The Ghyrrm are a physically delicate people who decompose almost instantly upon death and to whom a GalFed crew has been sent to provide assistance. The story makes much of cultural difference and the distrust and even fear the humans feel for their alien hosts, though that the Ghyrrm have similar concerns is made clear as the story progresses. Indeed, multispecies interaction is a favorite Gotlieb theme, and she has created numerous memorable and very alien life forms, such as the formless Lyhhrt, or the Yrln, which resembles "a bright blue bathmat with a fringe at one end" (*Judgment* 127), or the allosaur-like Khagodi (appearing in several GalFed stories), or Chrystalloid life forms (in *Heart of Red Iron*), or the Qsaprinli, crawfish-like creatures "formed mainly as heads surrounded by limbs" (*Emperor, Swords, Pentacles* 68), and others. Despite a dizzying range of alien life forms, however, GalFed constitutes a community in which these aliens have at least theoretical equality under law and struggle to work together.

However, if the Qumedni are by nature incomprehensible aliens, the far more common attitude towards human/alien relations in Gotlieb's work is in the attempt to bridge the gap. The importance of this idea is present even in an extremely early story such as "A Bone to Pick," in which Gotlieb shows the human characters coming to a provisional understanding of the Ghyrrm in part by making connections to human history. Thinking about the Ghyrrm's physical infirmities early in the story, Kappstein recalls the phrase, "*One long disease*, as one human life had been described" (49). Later in the story, he recalls the source of the phrase, Johnson's *Lives of the Poets*, specifically the life of Pope,[8] which Johnson, dealing with Pope's physical debilitations, suggested must have been "a 'long disease'" (65). Kappstein then thinks, "Well, here was someone who must have had something in common with the Ghyrrm" (65).

Evident here is a recurrent Gotlieb theme, the importance of the materiality of the body. Gotlieb is not simplistic enough to suggest that biology is destiny, but she does frequently play on the centrality of one's physical, bodily reality. This is evident even in "A Grain of Manhood" and its focus on the gravid body. Frequent moments in Gotlieb's stories comment on the link between one's physical and psychological nature, and in a story of creatures whose physiology is as frail as is that of the Ghyrrm, it should not be surprising to find that the idea assumes importance. But it is important in relation to the humans as well as the aliens. For instance, Kappstein finds himself at one point reflecting on the contrast between body and mind: he wondered "why, when the skin, bones, and ligaments were formed in such a fine body with the usual sensitivity of the Creator, the mind could not have been equally comely" (63).

Further consideration of Pope and the similarities between how he protected his infirm body and how the Ghyrrm behave leads Kappstein to recognize that the Ghyrrm are no more horrific than humans are; all the GalFed crew have their own demons too. This realization gives him the push he needs to help come to an accommodation with the Ghyrrm's alien and frightening reality, though Gotlieb is not so optimistic as to suggest that some degree of understanding is sufficient to eradicate all problems: the story concludes, "'At least it is a beginning,' said Kappstein" (71)—a concluding sentiment to which Gotlieb returns in numerous works.

More important than the recognition in "A Bone to Pick" of the complexities of multiculturalism, though, is how the story establishes a contrast between the idea of GalFed and its reality. The secretiveness of the Ghyrrm, which has contributed significantly to the human distrust and fear, arises, we learn, from their own fear that the truth about their practices (they employ vivisection in attempts to understand their own anatomy, having no choice in the matter) will alienate GalFed: "we find [...] so many nobilities in your laws, such reverence for all forms of life, and such care in its preservation—" (68), they note, that they greatly desire to be included in the GalFed community. The GalFed symbol, "three small gold emblems [...]: a star, a ringed planet, a circle divided by cross, ancient symbol both of Earth and of Creation" (*Caliban* 25), is in keeping with the aspirations expressed in the Ghyrrm understanding of GalFed. The story's human protagonist, Lazarus Emmanuel Kappstein, gently points out, however, that "the codes of law you have studied represent the essence of GalFed's aspirations, rather than the tally of its achievements" (70), while thinking privately, in response to the Ghyrrm's idealistic view of human political ideals, "*soap of the purest Jewsfat*" (68).[9] Whatever GalFed's ideals may be, Gotlieb suggests, one would do well to view governmental ideals with skepticism. Space is too huge, and the range of cultures too wide, for any easily workable and stable political system to be possible. One is reminded of Canada's own uneasy mix of federal and provincial levels of government in GalFed's complex relationships with its member worlds.

Indeed, the sheer vastness of space, though not a subject on which Gotlieb dwells, is crucial to an understanding of GalFed's difficulties in monitoring its worlds. Stories such as "Monkey Wrench" or "Phantom Foot" or "Blue Apes" or "Tauf Aleph" address the implications of isolation. Gotlieb has commented on the fact that Canadian literature has "a distinctive voice, a voice—like that of all Canada—wider-ranging than the English one because of our vastness east, west, and north" ("Alien at the Feast" 198). One is frequently reminded of the scale of space in the GalFed stories. The 1968 story "Monkey Wrench" (originally published in *Amazing* as "Rogue's Gambit"),[10] for instance, begins by telling us that GalFed has an enormous communications system "spread throughout the Galaxy, its orbit pacing the stars"; so far, GalFed might seem like a vast empire. The sentence continues, however, to note of that vast network, "it has not yet completed one twenty-millionth of that orbit" (110). GalFed may be vast, but it is also, in cosmic terms, tiny and therefore of necessity powerless. GalFed may have noble ideals and good intentions, but the sheer scale of a galactic organization militates against its success. There is too much space, there are too many places to hide, for GalFed to offer a utopian network with peace, happiness, and prosperity for all.

In "Monkey Wrench," the vastness of space and the paucity of humans available to manage it is not only a recurring motif but key to the plot. Doing all that needs to be done is stressful because "space is vast and lives by comparison are few and short. There was a chronic lack of manpower whether it came from Sol or Betelgeuse" (114). Space, we are told, is an environment so inimical that it can drive people mad; figures such as the protagonist Stannard, who likes the isolation, are rare. People are more likely to find the cold vastness of space unsettling, even literally maddening. The monkey wrench of the title is tied to this idea; Stannard recalls once subduing "a crewman who had gone spacemad and was laying about him with a wrench; but he never spoke of the incident, because it made him uneasy that a good, level-headed man could go wild working in the cool, quiet conditions he himself loved so well" (114).

The story deals with a crisis on a communications satellite. The satellite has stopped communicating, and Stannard, the closest thing to the local law, investigates, accompanied by a doctor and a pilot, Bugasz, who seems to have a greater interest in the satellite's man and wife team than he should. They find Hendricks, the satellite manager, dead and his wife missing. The debilitating influence of life in space is metaphorized in the story in Schoebl's disease, a parasitic infection akin to Elephantiasis that attacks the body, causing disfigurement. This physical disfigurement is contrasted with the mental disfigurement that can infect those isolated in the empty, sterile environment of space. Iris is a beauty who contracts the disease; when it disfigures her, she feels she can only marry a man who is also ugly. Hendricks is also physically disfigured; his features are asymmetrical and misaligned: "It was as if a noble marble head had been smashed by a child and glued together to escape detection" (116). But if Iris's disease is externally caused and no reflection on her character or moral nature, Hendricks's external ugliness reflects his nature: "'He was ugly,' the doctor notes, 'perhaps there was no one else in the world, he thought, who would have him ... such a person would be an ugly person inside, too, I think?'" (136). Despite Iris's disfigurement, though, "there was nothing twisted about her, inside" (137).

The real threat, though, is not twisted human passions like jealousy but rather the interpenetration of human and environment, specifically the computer that is essential to the station's function. Hendricks smashes much of the equipment at the station with a monkey wrench, but he himself is the real spanner in the works, as his own madness loops back into the computer.[11] The computer has become infected by Hendricks's mental imbalance, as Iris became infected by the virus: "Hendricks, damned fool, tangling himself up with his machine. People crying out of space for help. I, I, I. Hendricks, the I, was dead. Hendricks, the ugly man, Prince Frog, twisting his absurd passion for a beautiful young woman into the clean skeins of wires and transistors [...]" (130). Unlike the Frog Prince, though, he is irrecoverable.

In fact, in GalFed any peace or prosperity is hard-won and only precariously maintained. Numerous GalFed stories deal not with GalFed's colonists conquering or even taming alien environments but rather with their failure to do so, again a trend more evident earlier in the uncollected short stories than in the novels. Uncollected early stories such as "Planetoid Idiot" and "A Bone to Pick," as well as later ones like "Blue Apes" and "Tauf Aleph," and most of the GalFed novels, are set on worlds on which either colonies have failed or on which eking out a bearable life is a challenge. Furthermore, in GalFed even one's own home world may be a hostile environment, so much so that life is precarious, if not verging on extinction. This is the case in "A Bone to Pick" and "Planetoid Idiot," for instance, and one could make a case for the artificial environment that serves as the primary setting in "Monkey Wrench," which Gotlieb early in the story compares to "an anarchist's bomb, with a complex fuse of antennas for radar, maser and radio" (111). In the novels, the Ungrukh have an inimical home world (though in fact they are not native to it) and are dependent on GalFed almost for their very survival, while Dahlgren's world, Barrazan V, "has been scarred by hundreds of defeated colonies" (*Heart* 1) and indeed has been purchased by GalFed as an inimical environment in which scientists can work "to modify genetic strains of their home species to live on that world and many others just as repellant" (*Caliban* 8). Hellish as Barrazan V is, it is nevertheless preferable for some species than their home worlds, such as the Yefni, whose world "is one of sulfur and brimstone" (*Heart* 29). As Gotlieb notes after thus likening the Yefni home world to hell, though, "any kind of life is a miracle anywhere" (*Heart* 29); it is in the nature of life to be almost impossible. Home, in GalFed, may be where the heart is, but life is not easy. Gotlieb has noted that Canada is a nation of immigrants, and the search for a livable place figures large in her fiction; one must adapt to an intractable space, not force it into one's own image.

GalFed Central itself is a case in point. GalFed may administer "the affairs of thousands of worlds," but it does so not from "the hectic and dangerous center of the galaxy, but fitted into one of its armpits" (*Heart* 16). GalFed Central is made up of the twelve worlds of the sun Fthel, "but no more than six of the twelve planets are useful" (16). GalFed Central itself is no paradise but a plodding and hectic (if one can be both at once) bureaucracy, so the worlds under its administration can hardly be ideal. Indeed, there is a distressing mercantilism about GalFed. Economic exchange is the basis of its relationship with member worlds, and that economic concerns can be put ahead of social ones is a real danger in GalFed. In "Planetoid Idiot," for instance,

> It is better to believe, and probably the truth, that GalFed would have come to the aid of the Xirifri even if the survey ship had not discovered that the seas of Xirifor produced oysters that secreted pearls, huge, baroque and blue, more beautiful than any known before. Whatever the truth was, the pearls at least gave the peoples of the planet something to bargain with [9].

GalFed is inevitably interested in money, as money is something it always lacks. Even in the twelve worlds of GalFed Central, underfunding is a problem. The Port Central hospital there is a case in point: "because it was run by GalFed, [it] was naturally underfunded" (*Heart* 44). In fact, GalFed undertakes another expedition to the horrific Barrazan V in *Heart of Red Iron* primarily because doing so is underwritten by private financing—not quite Colombo's Crown Corporation model, but close. Frederick Havergal wishes to visit the system, ostensibly to continue the failed experiments of Edvard Dahlgren, and "he wants to pay quite a lot of money, to [Sven] and ... us" (17)—that is, to GalFed. Since GalFed also still needs habitats for colonists (especially ones whose home worlds are hellish), as well as needing money, they are willing to take Havergal's money and send GalFed employees back to this hellish world.

I noted the example of "Planetoid Idiot" in relation to GalFed's mixture of aid and profit; another example is Han Li, a profoundly mentally and physically handicapped young girl who "had been saved from the triple injustices of starvation, mental incapacity, and growth-hormone deficiency by a talent as mysterious as it was useful" (*Heart* 34), in that she is telepathic with Chrystalliod aliens. Would Han Li have been saved from a life of brutal suffering if she lacked this talent? Gotlieb implies not. Indeed, we first meet Han Li as she is undergoing the training and education necessary for her to become a GalFed *employee*; her talent is only useful if it can be used, of course, so Han Li must learn in order to "work for Galactic Federation" (35). Whether one should be heartened or disheartened that GalFed is not a welfare state is perhaps subject to debate.

This must make GalFed sound like a pretty unpleasant Galactic empire to inhabit, and Gotlieb's protagonists do often suffer much and profit little for doing so. Jane Donawerth's description of GalFed as a "capitalistic imperialistic megacorporation" (*Frankenstein's Daughters* 22) might seem apropos. However, I've also touched on other aspects of GalFed. While GalFed is certainly capitalistic, describing it as imperialistic is unfair. GalFed finds worlds and establishes colonies, and it exploits the resources of its worlds, but GalFed's relationship with its colony worlds and members is not coercive but persuasive and diplomatic. Indeed, one of GalFed's big problems is that it lacks the sort of imperial power that might make dictatorship possible but that also could empower GalFed to prevent the sort of exploitation and suffering that worlds and factions create on their own. GalFed does not ride into its worlds (or worlds that are not part of the Federation) to free the enslaved peoples. It negotiates and bargains. Where possible, within its limits, it improves things. In exchange for their brains being bottled, for instance, the Ungrukh attain the possibility not merely to survive but to thrive as a species. Like Canada, GalFed does what it can in dealing with fractious federated members with limited resources. The reality may often be problematic, but the ideals are admirable.

This point returns us to the first explicit GalFed story, in which the boneless Ghyrrm admire GalFed's noble laws. As Emmanuel Kappstein points out to them, there is a gap between the ideal and the reality. The reality, as we have seen, is limited, often unsuccessful and capable of committing great wrongs even with good intentions. But the reality also aspires to the ideal. Kappstein may be cynical and flawed himself, but he is also, in a way, Emmanuel: the savior. Gotlieb's GalFed is not unique in its multiculturalism, but its multiculturalism was more rare in the 1960s, when GalFed was created, and its granting of absolute equality to all sentient creatures is a crucial feature. GalFed progresses towards the ideal, much as many of Gotlieb's characters do, especially nonhuman ones. Mod Dahlgren the android becomes a citizen of GalFed. Spartakos the robot is instrumental in helping genetically created slaves, and even functions as a sort of surrogate mother for an embryonic Lyhhrt before also earning citizenship. O/G helps revivify a dying tradition and create a modest paradise. In GalFed little is accomplished, perhaps, but much is possible. What could be more Canadian?

GalFed's groundwork is laid in many of Gotlieb's early stories before being fully constructed in later stories and her novels, but a handful of other early, and mostly uncollected, short stories provide further insight into Gotlieb's interests and ideologies. Her third and sixth published stories, "No End of Time" and "Valedictory," are rare time travel stories (time travel features only tangentially in the Galfed stories, as an element in "Son of the Morning," the first Ungrukh story, which also makes up the first movement of *A Judgment of Dragons*); "The Dirty Old Man of MaxSec" is a bit of an oddity, a sort of hybrid dystopian/SF thriller tale.[12]

"No End of Time" brings the distant past and the distant future together.[13] The story is set in a far future world, not Earth but rather an intergalactic system known as Omegga, with several planets; Earth is the Mother of Worlds in this universe. It is a world in which life is highly regulated; the name "Omegga" suggests ending or finality, and indeed the culture (such as it is) of this world has stagnated. People are alienated from the fleshly and the animal. Though they still inhabit bodies, sexual difference exists merely for reasons of minor variations in personality, not as a biological necessity. It is all very mathematical, very antiseptic, and very unforgiving of even minor deviations from the accepted norm:

> All babies come from the store of protoplasm in the creche. They're nurtured in groups of ten and a dekurion is assigned to each group, or dekad. We still produce boys and girls equally for the minute personality differences between the sexes, because they give some harmless variety. At birth-time every dekad is examined carefully and if there's one imperfect child the dekad is scrapped. There are standards of weight, shape, and measurement [115].

Note the implication that variety could be harmful. Certainly, it is rigorously, even ruthlessly controlled, with an entire crop of babies wiped out if even one fails to measure up. The result is a world in which individuals are virtually indistinguishable from each other, anything linked with animal function is viewed with disdain if not disgust (the protagonist must wear a synthesized version of animal-based clothing to appear normal to the figure plucked out of time, and finds this disgusting, even though she knows what she is wearing is synthetic rather than genuine animal product), and deviation from the norm can cost one the right to reproduce and lead to exile.

The Omeggans have developed a machine, the Chronotome, which they can use to bring objects from the past into their world, for their own entertainment. One uses this machine to pluck Socrates into the future, at the instant before his death. Socrates is, in a way, what the world needs: a criminal. As Ashael, the protagonist, notes, in the pre–Omegga civilizations, "there were many condemned criminals who became the Anointeds and Enlighteneds of their people after their deaths: seminal minds, heroes of thought and action" (108). In Gotlieb, the choice of the word "seminal" in such a context can hardly be accidental, suggesting as it does the planting of a seed. In a highly regulated world where reproduction is controlled by the state, the idea assumes even greater weight. Ashael's growing fascination with Socrates leads her to question the premises on which her society is based, to see beneath its facade. The seed metaphor is solidified when Ashael later notes, "He had planted my mind with a fearful curiosity and budding flowers of love and hate" (117). Socrates questions, especially, the removal of the body from consideration as problematic: "I've always believed that the further Man is able to go away from the needs of the body, the nearer he will be to the heavens ... but in Omegga, where flesh is nothing, you haven't yet been able to see the faces of the Gods" (117–18). As she often does, Gotlieb makes the materiality of the body of key importance; abstraction from the flesh does not lead to a superior state of existence.

This is therefore a story of the inquisitive mind as criminal, hardly a unique circumstance in SF. It is, however, unusual to see the Socratic method specifically identified as criminal. Socrates can't imagine having any more success in this world than he had in his own; as he says, "I would ask a question too many and end up in a prison here, as well" (122). It is also unusual that Gotlieb does not create a dichotomy between an idealized past and repressive future, or vice versa; Socrates's ancient world is hardly lionized, and the Omeggan world has its benefits as well as its limitations. It offers virtual immortality in a crime-free world to its citizens. But it does not offer death, which Socrates desires, and Ashael grants him—not by killing him, but by not reanimating him when his body dies. To the Omeggans, this is a criminal act, and she is expelled from her dekad for it and denied the right to reproduce—but otherwise not punished. She is left recording her narrative in the hopes that some future savage, in a post–Omeggan world, will be able to learn something from it; a woman who learned something from an ancient savage (from her perspective) tries to pass something of that lesson forward to a future imagined savage, perhaps planting the seed for a different path for that unknown and unimagined future culture to grow. The lesson is to retain the animal; Ashael exits lying with Krisomer, "the length of our bodies touching in the rare human contact of Omegga. There is nothing else to do in this world" (126).

"Valedictory," Gotlieb's other early time-travel story, shares little with "No End of Time,"[14] taking a different perspective on how past may inform the future. This slight story imagines a future in which time travel is used for purposes of historical research by a group called Timesearch, and the protagonist is a young woman training to be such a researcher. One of the tests for potential researchers is to visit a period of their choice and discover some important piece of new material. Time travel has risks for the traveler, as well, since the temporal dislocation leads to a sense of detachment so profound that the investigators are not even entirely sure that one's full self makes the trip:

> We're not even sure that the whole physical body can go back in time [...]. When you're back there you feel an extremely strong sense of detachment—perhaps because the surroundings are so far removed from your everyday life, and it's certainly something you never experienced, but it's back there waiting for you [...] [47].

Given the story's invocation of the potential dangers of disrupting the past or of suffering a profound detachment, coupled with the quest-like narrative element—the narrator even refers to having "three tests to pass, like somebody in a stock fairy-tale" (48), this reference itself being almost a stock Gotlieb item—the narrative seems to be establishing the possibility for a typical time travel adventure in which the hero's actions have potentially dire consequences as she reclaims some key piece of information lost to time, while perhaps being lost to time herself. Indeed, the narrator almost does become lost. However, rather than an Ashael, who comes to question the foundations of her society, the unnamed protagonist of "Valedictory" has a far smaller revelation and accomplishment.

Her desire is to visit the time period of her own childhood for reasons she cannot entirely grasp herself, but perhaps to tell her younger self, "Look, kid, you're having a tough time now, but it'll turn out all right" (50), since her recollection of her own past is of how tough she had it. Time travel here could become a sort of bootstrapping on a far smaller (and more plausible) level than in Heinlein's "By His Bootstraps" (1941)—not complete self-creation via the exploitation of time paradoxes but rather a gentle boost to the self from a superior vantage point. However, rather than the future informing the past, the story instead inverts this concept of self-help by having the narrator discover that her young self is *not* living the life of misery she remembers. Or, perhaps more accurately, she has remembered only the bad, not the good, from her childhood. This is a revelation, making her see the world of her past anew, both literally—she is there as a time traveler, after all—but also psychologically. Ironically, the shock of finding a younger self with complex "reality and vitality" (51) almost disorients the narrator enough for her to forget how to find her way back to the future (the closest thing to conventional drama in the story). Only her immersion in her forgotten memories—all the good she had forgotten in "[t]he injustice I had committed against the past" (52)—allows her to reorient herself and find her way back. Justice here, in contrast to the justice meted out in "No End of Time," is purely private and personal. Time travel becomes a means of self-reclamation.

Gotlieb's final story of the 1960s, "The Dirty Old Men of Maxsec," was published in the November 1969 issue of *Galaxy*, and it represents one of Gotlieb's rare cover appearances, where its placement in the upper left, just below the magazine title, gives it pride of place and primary newsstand visibility—in an issue also featuring the first installment of Robert Silverberg's *Downward to the Earth* and Harlan Elison's "Pennies Off a Dead Man's Eyes," as well as the conclusion of *Dune Messiah*—good SF company to keep. This odd spy pastiche is one of Gotlieb's most anomalous stories. Though set in an unspecifiedly distant future, it is one of the few stories that does not, apparently, fit in the GalFed universe; certainly there is no explicit or overt reference to any of the peoples or planets of that universe, nor do its subject or thematic concerns fit into the typical GalFed scenario. It is the only Gotlieb story to make concerted use of dystopian motifs. Furthermore, though literary self-consciousness and intertextuality are major motifs in Gotlieb's work, this is the only story that is self-conscious to the point of verging on metafiction, in its commentaries on narrative tropes and on the use of story to guide perception.

The protagonist, Fenthree, is a programmer whose job is to set the parameters for computer-generated children's stories. He is also a part-time spy (shades, perhaps, of Ian Fleming, real-life spy and spy fiction master, as well as the author in 1964 of the children's novel *Chitty-Chitty-Bang-Bang*, the film version of which came out the year before this novelette was published). Fenthree is sent, much against his inclination, on a mission to Maxsec, a prison facility that seems to function by virtue of isolation from the urban world of the dominant culture, rather than because it is walled or enclosed. Rather than a prison contained within the larger world, it functions instead as a sort of alternate social environment to Fenthree's familiar world, on the well-established model common in dystopian fiction of contrasting social models. Typically, though, Gotlieb plays with the conventions of dystopianism, with neither model ultimately emerging as ideal. Whether the story is rendered more complex or less focused by its additional metafictional play is perhaps open to debate, but the end result is arguably a qualified success rather than one of Gotlieb's great works.

Fenthree's society is, like that of the Omeggans in "No End of Time," in some respects what might be conceived of as an ideal. It is one in which a rejuvenation process allows humans to live for hundreds of years. However, its dystopian traits predominate. Even character names, which are consistently based in numbers—Fenthree, McAllifive, etc.—suggest a dystopian landscape such as that in Zamyatin's *We* (1921), in which individuality is overwritten. Despite the apparent benefits of extended life, citizens live in crowded and straitened circumstances: Fenthree "rubbed his eyes wide open, peered at the clock, and reached to punch the chord on the keyboard that would allow him simultaneous possession of the kitchen and bathroom for twenty minutes. He paid a lot of rent for the twice-a-day privilege. At other times he used them singly. Right then they had been sealed and folded in some storage space in the vast building" (54).

Ironically, the prison he infiltrates is a place of greater wealth than the "free" world. Maxsec is a sort of "artificial oasis in the midst of an eternal desert" (71). It may be artificial, but the desert by implication is the outside world. Furthermore, "the gardens were green and fresh and the air was pure and gold, not sodium yellow and fluorine blue" (71); the prison is more idyllic than the free city. The prison also has more luxurious living space than the free world: "The ceiling was high—the floor was far below. Where [Fenthree] had come from, six tiny expensive apartments would have been crammed in the intervening space. Squeezing his way from kitchen to bedroom in his amorphous City LivUnit he had not been able to imagine this kind of dwelling place" (61).

Furthermore, there is something Orwellian about the free city. Fenthree is referred to as a volunteer, for instance, but we quickly learn that this is a euphemism: "The Obligations Act had been passed many years ago and no one had volunteered for anything since. The force of habit and the glory of [McAllifive's] rhetoric had put him seventy-five years out of date" (55). Calling a conscript a "volunteer" is on par with calling the war office the Ministry of Peace. Nor is there much sense that the government is competent. Again, as in "No End of Time," extended human life has led to stagnation and the loss of novelty or original ideas: "We haven't had a new idea for three hundred years," McAllifive reports (55). This manifests itself amusingly (and metafictionally) in the fact that Fenthree is sent on his mission in a cliché spy outfit rather than in something appropriate to the environment and the job: "the fleabrains at HQ had not considered how cold it would be. Spies had always worn black jerseys—at least ever since anybody could remember" (54). Indeed, and ironically, part of Fenthree's mission in the prison is to find "new ideas [...], new combinations of ideas, new experiences" (57) because, in fact, the government realizes that it has been wrong, but it cannot so admit; the repressive system, including MaxSec, must be maintained, even if in fact MaxSec offers more in the way of hope for progress than the "free" world.

MaxSec is a prison for criminals, but also for dissidents; those who have made the mistake of speaking too vociferously against the regime end up there. Others have chosen the literal prison of MaxSec over the metaphorical prison of the City, a place where the fear of aging and death has led to repression. The prisoners are working on developing new science that will reverse aging on the one hand, and neutralize the current rejuvenation formula on the other, to disrupt the current repressive model. However, despite the ways it seems an environment superior to the free world, it is not really like the utopian contrast held up in the typical dystopian work. Gotlieb does not provide an either/or dichotomy. Fenthree realizes that "MaxSec may have been busy but it was not cheerful and vital, as McAllifive had been led to believe. It was running on pain, hate and anger—conditions of life the City could not live with or tolerate for humans anywhere. It would have to find new ones or die" (94).

Nevertheless, his experiences in the prison change Fenthree, much as the typical dystopian protagonist's discovery of an alternative to the state he accepted without question at the beginning is transformative in dystopian fiction and often turns the good citizen into a rebel. When Fenthree makes an idle remark to the helicopter pilot taking him away from the prison about how the prisoners don't seem any more fond of the idea of dying than do the inhabitants of the City, the following exchange occurs:

> The pilot gulped and said, "Hey, watch the language there, fella. That could get you into bad trouble."
>
> Fenthree stared at him. Uneasiness swept into him like a cold sweat. The words had not seemed out of order. Had he changed somehow in the scarcely more than two days he had been away? [93–94].

Even a brief exposure to an alternate model causes Fenthree to rethink his ideology, and he decides to manipulate his report, using his fiction-making skills to try to mislead the world of the City, thereby helping to bring about change from within. In effect, he becomes a sort of MaxSec Fifth Columnist, working from inside the machine to help gum it up:

> McAllifive wanted a story from him. He thought about that. And about his experiences as a coder of children's books—about how he took random plot elements and fed them into a machine and got stories neat as strings of sausages in return.
>
> He wondered what the machine could do with that list of the products and equipment sent to MaxSec. He wondered what he could do with it, since he knew how the process worked.
>
> His mind began to spin, tentatively at first, then busily. To do what he planned would take courage—perhaps more than MaxSec thought he had. He grinned [95].

The story ends on this note, rounding out Gotlieb's 1960s short fiction output with a tale that ends up explicitly commenting on how fiction might infiltrate the minds of readers and encourage change. Gotlieb's fiction is not usually this self-conscious, but it is always conscious of the possibility for change and eager to help bring it about.

These early stories, then, lay the groundwork for Gotlieb's subsequent career. Some, such as "Valedictory," "No End of Time," or "The Dirty Old Men of Maxsec," represent experiments or paths ultimately not taken, though even in these stories we can see the seeds that will flourish later. "A Grain of Manhood," by contrast, is literally seminal. Though not necessarily a GalFed story, nothing in the narrative prevents it from fitting into the GalFed universe, and it lays out some of Gotlieb's career-defining thematic interests. Key here is Gotlieb's interest in reproduction and maternity, as reflected in Lela's odd pregnancy; also key is her interest in the relationship between self and body. The tale's literary allusiveness also speaks to the density and sophistication of Gotlieb's best work. The most significant stories, though, are the ones explicitly set in the GalFed universe, in which Gotlieb lays the foundations for the fictional environment that was to dominate her career, being the universe in which all but one of her published SF novels and many of her short stories are set. GalFed becomes the landscape in which Gotlieb explored most fruitfully her interests in essentialism versus constructivism in relation to identity, the limits and borders of identity, and the central role reproduction plays in cultural and self-definition, as well as the problems and complexities inherent in social organization. As a sort of galactic empire replete with sentient life forms of various kinds but lacking a powerful, autocratic central authority, GalFed allows for diverse thought experiments. However, Gotlieb's major work of the 1960s, *Sunburst*, is not set in the GalFed universe, despite exploring many of the themes Gotlieb elaborates in her GalFed tales. We will turn to that novel now.

Two

Sunburst

Sunburst, Gotlieb's first novel, was serialized in *Amazing* in 1964 (volume 38, issues 3, 4, and 5; the March, April, and May issues) in abridged form. One of Gotlieb's rare SF magazine cover appearances, the story is mentioned on only the first of the three successive *Amazing* covers. The editorial head note in the March issue introduces the novel thus:

> Not since, perhaps, Stapledon's *Odd John* and Mark Clifton's poignant *Star Bright* have we read as gripping and insightful a story of children with strange powers. Those in Phyllis Gotlieb's violent and touching narrative are not all supermen—some, indeed, are sub-men. But all are too human [26].

This is an accurate enough description—it avoids, at least, the hyperbole of the first paperback edition—but demonstrates that from the beginning what the book was about was not really understood. The novel is not about super- or sub-human characters, though those concepts certainly are addressed in the novel. The concept of the superhuman is rejected, but not simply by the convenient device of treating the strangely powered as monstrous. The reference here to Stapledon's *Odd John* (1935), indeed, helps contextualize the novel. *Odd John* is a book that plays on the super/subhuman possibilities of the mutated child, and it is an intertext explicitly invoked by Gotlieb, though she challenges its depiction of the superhuman by adopting some of the novel's elements while modifying others as she stakes out her unique territory.

Sunburst remains Gotlieb's best-known and arguably her most highly regarded novel. It has been published in multiple editions, notably in a 1977 edition from Fitzhenry & Whiteside, a facsimile edition of the Fawcett paperback designed for use in grade schools (including a brief introduction, chapter by chapter study questions, general questions, suggested essay topics, and suggested additional readings), a 1978 Gregg Press edition (also a facsimile of the

Fawcett edition but including a longer useful and insightful introduction by Elizabeth A. Lynn), and a 2000 edition published by Bakka Books, with a foreword by Terence M. Green,[1] as well as in a French translation (under the title *Psycataclysme* [1976]). In addition, it has received occasional academic attention, such as Douglas Barbour's consideration of it in relationship to Gotlieb's poetry, or Dianne Newell and Victoria Lamont's discussion of it in relationship to post–Armageddon SF by women (though the novel is not, strictly speaking, post–Armageddon, as the nuclear disasters that have caused children to develop remarkable abilities have been carefully contained; most of the world remains unaffected). Its importance to Canadian SF is reflected in the fact that the juried Sunburst Award for Excellence in Canadian Literature of the Fantastic (established in 2001) is named after Gotlieb's novel and presents cash awards in two categories, adult and young adult.

David Ketterer's point, cited earlier, that Gotlieb's Canadianness is reflected in the position she occupies, mediating between the pessimism of British SF and American power-fantasy SF as exemplified by A. E. Van Vogt, is perhaps a good beginning point for a consideration of *Sunburst*. The comparison to *Slan* is illuminating; *Slan* and *Sunburst* both fall squarely within the general category of novels of the superhuman child and both are superhuman bildungsromans,[2] but they do, as Ketterer notes, present fundamentally different conceptions of the superhuman as hero. What Ketterer does not comment on, and what I would argue serves even more clearly as a marker of Gotlieb's Canadianness than her compromise between optimism and pessimism, is her compromise in the figure of Shandy Johnson between the horror of the nuclear monster and the wonder of the nuclear superhuman.[3] Shandy is not superior to *Homo sapiens* in any of the spectacular ways—either positive or negative—normally associated with stories of super-powered humans (especially super-powered children). Instead, Shandy's superiority resides in her slow maturation and her manifest emotional and intellectual balance; if she is super in any way, she is super*normal*. A more Canadian ideal of human evolution is difficult to imagine.

Regardless of its Canadianness, *Sunburst* is a significant novel in the evolution of stories of superhumans. The idea of the superhuman has been widely and repeatedly explored in SF; as Casey Fredericks notes, "The concept of the superhuman has remained central to speculative fiction" (122), while Erik S. Rabkin has identified Olaf Stapledon's *Odd John* as

> The fountainhead of all those SF works, like A.E. van Vogt's *Slan* (1940), Theodore Sturgeon's *More Than Human* (1953), and Robert A. Heinlein's *Stranger in a Strange Land* (1961), which show mankind stepped up to a higher consciousness in which

individuals can merge their thinking with that of their fellows in order to achieve a new order of mind, a group mind. Like the protagonists in those other novels, and like Frankenstein's demon, John is persecuted for his oddity and superiority; indeed, John is finally destroyed [239].

Van Vogt's *Slan* is just one example of such an exploration which predates Gotlieb's by over 20 years, but it is hardly the first such novel, nor is it Gotlieb's most direct influence, though as one of the best-known such novels, it makes a handy comparator in general terms.[4] A few basic assumptions are common to such stories. First, the superhuman is invariably imagined as spectacularly different from the "dull normal," as Shandy defines the average human being. Van Vogt's Slans, for instance, are not only telepathic but also super-intelligent, super-strong, and tireless, and they differ visibly from humans, for they have golden tendrils on their heads. Second, the telepathic superhuman (Fredericks notes, "ESP attributes are introduced as an attribute of the superhuman by almost all the writers" [122]), despite a consistent treatment within SF narratives as sympathetic, remains "among the most effective monsters the genre has produced" (Wolfe, 217), consistently being seen by the normal humans within the story as a threat. Even when readers are not invited to share this perception that the superhuman is a threat, the *idea* of the threat represented by the superhuman is a constant feature of such texts. Third, the kinds of power associated with the superhuman (ESP, telekinesis, etc.), even if threatening to normal humans, are generally understood as advances beyond the level of normal humanity; indeed, the threat posed by the superhuman is as often as not the superseding of normal humanity, rather than the tyrannizing of humanity by those with superior powers. Van Vogt's Slans are feared as monsters but in fact represent the natural next level of human evolution; for instance, "the distinction between superiority and monstrosity is of course simply a matter of point of view," according to Mark Rose (179), though the point of view of the narrative and that of the characters within it will not necessarily agree. Fourth, such stories frequently explore how the human and superhuman can come to an accommodation; as Gary K. Wolfe suggests, "If the unknown mutation can be subsumed into a knowable pattern of evolution or history, the imbalance caused by the presence of such a creature is corrected" (221).

These general traits of the superhuman story are not absent from *Sunburst*. However, they are employed with both skill and care in unconventional ways. The superhumans in the novel are referred to as Dumplings by the normal humans, because of the dump in which they are contained to damp their powers. They are spectacularly powerful, possessed of a wide range of paranormal mental abilities; they are variously possessed of telepathic, teleportative, telekinetic, and pyrotic talents. Furthermore, they are not merely *perceived* as a threat by the novel's humans but are in fact genuinely dangerous: when the novel opens, they have been locked away for years, since their destructive rampage on the night they formed a telepathic gestalt, in a dump surrounded by an electronic field that dampens their abilities and protects the community of Sorrel Park, as well as the rest of the world, from further attack. So far, Gotlieb's novel lies well within the norm for novels of this type. However, in her handling of the idea of the superhuman's evolutionary superiority and in her handling of the necessity of human/superhuman compromise, Gotlieb twists and expands the conventions. She does so in large part by invoking only to problematize Olaf Stapledon's *Odd John* through her own protagonist, Shandy Johnson, who, in contrast to John and to Gotlieb's own superpowered children, possesses *no* super powers.

At one point, one of *Sunburst*'s characters, Helmi, herself a psi (and indeed pregnant, so with an especially compelling reason to wish to protect psis from non-psis) asks Shandy if she has read *Odd John*. She then briefly describes the scene in which John kills a police officer, since "in comparison with him, the man was an animal"; Shandy's response is to assert, "That's a filthy argument to base an ethic on" (111). Though many novels of the supernormal human being lie between these two books, many of the key elements of Gotlieb's treatment can be traced to Stapledon's work. However, Gotlieb interrogates Stapledon's underlying assumptions—and those made by many of the intervening texts—by offering an alternative to Stapledon's ultimately pessimistic vision of the supernormal as not merely superhuman but as necessitating a destruction of the human through transcendence of it. As Roy Arthur Swanson has noted, Stapledon's vision complicates a reader's response by making full sympathy with his protagonist difficult: "Readers will sympathize with Odd John as they wishfully contemplate the elevation that will transmute Homo sapiens into Homo superior. They will withhold their sympathy if they qualify their wish with an unwillingness to be what John actually is, that is, to be something other than human" (287). Swanson further points out that John becomes, from a human perspective, monstrous. John Kinnaird suggests that "we are made to identify with the hero even as we recognize that there is something terribly wrong, or at least morally problematical, in his actions, even at their most heroic" (56). This is not a comfortable model of the superhuman, and Stapledon is unusual in that he does not fall into the simple binary of the superhuman either as monster or superior, but rather something of an admixture of both. Nevertheless, Stapledon allows only two possibilities: either the supernormals will supplant humanity, because they are superior, or humanity will destroy them, because they are a threat. The only relationship possible, on anything other than an individual level, is antagonistic. Indeed, at one point, John asserts, "Well, if we could wipe out your whole species, frankly, we would" (121), in the same way that humans would destroy vermin or harmful animals such as wolves. John is to human as human is to animal—and he defines the human as a dangerous, predatory animal, at that.

Gotlieb does not ignore the monstrous possibilities of the "super" powers possessed by John, but she redefines them as associated not with transcendence but instead regression; the genuine supernormal will not, Gotlieb argues, transcend human morality but will instead direct its development. Nor does she ignore the negative aspects of humanity, that humans might be seen to represent as much a threat to survival as the superhumans might, albeit in different ways. Gotlieb's key modification, perhaps, is her bifurcation of John's elements, ascribing some to Shandy, some to the Dumplings, thereby allowing both the admirable and the monstrous to be retained but in different figures. In some key respects, Shandy and John are parallel characters. Even her surname—Johnson—suggests his name, a fact to which she draws attention near the end of the book when she looks in the mirror: "Hey, Odd Johnson," she jeered, "where's your coltish grace?" (157). She also shares with John a slow maturation process. John—and all the supernormals in *Odd John*—physically mature and age far more slowly than *Homo sapiens,* or *hom. sap.* as John dubs them, playing on the meaning of "sap" as fool or simpleton, rather harsher than Shandy's term "dull normals." As a child of four, for instance, John looks like "an extremely bright six-months infant" (9). Mentally, however, John is remarkably precocious. We learn, for instance, that he remembers his own birth, and a recurring motif in the novel is his frustration as his body does not keep up with his mental and psychological maturation. Shandy is similarly precocious mentally but slow physically. Her condition is referred to later in the novel as "extended foetalization" (120), and though she is thirteen years old, she has not yet shown signs of puberty. Also like John, however, her psychological development is accelerated; we are told that she had a fully developed personality by the age of 3½, and the only time she reports crying or being upset as a young child was "when my hands or body wouldn't work the way I wanted, or I couldn't find out something I wanted to know" (22–23). Both characters are defined in part by mental precociousness but physical retardation.

Furthermore, both Shandy and John take an anthropological approach to understanding the human race to which they only partially belong. John "set about studying our conduct and our motives, partly by questioning us, partly by observation," we are told (15). In his teens, especially, "this study became much more earnest and methodical than it had been, and took the form of a far-reaching examination of the normal species in respect of its nature, achievement and present plight" (53); "he had to behave as a naturalist who studies the habits of some dangerous brute by stalking it with field-glass and camera, and by actually insinuating himself among the herd under a stolen skin, and an assumed odour" (53–54). Shandy's unique feature—she is an Impervious, or Imper, as she is referred to in the novel,[5] one who can't be read by telepaths or even much noticed by anybody—makes her almost the ideal concealed observer. This unnoticeability is used by Shandy to observe her surroundings and other people to learn from them. Shandy repeatedly refers to Margaret Mead, even having a sort of refrain, "what would Margaret Mead have done" (29), which she repeats when she decides to solve the puzzle of the Dumplings: "She would find out what made Dumplings tick, how to handle them, what Margaret Mead would have done, and more. And when she had done that she would be a step closer to knowing what she herself was" (98).

Mead is an important touchstone for Shandy in the book. Even the code established to break the hypnotic control placed on several characters to prevent the Dumplings from being able to read them, during the search for them after they have escaped, comes from Margaret Mead: Urquhart tells Shandy,

> "The code-phrase is: *new insight carries new delight*. Something you wouldn't be likely to say over the back fence."
> "New insight carries new delight ... did you choose that?"
> He blinked. "No. Jason did. Why."
> "It's out of Margaret Mead." [...] "From a passage I liked very much. He knows I read her books, but I never mentioned that bit to him" [131–32].[6]

Margaret Mead was a significant anthropologist, not only for her groundbreaking studies but also as a popularizer of the anthropological approach to studying the human condition. By the time Gotlieb was writing *Sunburst*, Mead was a popular public intellectual. Her books were published in mass market paperback editions, she gave public lectures, she wrote advice columns in popular magazines, and she even wrote books on anthropology for children. Mead consistently turns to wonder and curiosity to describe humans' reaction to their environment, and the importance of such traits to the growth of knowledge. Shandy might have found such ideas in several places in Mead's work, but a likely place for the child reader to find them at the time the novel was written would have been in Mead's *People and Places*, an anthropological tour of the world designed for children. Her description of intellectual inquiry sounds very much like Shandy:

All through history man has wondered about many things and has tried to find satisfactory ways of explaining them. Wonder is very important, because if we never wondered, we would never get to the point of asking questions. Yet wonder may lead people to write poetry or to paint pictures or to pray, as well as to ask the kinds of questions about the world and themselves that can be answered by science. Science means asking a question and keeping that question in one's head while one watches, over and over again, what happens until one finds an explanation—watching and watching again to see if the explanation works [61].

Shandy watches and wonders, determined to discover how things work—to do what Margaret Mead would do.

As is perhaps clear from what we're told of John's and Shandy's anthropological endeavors, however, though their methods are similar their ends are different. Both study humans in part to understand themselves, but in John's case humanity is clearly the enemy. *Sunburst* also offers up an antagonistic relationship between normal (or "dull normal") humans and the psi-powered children; the Dumplings are, plot wise, the enemy in *Sunburst*. However, whereas John is one of the super-powered and allied with their perspective against the human, Shandy occupies a liminal space. She is not one of the Dumplings, allying herself with the human side in the conflict, but she also feels a kinship with the Dumplings, in contrast to John, who may be fond of individual humans but who has contempt for the species. Indeed, *Sunburst* stresses the connections between the Dumplings and the dull normals as well as the differences, whereas in *Odd John* the differences are ultimately irreconcilable.

This contrast links with the fact that both John and Shandy are defined, as well, as beings with some sense of destiny. Though John is not unique—there are numerous other supernormals with powers similar to his—he is unquestionably their leader, the one who develops the idea of the supernormals creating a new world. The book makes much, early on, of his sense of difference and of his sense that he is to become something, but he does not know what. For instance, in an early dialogue, when a character suggests John will go a long way, he replies, "I want to, terribly [...] but I don't know *which* way yet" (25). He's aware of his difference, but, he says, "I didn't clearly know what it was in *myself* that made me different from you" (30). Eventually he comes to feel that he is meant for some purpose or job: "*What* that job is I'm not yet sure about, and can't possibly explain, but it begins with something very *interior to me*. [...] I don't matter on my own account, but I have it in me to do something that does matter" (70). Shandy, similarly, is marked by a sense of otherness and potential. Even others recognize this in her. When Shandy protests that she has no psi, for instance, Urquhart notes that despite her age she is not yet physically mature, and continues, "Who knows what you might be able to do later?" (24). She wonders herself shortly afterward whether she might have a purpose despite not knowing what it is: "Just because *I* don't know what it is doesn't mean there may not be one hidden inside me" (31). This idea is echoed again and again in the book; even at the end, when it is determined that Shandy is indeed the true supernormal, the key point in the supernormal's development is defined as self-discovery: "To find out what he was" and then to find a place in society (155). The potential for Shandy to become something dangerous—like the Dumplings, or John—is hinted at early in the novel, but ultimately Shandy's relationship with *Hom. sap.* differs fundamentally from John's.

Despite this shared sense of destiny, or a job to fulfill, between Shandy and John, Gotlieb stakes out different territory with the concept. John ultimately determines that his purpose is to supercede humanity. He comes to see the supernormals as superior to *Hom. sap.* and expresses a willingness, even a desire, to eradicate humanity as humanity might eradicate pest animals: "*Homo sapiens* is at the end of his tether, and I'm not going to spend my life tinkering a doomed species," he says (70). Shandy, by contrast, comes to see the function of the supernormal as more or less just the sort of tinkering that John scorns. Rather than annihilating or superceding *Homo sapiens*, the genuine supernormal would strive to be inconspicuous, to fit in, and ultimately to bring about change incrementally, by being a member of society, marrying, and reproducing: "you'd want him to be an organic part of humanity, to give his qualities to his children—if he could transmit them" (152).

This model contrasts, of course, with the sheer destructiveness associated with the Dumplings, but it also contrasts with John's agenda of, at best, separation and ultimately replacement of *Hom. sap.* by his own species. In fact, as noted above, Gotlieb in a way splits John, making him and Shandy akin in some ways but making him and the other supernormals akin to the Dumplings in others. For instance, both Stapledon and Gotlieb use animal imagery in their books to some extent similarly but ultimately to different ends. The otherness of John and his cadre is frequently imaged in animal terms. His fingers, for instance, are described as "tentacles" (39) or, more grotesquely, he is described as having "tarantula hands"; he seems "something fiendish. Crouched and clutching, he seemed indeed a spider preparing to suck the life out of the tortured boy beneath him" (18). This comparison to a spider is repeated. The animals Stapledon selects for such comparisons are consistently ones that tend to inspire fear or revulsion in people, stressing John's physical grotesqueness or monstrosity. John and the other supernormals are explicitly likened to monstrosities several times; terms like "hideous" (18), "grotesque and repellant" (47), and "ghastly" (92) recur; one supernormal is described as "a freak" (111); another is literally a grotesque, combining human and animal features, having "no legs, and arms like a newt's arms" (92); they're described as a group as "goblins" (132) and their remote retreat is referred to as "an island of monsters" (135).

The comparator characters in *Sunburst* are the Dumplings, many of whom are similarly physically grotesque. Even one of the "good" psis, Jason Hemmer, is likened to a bull and a monkey (5) when we first meet him. One of the worst of the Dumplings, LaVonne, is "a dwarf with a twisted compressed body and a mind equally ugly" (36–37); Donatus Riordan "is a hunchback with *spina bifida* and the children called him Doydoy because of his awful stutter" (37). Shandy herself is not grotesque but imaged in terms that suggest physical oddness: "She was still a very tall cranelike girl, rather sallow, with narrow torso in a navy sweatshirt and long bluejean legs like articulated stovepipes. A high forehead and pointed chin gave her face the look of a brown egg poised on the small end..." (5). However, many of the Dumplings and other psis are physically normal, and even those others are more often othered metaphorically rather than literally. Gotlieb does associate physical animality, warping or at least oddness with the Dumplings, but she also associates it with Shandy and various other humans. For instance, we're told that Mrs. Baggs's "pig-face opened in a grin, remarkably like LaVonne's" (96). There are numerous other examples, but this one is especially telling as it makes a dull normal a reflection of a Dumpling—but not in a way that suggests opposition so much as kinship. The dull normals and the psis are not poles apart as they are in *Odd John*.

Furthermore, and even more significantly, *Odd John* treats the supernormals as monstrous, but stresses that they are monstrous from a human perspective; humans are, from the supernormals' perspective, mere animals. Hence John's willingness to kill the policeman or to consider simply annihilating humanity. He compares wiping out humans with humans killing "wolves or tigers so that the far brighter spirits of men may flourish" (121)—John and his ilk being, in this construction, as superior to humans as humans are to, say, wolves. This notion is extremely common in fiction about the development of superhumans; they are almost inevitably superior to, better than, mere humans. The psis in *Sunburst* are monstrous from a human perspective as well, but this is not, or not merely, the subjective matter it is in *Odd John*. The novel articulates a theory that those with psi powers are on some level atavisms, throwbacks to an earlier stage of development; they represent regression, not progress. John would kill humans as if they were no more than wolves; in *Sunburst*, the Dumplings manifest as a pack, complete with a top dog. They *are* the wolves, in a way.

Gotlieb, however, refuses to accept the ethic of *Odd John*. Helmi, the psi who reminds Shandy of Stapledon's novel, speaks from the perspective of a psi—the superior being from *Odd John's* perspective. She suggests, therefore, that the psis in *Sunburst* might reasonably choose to act similarly—and given that the dull normals have imprisoned most of them, her taking such an antagonistic view should not be surprising. Shandy, however, rejects the premise. Rather than seeing such an act as merely an act of rational self-preservation from dangerous inferior creatures, Shandy points out, "'In John's own terms, first he baited an animal, and then he killed it because its rage endangered him.' She snorted. 'No wonder his species ended up blowing themselves up!'" (111). Rather than the binary opposition between human and superhuman, Gotlieb presents a third thing, a different model of the supernormal, not as possessed of fantastic abilities such as telepathy, telekinesis and so on, but rather possessed of intelligence and morality; the supernormal would be defined by a "stable moral equilibrium" (152), in contrast to the immoral, amoral, or even sociopathic characteristics that define the Dumplings and, arguably, John and his compatriots in *Odd John*. Here's John, commenting on how he was coming to view humanity as he matured: "I was living in a world of phantoms, or animated masks. No one seemed really alive. I had a queer notion that if I pricked any of you, there would be no bleeding, but only a gush of wind" (30). While he may, as noted, feel affection for individual humans, his general view is contemptuous, and even the humans he supposedly likes, he has no qualms about using to his own ends. The novel's narrator he calls Fido, and the narrator himself seems content to accept a role as John's lapdog.

The analogous characters in *Sunburst* would be the worst of the Dumplings. Shandy sympathizes with them and wants to come to understand them, as we've seen, but they themselves are amoral at best. Psi is inherently dangerous: "Its danger threatened not only the powerless, but the psyche of its user. Only a psychopath could use it without damaging his spirit: a psychopath had no conscience" (92). This does not of course mean that the Dumplings are all psychotic, but the novel does explicitly and repeatedly associate them with juvenile delinquency and makes an argument for nature, not nurture, directing one's propensities. Shandy suggests, "The psychopath started out being one in his mother's and father's chromosomes" (115), in her attempt to define why psi manifests primarily in certain types: it is a significant component of a predilection towards antisocial behavior, if not inherently linked to such a predilection. Were Shandy like John, her solution would be to propose simply wiping out the Dumplings and anyone with such powers. Indeed, she fears this possibility: "I'd even be sorry if anybody found out an absolutely definite way of identifying them because then you'd have some crank yacking that they ought to be sterilized, and that'd be awful. I don't know what ought to be done for them—but I think there ought to be better ways to weed them out and handle them when they're young and dangerous—without being either cruel or soppy—until they're fit to live in society" (151).

Sunburst, then, echoes *Odd John* in several respects, but it does so in order to challenge that novel's perspective on the superhuman and to propose its own counter model. Shandy and John are superficially alike but very different under the skin. Shandy is, as noted, a gangly, unpromising-looking thirteen-year-old girl. Jason Hemmer whistles at her at the end of the novel's first paragraph, leading to this passage:

> She glanced into the plate glass window of Fitch's Joint to see if she had turned within the last moment into something rich and strange; she hadn't. She was still a very tall cranelike girl, rather sallow, with narrow torso in a navy sweatshirt and long bluejean legs like articulated stovepipes. A high forehead and pointed chin gave her face the look of a brown egg poised on the small end [5].

The passage, with its echo of Shakespeare's *The Tempest*,[7] and the subsequent presentation of Shandy throughout the book, invites the reader to expect the transformation absent here.

Shandy's physical awkwardness is a recurrent motif serving to distance her somewhat from the rest of society. We are reminded at various points of her physical oddness, which serves as an estranging device, especially when Gotlieb uses it to hint at the ultimate revelation about Shandy: "I know I'm bright—what else is different about me," Shandy wonders, "'besides this?' She indicated her stringbean proportions" (13). The text reiterates repeatedly that Shandy's potential remains undeveloped, unknown. At the same time, however, the transformation into something noticeably rich and strange never occurs. Shandy is not like the other normal humans, but neither is she like the psis. Given the novel's premise, that children of irradiated parents have developed spectacular (and dangerous) psi powers, and given that Shandy's father is one of those irradiated (the *Sunburst* of the title refers not only to the nuclear disaster that led to the closing of Sorrel Park but also to the radiation scar on Shandy's father's back), and given, finally, that the novel begins with Jason Hemmer, psi-hunter for the military, on Shandy's trail, we expect a climactic revelation of Shandy's own powers. Comments such as Urquhart's about Shandy's unknown potential, and Shandy's repeated wonderings about what her purpose is and what she will become, keep the idea of Shandy's mysterious possibilities before us throughout the novel.

The concern shown by Shandy (and others) about what she will become when she matures is consistent with the novel as bildungsroman, but it also invites us to consider Shandy as akin to the fair unknown of medieval romance, the figure whose true identity and power usually remain concealed until the climactic moment. The fair unknown is a character type which recurs frequently in medieval Arthurian romance, as well as in other contexts. Though the character may or may not know his ancestry (e.g., Arthur does not know he is the son of Uther Pendragon, but Gareth knows his parentage and chooses to disguise himself to prove himself on his own merits, rather than merely by birth), he is not generally known or recognized; his nobility is concealed, either due to an obscure upbringing or deliberate concealment. However, such tales are ultimately essentialist in their view of character, as regardless of nurture, the true nature of the character ultimately shines through, generally in the form of some unique victory or accomplishment. For instance, despite his apparent lack of nobility, Arthur is the only one who can draw the sword from the stone, thereby proving his right to rule England. Rachel E. Moss points out that "what is particularly striking in these narratives is how little these heroes know about themselves, and how driven they are to find self-knowledge" (99), a trait we see in Shandy, as well. As Andrew King notes, the fair unknown "story has taken a number of forms, such as the narratives of Moses, Jesus, Luke Skywalker, and Harry Potter, and in all its manifestations the hero's eventual success is fundamentally a gift (through blood), no matter how much the hero struggles toward and seems to merit his final reward" (151). As is also evident (even from my pronoun use above), such heroes are frequently, if not always, male. However, there are female unknowns, even in medieval literature, who Jane Bliss asserts, "are as likely as male ones to wonder about who they are" (56)—as Shandy does.

In many respects, despite her unprepossessing appearance, Shandy follows the path often followed by the questing knight, whether a fair unknown or not. Like the typical fair unknown, though, Shandy is an orphan, raised in obscurity by unpromising foster parents, faces numerous tests and challenges, acquires helper figures, undertakes a quest, and even faces a quasi-death before being revealed for what she truly is, as we would expect of the romance hero. Though she is not, as the fair unknown is, someone of noble birth raised in humble circumstances, she is nevertheless, in a way, the sort of society-transforming superhuman the fair unknown usually proves to be. What makes her different is also a matter of heredity, the effect on her physiology of the radiation absorbed by her father, on whose back the sunburst scar of the title appears, so paternity is of import, as it typically is in fair unknown narratives. Indeed, Sorrel Park is akin to the wasteland of romance, "a patch of carrion land" (7) in which life is stagnating. After the disaster that closed it off when the military intervened and put up the barbed wire, "the place withered and shrank back on itself. A generation had been cheated. With twisted spirits they began to cheat in return" (8–9). The place becomes a metaphor for its twisted, stunted inhabitants—not just the Dumplings but the entire town. Even the local name for it, the Sore, suggests a wound that must heal. To heal, a sore must be opened to the air and allowed to drain, as Shandy suggests, "If the Sore's going to be opened up you need help right now" (48). Clearly, it as well as Shandy needs to undergo a restorative transformation.

That Shandy *will* undergo some form of transformation is evident enough, even from the egg image associated with her head in her initial description; she is waiting to hatch. Associating the egg with her head locates the aspect of the self that will develop in Shandy: her mind. Shandy is literally an egghead. Gotlieb returns to the point at about the midpoint of the novel:

> Her anterior fontanel had not closed until she was seven years old, and as a very small child falling asleep she would lie touching the faint depression where her pulses moved openly between brain and membrane. She had had the fancy that these were the thoughts moving about in her head. [...] It had not occurred to her how much more vulnerable than other children she had been, since a comparatively light blow on the head would have killed her [79].

The appropriateness of the implications of the fragility inherent in the egg image is clarified by this passage. So, too, is the idea that Shandy's development is not only unusually slow but specifically associated with mental development; physical development is secondary to intellectual development in Shandy (she remains prepubescent at the novel's conclusion, though it does anticipate her sexual maturation). Even the fact that her term for regular humans is "dull normal" (not quite as insulting as John's *Hom. sap.* perhaps, but in the same territory) stresses her brightness as key. Indeed, Shandy's intellectual precociousness is the key marker of her uniqueness. Her desire for knowledge is a driving force—she "exercised her intellectual suction pump for years on illegally borrowed books" (49), we're told—but her familiarity with figures such as Margaret Mead or with core psychological and sociological texts suggest an intellect far beyond that typical of adolescents. For instance, we learn that she's been studying Beck's *Rorschach's Test* (1952), and she can cite familiarly figures such as William Herbert Sheldon, who created the idea of somatotypes as psychologically significant,[8] or the criminologists Sheldon and Eleanor Glueck, whose work on juvenile delinquency built on Sheldon's theories and also figures strongly in the novel.

Gotlieb's use of figures such as Sheldon and the Gluecks, who were among the numerous figures who studied the causes of juvenile delinquency in the 1940s and 1950s, has troubled some readers. Elizabeth A. Lynn says, "The theories in *Sunburst* about the roots of juvenile delinquency may be questionable" (xi). Less academic respondents can be more blunt; Ian Sales's review on the *Mistressworks* website, for instance, asserts that the novel's conclusion that "juvenile delinquency is genetic and most often to be found in immigrant families is offensive nonsense." However, it is important to remember that the novel was conceived and written in a period in which juvenile delinquency was a pressing social concern, leading almost to public hysteria. Jason Barnosky, for instance, notes that "polls from the mid-to-late 1950s suggest that Americans were concerned about juvenile crime and considered it a problem" (320), noting that entertainment media helped fuel the panic; "movie studios addressed the issue, making 60 films dealing with delinquency over the decade" (320). That these include classics such as *Rebel Without a Cause* (1955) or *The Wild One* (1953) hardly mitigates the fact that they fed on a contemporary fear. The Senate Subcommittee on Juvenile Delinquency, established in 1953, is perhaps the best-remembered manifestation of this hysteria, given that its investigations contributed to the decimation of the comic book industry and the elimination of comics dealing with crime or horror. Fredric Wertham's *Seduction of the Innocent* (1954) was a seminal book arguing that comic books caused delinquency, though his methods and findings have recently been thoroughly debunked (see Tilley).

Furthermore, Gotlieb's conclusions about the subject are not merely a matter of the long-standing literary tradition of using physical characteristics as a component of characterization, but are derived from contemporary psychological and sociological theory that attempted to determine whether there is some sort of correlation between psychology and physiology, as her citation of figures such as Sheldon and the Gluecks reveals—nor were they the only people studying the subject and positing explanations. Sheldon, the Gluecks, and others argued repeatedly that physiology as well as cultural factors played a role in delinquency, and though their conclusions were not universally accepted, they were given serious consideration. Though they were careful not to make prescriptive pronouncements, the Gluecks, for instance, found that delinquents differed generally from non-delinquents in several categories, including the physiological, delinquents likely being

> *Physically* [...] essentially mesomorphic in constitution (i.e., solid, closely knit, muscular); *temperamentally* [...] restlessly energetic, impulsive, extroverted, aggressive, destructive (often sadistic)—traits which may be more or less related to both their bodily structure and their erratic growth pattern with its physiologic correlates or consequences [*Delinquents in the Making* 185].

However, the aim of such studies was not to provide a biology = destiny argument but rather to determine what factors might contribute to delinquency and then to develop social policy to help prevent delinquency from developing. The sort of final solution proposed by Stapledon's John and even underlying *Sunburst*'s treatment of the psis is far from the mind of either the Gluecks[9] or Gotlieb. Indeed, that Gotlieb has the humans treat the psis as rubbish, putting them in a Dump, and that she makes clear that the sort of repressive model adopted towards them fails to address the core problem, suggests that Gotlieb's views were, given the tenor of the times in which she wrote, relatively progressive.

Shandy contrasts physically with the majority of the Dumplings, as an ectomorph herself. Her intellectual development is also explicitly contrasted with the mental development of the Dumplings. For one thing, she is in a sense the polar opposite of the Dumplings when we first meet her, in that, as noted earlier, she is an Imper, not only lacking psi powers of any kind but also undetectable by telepathy or by instinct, as Jason Hemmer points out:

> Most normal people have latent or vestigial psi. It's a lot stronger in babies and little kids, but it's a kind of clumsy and inarticulate thing and it withers away when better methods of communication develop. But adults can still feel the presence of people they can't see, most of the time unconsciously, or nobody could ever hide. With you it's different. Anybody who notices you has to practically tread on your toes first.... You're the first complete Imper I've ever come across [16].

This passage is significant for several reasons. First, it establishes Shandy's most evidently abnormal aspect, her unobtrusiveness; she is anything but spectacularly noteworthy. Second, and more importantly, it suggests that Shandy represents a new variation, neither a "dull normal," as Shandy dubs the mass of common humanity among whom she has been raised so far and as represented by the Slippecs (cf 20), nor a super psi-powered prodigy/danger, as the Dumplings are. Shandy's difference is not defined by her power but by her radical *powerlessness*, in contrast to protagonists from *Slan*'s Jommy Cross to Odd John himself. Or, if she has a power, it is simply the power not to be noticed, an extremely passive power rather than the actively dangerous powers possessed by the Dumplings (though it does come in handy more than once).

A third, and more crucial, point emerges in the passage, however, for in it Hemmer not only comments on Shandy's uniqueness but also establishes the novel's perspective on superhuman psi powers. The uniqueness of Gotlieb's perspective has been noted by Douglas Barbour, who rightly asserts that the book is "deliberately at odds with every psi story since *Odd John* [...] in its analysis of the meaning of fully developed psi powers to the individual" (75). As Susan Stone-Blackburn notes, psi is usually presented in SF as a clear advance over linguistic communication (248). Gotlieb, however, asserts the opposite: psi is not a mental advance but is instead a throwback to something the species has outgrown. It is animalistic. As Shandy notes, "When you think of psi it looks so terrific, but when you think of the types that have it—" (44–45). Even Jason Hemmer, the least powerful of the psis and employed by the army to help catch and contain new psis, is described upon his first appearance as monkey-like; later, we are told he is "like Neanderthal at his best" (9). Far from being a manifestation of superiority, psi in *Sunburst* is atavistic, anti-progressive: "*Their minds seem more primitively organized*," as Shandy notes (115). The reality of psi contrasts vividly with what has been imagined about it before, both in SF in general and in the world of the novel; as Urquhart notes, "People have had some pretty wild romantic dreams about psi over the years. I'll admit the Dumplings aren't anybody's dream come true" (151). In short, the novel associates superhuman powers consistently with infantile, primitive, even animalistic traits.

Gotlieb addresses the link and divide between the animal and the human frequently in her work. The most productive use of animals in her work interrogates the concept of the human by juxtaposing it with variations and iterations on animality in ways that require her readers to break down the conventional binary opposition between the two. Gotlieb's SF—and even her poetry—is heavily populated by various "animals" (human and otherwise) engaged in a complex symbiotic relationship. A complex and encompassing view of the "human" (or sentient) as extending well beyond the parameters of human flesh is central to Gotlieb's work, from *Sunburst* (though here, animal imagery is used relatively conventionally to depict those who fail as human) to her mature work, in which the concept of the human is almost entirely superseded in a universe in which even being sure what *is* an animal is problematic. Via the tropes of SF, Gotlieb literalizes the moral and ethical problems inherent in being a thinking animal.

"Animals are ideas as well as living, breathing creatures," as Ralph H. Lutts observes, and "people and cultures have given them special meanings and responded to them in terms of those meanings" (2). Explicit in this observation is that what animals mean is determined by humans, not inherent in animals themselves. Divine, terrifying, important, trivial, animals are what people say they are; the relationship, as Randy Malamud points out, is hierarchical: "The predominant Western moral code positions humans with regard to animals as unilaterally supremacist" (3). While animals may function in art and literature to reveal things about ourselves, they do so in our own terms, not theirs. However, as Marian Scholtmeijer points out, "Anthropomorphism received a severe blow with the advent of the theory of evolution" (6): as we have come better to understand our origins through scientific investigation, we have discovered continuities as well as disjunctions between human and nonhuman animals and have been faced with the challenge of coming to terms with our literal animal heritage.

If science has modified our understanding of our relationships with animals, SF has explored speculatively some of the ramifications of our modified understanding, and Gotlieb is hardly unique in her interest in non-human life. There is a strong historical association in SF between the alien and the animal. From H. G. Wells's Martians on, aliens have frequently been presented as chimerical combinations of various Earth creatures, and the less humanoid they are, the less good they are.[10] Despite its interest in the alien, however, there is a strong anthropocentric streak in SF, so the alien, animalistic, and monstrous commonly coincide. Indeed, one can almost find an equation— alien=animal=monster—in much SF, especially in SF written prior to the 1970s. As Gary K. Wolfe has asserted,

> Still today the icon of the beast [in SF] suggests the flow of unreason that underlies all rational structures. [...] In a genre in which the humanness of man is often overshadowed by wonders of technology and vast historical patterns, the beast stands as an inescapable and extreme reminder of our own animality, of what we may have been and what we may yet become [86].

Though her career began in the late 1950s, however, Gotlieb never really embraced such a simple conception of the alien, animalistic, or monstrous. Indeed, her most "monstrous" characters are also often her most human ones, while her animals/aliens are often her most complex and civilized ones. *Sunburst* represents an early instance of how she uses the idea of animality complexly, albeit only metaphorically. As we shall see in later chapters, she comes at the question far more directly in later works.

The cover copy of the first edition of *Sunburst* sells it as a conventional story of "a new race of monster," and there are elements of the novel that capitalize on the conventional association of the mutant with the monster, in ways that invoke animal metaphors. We saw earlier that Jason Hemmer, for instance, is imaged in animal terms. Here is a fuller quotation of his first appearance:

> He had a boxcar-crouching bullethead set on a bull neck, thick arms, and a barrel chest tapering into short legs and small feet. But he was so obviously an extreme of his type she began to wonder if he hadn't escaped from a zoo. He had a longlipped chimp mouth, and best of all, one fantastic black eyebrow curling around his eyes and across the bridge of his nose [5].

The predominant impression created by this passage is that Jason is or resembles some sort of a simian, which clearly ties in with the novel's idea of psi as atavistic. The Dumplings are described by Shandy as like animals, and animalism in these terms is fairly clearly negative, since the Dumplings are also generally destructive and criminal. The conventional human/animal hierarchy is invoked, with humans represented as more developed than animals and jettisoning things that as humans—logical, rational creatures—they no longer need from their animal roots. Shandy suggests, "For herd animals that have to stick together [telepathy] might be useful, but I bet a human being born with it could never separate his mind from everybody else's long enough to develop a logical idea" (151). So far, animalism is associated with the primitive and irrational and therefore with the monstrous and dangerous in the novel.

However, the first example I cited, Jason Hemmer, is also an exception. He may seem physically simian—an atavistic throwback—but he is as human and sympathetic a character as is Shandy herself. Nor should we forget that Shandy herself is also a mutant, and in some ways even stranger and more alien than Jason and the other psis. Like Jason, she is also imaged in estranging terms when she is first described, as we have seen. But if Jason Hemmer is simian, Shandy is avian, linked in her first description with a bird (a crane, admittedly not the most elegant or aesthetically pleasing of birds) and with an egg. The simian associations suggest brutishness and violence, whereas the avian ones suggest, in addition to awkwardness, fragility and a strange kind of beauty. The egg image also suggests potential; Shandy is a kind of embryo, a bird still in its shell, waiting to hatch, an idea we've seen is explored in the novel as Shandy discovers the truth about herself. It is also worth note that Hemmer's simianism is not, or not simply, a fact about him but is a reflection of how Shandy sees him: the initial description of him is narrated in the third person, but is filtered through Shandy's perspective; arguably, she sees him, in part, as an enemy and as associated with the thuggery of the authorities as Shandy then understands them. Similarly, the initial description of Shandy follows her own gaze, as she looks at her own reflection in a plate-glass window. The objective physical reality of the characters, therefore, is tempered by subjectivity, and the animal associations are therefore somewhat qualified. Furthermore, an image reflected in a window is translucent at best; in looking *at* herself, Shandy is also looking *through* herself. The insubstantiality of the image suggests the problematics of perception. When looking at a reflection—and when reflecting—what is one doing? The image's transparency suggests further that the process of examining the self—and the other—requires not merely looking at what is on the surface but seeing through the superficial to what lies beyond.

Certainly, what lies beyond literally in this novel, the Dumplings, are imaged in negative animal terms. The description of the first full manifestation of their power likens them to a pack, and there are numerous other instances of explicit animal associations, which translate into how they are treated when they are trapped and caged. This passage from the sequence describing the Dumplings' coalescence as a powerful and dangerous group makes the animal metaphor explicit: "Every ugly thought locked in the mind broke free and dragged with it the animal hates and terrors of childhood, the horrors of the Blowup, and all the small bestiaries accumulated by even the sanest mind living the calmest life" (37). Here we see the Dumplings manifesting the conventional negative associations of animals: hate, terror, violence, and so on. However, it is crucial to note that these beasts remain resolutely human and manifest animal traits found in "even the sanest mind living the calmest life." If the pack unleashes something, it is not something that can be scapegoated, cast off and caged. Rather, it is something inherent in humans, merely clarified and exposed. The animal, then, is not ultimately other but rather inherently human. Even the name of the town, Sorrel Park, may hint at the essential animality of all the inhabitants, as "sorrel" can refer to a type of horse. The novel renders the animal link between the Sorrel Park citizens and the Dumplings explicit later on, when the townsfolk themselves form a mob, as did the Dumplings earlier. When Shandy comes upon them, she hears them "raising their voices in the dark animal cry of the mob" (99), which manifests itself in a quite ugly parallel enactment of the Dumplings' initial outbreak when Fitch's Tabernacle of the Latterday Evangelical group attempts to take over Sorrel Park and comes close to killing Shandy. One of their leaders is even named Fox; Gotlieb here engages in a conventional example of characterization by comparison. Fox, as the fox is traditionally seen, is a sly, treacherous, predatory vermin. Animal images proliferate in this section. The mob is like "ominous beeswarms" (101), for instance, Fox delivering Shandy is compared to "a dog bringing home the evening paper" (102), Fitch "gaped like a fish" when he sees Shandy (102), and so on. Though the members of this mob come "from the opposite end of the spectrum that produced the hoodlums and the Dumplings" (99–100), they are just as capable of animalistic, subhuman behavior, from which Shandy is rescued, ironically enough, by one of the psi-powered children unknown to Dump officials. The "dull normals" may be less inclined to antisocial behavior than the psis, but it remains well within their grasp; Shandy represents an alternative to them as much as she represents an alternative to the superpowered, subhuman psi children.

The Dumplings may be dangerous, then, but so are the "normal" humans. Consigning these mutant children to a prison, the Dump—the name of which of course suggests that its inhabitants are refuse, garbage, discarded by the culture that produced them—fails as a humane, or even sensible, solution to the problem they represent. As Shandy points out, "If there's bars around you, you feel you have a right to try to squeeze through them, and if there's guards in front of you, you have to outwit them. Doesn't matter how much people feel they have a right to put you there. From your point of view they have no right at all. Ever" (48). Though it may be the case, as Newell and Lamont suggest, that the "state of martial law is later vindicated when the psis pool their strengths," escape, and wreak havoc (429), it may equally be the case that imprisoning them and placing them in a Darwinian dog-eat-dog environment in which only their most base instincts could be encouraged merely exacerbated the negative characteristics it was trying to control. The novel ultimately seeks a model for controlling and reintegrating the Dumplings into the larger human culture, rather than suppressing and alienating them, and in doing so its perspective anticipates the more complex and nuanced treatment of the animal other in Gotlieb's later works.

Psis, therefore, are animalistic—subnormal—in Gotlieb's treatment, and therein lies much of the novel's originality. However, Gotlieb carries her exploration further, through her alternate to the "dull normal" human, Shandy. The psis are subnormal, regular humans "dull normal"; Shandy might be dubbed supernormal.[11] There is a link in the novel between the psis and the normal people as described by Jason Hemmer; the atavistic Dumplings possess psionic powers under their conscious control. "Most normal people," as we have heard Hemmer assert, are also possessed of vestigial psi powers of which they are generally unconscious. Insofar as they possess such powers, they remain linked to the animal world of instinct. But to argue that the "normal" humans are significantly better than the Dumplings is problematic at best. Shandy fears the implications of the Dumplings being treated as animals. Odd John may be willing simply to kill humans as if they were animals, but Shandy asserts that such easy differentiations are dangerous. Even if the possession of psi might be seen as revealing the animality of the Dumplings (as the novel suggests it does on page 117), Shandy notes that the animal conception can be applied in other contexts:

> I once read a zoologist's description of a couple of bunches of apes—what he called primate hordes—threatening each other on the borders of their territories, and it sounded very familiar. The parents're always saying, "My Joey was always such a good boy till he started running around with that gang." They never figure that's what their Joey was waiting for all his life—some of his own to run with, and a herd leader instead of an old drunk of a father. And something to bust. They can't get along with ordinary people. The world's a zoo to them, and they have to throw themselves at the bars [118)].

Here, the dull normal human is again clearly the animal as much as is the psi. And Shandy wants to make sure that the question of what is human and what is animal is fully answered before any final solutions are proposed: "Maybe someday we'll have to kill some animals, but we'll damn well make sure we know what's an animal first" (112).

Shandy remains separate from both the Dumplings and the regular humans, though she allies herself with the "dull normals," the representatives of an attempt, at least, at social order. In her discussion with Urquhart after the climactic battle with the Dumplings (in which the superpowered Doydoy, not Shandy, performs the conventional heroic role by defeating power with power, though he is socially non-functional), Shandy defines the "supernormal" in terms very different from those that apply to the psis. Intelligence and moral equilibrium are the primary traits she associates with the genuine superhuman, or supernormal. Most important, though, is the fact that the superhuman Shandy defines must of necessity fit invisibly into the social world:

> If he looked too beautiful or noble or eccentric he might be picked out and pushed aside. You'd want him to be an organic part of humanity, to give his qualities to his children—if he could transmit them. [...] I guess he'd keep out of the way and stay inconspicuous until his building materials were permanently arranged. [...] He'd have the same emotions and the same hopes [as normal humans]. [...] You couldn't expect an advance to come in a single impossible leap to the summit [152–53].

"It's a modest superman," as Urquhart observes (153). The superiority is defined not by radical difference from human norms but rather by a closer adherence to them than normal humans are capable of. Such a superhuman would mature slowly, quietly, inconspicuously, virtually invisible in the whirlwind world of human action and emotion, as Shandy was in the Slippec household. Such a superhuman would not transform the world quickly or radically, as would the superpsi that Shandy imagines as simply too radical a leap to be achieved in a single step. Instead, such a superhuman would work more by long-term influence and the dissemination of a genetic predisposition to intellect and emotional and moral balance. This superhuman would come to an accommodation with normal humanity simply by being absorbed into it quietly and unobtrusively rather than by challenging or supplanting it. Gotlieb proposes a step, not a leap, a modest extension of values such as stability and balance, as the first move forward in human evolution; she imagines an intensification of what she perceives to be the human norms, imagining a supernormal (and the term is hers) as the next evolutionary step. Here, the idea of the supernormal is not associated with the possession of abilities superior to those of normals but rather with an intensification of the traits deemed normal; the term might be paraphrased "extremely normal," rather than "above normal."

In conclusion, then, we can see that Gotlieb works within the tradition of the superpsi novel to some extent, but that she ultimately inverts the conventions. *Sunburst* rejects the idea that psionic powers are inherently superior to the normal range of human powers, arguing instead that they are inferior. What is superior, the novel argues, is the rather more abstract power of the human mind to create order, balance, and stability, in thought and emotion. The true superhuman, or supernormal, in the novel's terminology, will quietly help lead humanity towards a self-realization that leaves behind the herd and mob mentality associated with the subnormals and the dull normals. It's a lonely job, as the novel asserts in its conclusion, but that conclusion suggests, as well, that the stress in self-realization will fall on the *self*, that progress depends on the ability of humans to dissociate themselves from the undifferentiated mass of humanity but continue to function communally and cooperatively.

Three

The Dahlgren Diptych

Gotlieb's second SF novel, *O Master Caliban!*, was not published until 1976, some twelve years after *Sunburst*, though her mainstream novel *Why Should I Have All the Grief?* came between these two books. *O Master Caliban!* was followed by a sequel, *Heart of Red Iron,* in 1989, with the Ungrukh Chronicles appearing between the first and second book in this pair. Though they received hardcover treatment, unlike *Sunburst*, neither has proved as popular as that novel. *O Master Caliban!* was reissued in paperback in 1979 but remained out of print subsequently until its recent publication as an ebook by Event Horizon Books; it has also been translated into German (as *Oh, Meister Caliban*! [1982]). *Heart of Red Iron* received no paperback release and remains out of print.[1] Nevertheless, they are—the first especially—complex and accomplished novels, arguably more fully mature works than *Sunburst*, if not, perhaps, as innovative as that novel. *O Master Caliban!* is the first novel set in the GalFed universe, though Gotlieb had fleshed that universe out fairly thoroughly in several short stories published prior to the novel's appearance (see Chapters One and Four). What became characteristic Gotlieb themes and devices are on full display here, from the metatextual elements (the novel's debt to Shakespeare and Browning is akin to the debt "A Grain of Manhood" owes to Milton, for instance) to Gotlieb's interest in reproduction and the knotty questions of identity as psychological and physiological phenomenon. *Heart of Red Iron* is far from a sequel that merely reprises its predecessor, but it revisits key themes of the earlier novel from different perspectives.

Both novels are set on Barrazan V, a decidedly hostile planet. If Sorrell Park is a limited and depleted environment which twists its inhabitants, Barrazan carries the idea much further. It is not merely a wasteland-like environment, but is threatening to life, sort of a Gotliebian version of Harry Harrison's

Deathworld (or one of them; Harrison wrote *Deathworld* [1960], *Deathworld 2* [1964], and *Deathworld 3* [1968], all about different yet similarly hostile planets), albeit not as actively threatening. Numerous colonization attempts have failed, as the planet is not fit for higher life forms: "It blew with dust clouds and rainstorms, stank with jungles, swarmed with diseases; the polar icecaps were small because of the dust cover, and the seas were poisonous. It neither grew nor attracted intelligent life" (*Caliban!* 7). *Heart of Red Iron* paints an even bleaker picture, suggesting through personification that the planet is actively hostile to life: the planet "turns sullenly more as if away from the light than toward it. Hunched and surly, it looks like the creation of a malevolent god" (1). However, the planet's value to GalFed is precisely that its inimical environment is one in which experiments to help develop life forms capable of inhabiting such environments can be carried out. Ironically, this deadly planet is acquired by GalFed to serve as a cradle for new life forms. The setting on a planet hostile to life ties the novels in to the characteristic Canadian literature theme of survival, as identified by Margaret Atwood. By "survival," Atwood does not mean surviving some active antagonism but simply surviving the environment one inhabits, in which the threat comes "not from an enemy set over against you but from everything surrounding you" (*Survival* 25): from the world itself, in effect. Barrazan V is such a world, rendered even less survivable by the active threats engendered there.

O Master Caliban!

We've seen the importance of reproduction as a theme in Gotlieb's work from the beginning. It was important in *Sunburst*, though Gotlieb is more interested in that novel in exploring the implications of evolution and the potential of the superhuman than she is specifically in issues of reproduction. Nevertheless, the novel's key elements are rooted in genetics and in the ways parents can influence their children. In *O Master Caliban!*, though, reproduction takes center stage on several levels, and in ways that are far more problematic and frightening than in any of her work hitherto. The mutations in *Sunburst* are accidental, at least, but in *O Master Caliban!* Gotlieb gives us not one but two figures with disturbing reproductive agendas. Though the novel does not explicitly cite Mary Shelley's *Frankenstein* (1818), both Edvard Dahlgren and erg–Queen, Dahlgren's rebelling robot who sets out to emancipate the machines and control the humans, can be seen as Frankensteinian figures in some respects, and this novel offers Gotlieb's most extended exploration of Frankensteinian motifs.[2] Indeed, the novel is rich in intertextual references, as the title suggests.

In *O Master Caliban!* we learn that the scientist Edvard Dahlgren's experiments on Barrazan V to "warp [...] life forms with radiation" (8) in an attempt to develop "genetic strains [...] to live on that world and many others just as repellent" (8) have gone disastrously wrong. Dahlgren is attempting to bio-engineer mutations capable of living in hostile environments, so he's not literally a parent of his experimental creatures, but his agenda is procreative. The few human and alien experimenters who have carved out a relatively habitable space on the planet's surface have "a thousand ergs" (8)—sophisticated and in some cases intelligent machines—to handle the hard labor. Dahlgren is a cold and distant man who ultimately alienates his wife, who leaves him but whose ova Dahlgren uses to create a test-tube baby son. The ergs interfere with this process, producing in the son, Sven, a four-armed mutant; ultimately, the ergs rebel, wiping out most of the human and alien scientists, keeping Dahlgren and allowing Sven and a crew of genetically modified animals to relocate to a small enclave in the distant jungle.

In these actions, the ergs behave in keeping with what Allan Weiss has identified as particularly (though admittedly not uniquely) characteristic of the representation of robots and AI in Canadian SF: "there are very few machines in [Canadian] fantastic literature that do not enslave or at least dehumanize us" (68). Weiss points out that robots and androids are generally uncommon in SF of the 1960s and 1970s, and that "the robots that do appear are anything but lovable or benign" (72); he cites *O Master Caliban!*'s ergs as an example. Their actions here certainly are neither lovable nor benign. However, as the novel proceeds, the extent to which the ergs function merely or simply as monstrous others becomes open to debate. The ergs do (or try to) both enslave and dehumanize their human creators, but they also become complexly interconnected with those humans. Gotlieb deepens and complicates the convention of the enslaving/dehumanizing machine.

Though the erg interference in the breeding of Sven rationalizes Sven's mutation and frees Dahlgren from the taint of being a deliberate monster maker (and Sven suffers considerable trauma as a result of his belief that his father "made him a monster out of revenge against his mother" [36]), the thematic and symbolic implications of that mutation depend on Dahlgren's nature. Though feminist utopian fiction can imagine that "when everyone—males as well as females—can become mothers," the result will be "equal relationships with warm, nurturing men" (Barr, *Lost in Space* 72), Gotlieb is not so sanguine. Like Scarpino in Gotlieb's poem "ms & mr frankenstein,"

Dahlgren is cold and distant; his wife leaves him because "the inside of you isn't worth that awful thickness of the surface" (38–39), and she is explicitly relieved that their union produced no children. The union produces a child nevertheless, but according to Dahlgren's "hard clear" (23) logic, the logic that determines his will to mastery and the self-conception that leads others to view him as "little god [...], Dahlgren-with-a-world-of-his-own" (38). The little god Dahlgren creates a son, the genetically scrambled Sven, modified by the ergs.

If Sven is Dahlgren's biological child, the ergs are, in a way, the offspring of his mind. The ergs clearly model themselves on Dahlgren. We are not given a clear picture of how exactly the ergs acquire the ability to act independently, not surprisingly, perhaps, given the general failure to explain machine consciousness in such fiction, as noted by Russell Letson (103–104). However, the novel strongly suggests an almost osmotic acquisition of their defining traits from Dahlgren himself: "Being with Dahlgren, alongside him, building new machine forms at the same time he built or changed life forms ... they picked up a pattern" (15). That is, the ergs' self-replication and desire of mastery reflects the character of Dahlgren, who becomes thereby in a way their creator—their mother. In fact, when Dahlgren asks what motivates them, erg–Dahlgren responds that they desire "to do what you would do. Make worlds. Create, destroy, and own, like all men" (39–40). Note the sequence. Note as well the assumption that as is Dahlgren, so are all men. And though arguably the word "men" might here be taken to mean "humans," it is arguably no accident that the erg model is specifically male, not merely human. As a poet as well as an accomplished fiction writer, Gotlieb is very sensitive to nuances of language. Indeed, one of her strategies to establish the kinship of sentient creatures, human and otherwise, throughout her GalFed works is to ascribe human terms (e.g., man or woman) to aliens who from a human perspective more closely resemble animals.

More noteworthy than the general implication of the ergs comparing themselves to "men," though, is the explicit and extensive parallel between the ergs' grotesque and perverse agenda of creation and Dahlgren's own. We have noted already that Dahlgren's primary experiment involves the creation or mutation of new life forms, and that his son specifically is such a creation. Sven himself suffers, much as Frankenstein's monster does, as a result of being created and abandoned, though Sven's physical monstrosity is actually the result of erg interference and only metaphorically a representation of his sense of alienation and abandonment.

Dahlgren tries to differentiate between himself and these mechanistic monsters by considering that "he had manipulated flesh, flexed limbs. But I did not do that to torment. Did you not, Dahlgren? Only to be powerful" (162). As the internal dialogue suggests, Dahlgren himself comes to question the purity and benevolence of his own motives. Indeed, since the ergs explicitly model themselves on Dahlgren, the pain, torture, and death they cause are linked, if not to Dahlgren's intentions, at least to his practice: "Dahlgren had made and marred at will; so had they" (192). The ergs imitate Dahlgren's creational agenda in various ways. For instance, they have also created mutations, living grotesqueries they keep in a pit. They have also created clones (male and female) of Dahlgren, creatures that do nothing but eat, fight, and copulate, though they are apparently sterile (as, apparently, are the other mutated creatures the ergs have created). These clones are a bestial reduction of humanity, and yet, shockingly, entirely recognizable as images of himself by Dahlgren. Dahlgren is forced to confront his facile self-justifications and see anew his reality when the ergs treat him the same the way they treat their animal experiments and lock Dahlgren up in a pit with these creatures. The most dangerous creatures in the pit, however, are not the ones derived from animals but rather the clones of Dahlgren produced by the ergs as their first attempts to produce their own version of Dahlgren. These clones are animalistic parodies of the human. Nevertheless, Dahlgren immediately recognizes them as reflections of himself. He sees himself in the base monstrous version of humanity more than he sees it in his physical duplicate, erg–Dahlgren, or in his biological offspring, Sven. The easy hierarchizing of self and other, human and beast, falls apart. So does the idea that one can exert meaningful control over the vital principle: though one of the consistent factors in the erg creation of biological entities is their inability to render them fertile, one of their creations has developed a parthenogenetic mode of reproduction, as Dahlgren discovers. The urge to reproduce can overcome much.

The ergs' imitation of Dahlgren the maker of life is manifest most clearly in the figure of erg–Dahlgren, however. The ergs create an android duplicate of Dahlgren in order to fool and infiltrate the outside world of GalFed. It is during his (assuming we can safely label as male a mechanical construct) creation that the ergs are first associated with a hive and we get the first hint of the erg leader, Mod 777, as being like a hive queen. The implications of this biologizing and gendering of the erg leader will be considered shortly. Erg-Dahlgren is created physically as an exact duplicate of Dahlgren, and their physical mirroring of each other is brought up repeatedly in the book. In this figure, Dahlgren is confronted, literally, by an image of himself. Though human, he is machine-like in numerous respects, so much so that the ergs are sure that erg–Dahlgren could well fool anyone not intimately familiar with Dahlgren. Dahlgren's confrontation with erg–Dahlgren, by contrast, is associated with his turn back toward humanity: "Am I becoming a man again?" (28), wonders Dahlgren, when he first sees erg–Dahlgren and feels contempt, then fear. Confronted with an image of himself as machine, Dahlgren begins to reclaim his humanity.

Technically, of course, erg–Dahlgren is not a mirror image of Dahlgren, as Dahlgren himself reflects on in a passage in the fair copy typescript but cut from the final version of the novel (it would have appeared on page 113 as part of his thoughts about recognizing himself in the caged bestial clone versions of himself):

> If he had thought about it, he might have said that erg–Dahlgren would never completely be his mirror image because that face did not have his own symmetries reversed; nor was he a camera image, because that is only a representation accepted as truth by complicity, as a stick man equals an anatomical chart; he would have said, in sum, that he did not look in mirrors much, nor did he like to be recorded by camera [149–50].

More than enough remains in the novel as published to get a clear sense of Dahlgren's coldly analytical and yet not self-reflective mind, but this passage would have provided not only an amusing instance of his thought processes but also some incisive suggestions about the relationship between the real and the copied.

The irony of the machine-like Dahlgren beginning a move back towards humanity when confronted with a literal externalized representation of himself as machine is echoed and enhanced by the trajectory within erg–Dahlgren himself. Erg-Dahlgren is the creature of Mod 777, who assigns him the task of learning as much as possible about Dahlgren in order to be able to mimic him effectively. An unanticipated corollary of this task is erg–Dahlgren's growing autonomy and desire to become human himself. As erg–Dahlgren learns, he develops feelings, just as Dahlgren begins to reacquire feelings when he first sees erg–Dahlgren. He also develops desires: "I have discovered, Dahlgren, that I can feel. I wish to maintain my being, and the threat to it induces what I call fear. I find I have wishes and wants. I want to live, and also I want to know" (130). He and his "mother," the erg–Queen, are contrasted: "Erg-Queen. The machine that wanted. Erg-Dahlgren, the machine that wished to be flesh" (188). Erg-Dahlgren desires a place in the human community. Frankenstein's monster learns human behaviour by observing, in secret, the simple life of Felix and Sophie; ironically, erg–Dahlgren, the machine, learns human behavior by observing and interacting with the machine-like Dahlgren.

It's worth noting that automata, from Pinocchio to Data on *Star Trek: The Next Generation* (1987–1994 as a television series, followed by several movies ([1994–2002]), frequently desire to be human, in what might be termed the Pinocchio Syndrome,[3] and erg–Dahlgren fits into this pattern. However, this is not an instance of the anthropocentric assumption so frequent in SF that being human is the ultimate accomplishment, though it is the case that erg–Dahlgren is gratified to be seen as human. Rather, it is reflective of Gotlieb's exploration of the implications of reproduction, in that the created is torn between a desire to love and be loved by the creator, enacted in its desire to become like that creator itself—as the ergs have become like Dahlgren, for instance—and the necessity of self-definition against that creator—the seeds of rebellion that Dahlgren notes are endemic in family relations (256). The ergs imitate and attempt to supplant their maker, in a manner of speaking. Sven is torn between love of his father and resentment, even hatred, of the man who he believes made him a monster and abandoned him. Erg-Dahlgren ultimately rebels against his immediate creator, Mod 777—his mother, metaphorically—in favor of his own mirror image, a father on one level but more akin to a brother on another.

The theological undertones here are consistent with SF tradition. The creator/scientist as rival to God is one of the fundamental Frankensteinian motifs, and it clearly applies to Dahlgren. Certainly, *O Master Caliban!*, like *Frankenstein*, posits metaphysical implications for the creation of life. Indeed, a passage cut from the typescript of the novel's fair copy offers an overt religious echo as well as the closest thing to an echo of *Frankenstein* in the book. When contemplating in chapter eight that there is no arguing with a machine, Dahlgren likens the machine's refusal to argue with him with the scientist's distance from the experiment: "Did you discuss biogeny with mutant rats? Or vascular dynamics with embryo chicks?" (54). The contemplation in the novel as published then moves to Dahlgren's recollection of his own father, with whom he had a fraught relationship and with whom he never reconciled. However, in the typescript, the reference to embryo chicks is followed by this sentence: "Does the clay say to him who fashioned it, 'What are you making?' or 'your work has no handles'?" (71). The reference to the divine creation of life is explicit, and one might recall that Shelley's epigraph for *Frankenstein* consists of the clay's rebellious words to the creator, as drawn from *Paradise Lost* (1667). Gotlieb elsewhere (notably in "Tauf Aleph") works more extensively with the idea of the golem that underlies this reference.

There are enough other references retained in the novel to keep the point clear. Dahlgren's experimentation has led to the creation of autonomous creatures, as has the creation of the ergs, and this is cast in metaphysical terms: "[the ergs] had grown themselves souls, like Esther and Yigal" (172). Esther and Yigal are a gibbon and a goat, respectively, who have developed intelligence, Esther as the result of genetic engineering and Yigal as the result of mutation—the two branches of Dahlgren's experimentation. The use of animal metaphors Gotlieb engaged in in *Sunburst* is carried farther here, in the conversion of animals to sentient beings, a device that will become central in the Ungrukh Chronicles. These animals are of course anthropomorphized to some extent, by virtue of the genetic modifications and mutations (radiation again plays a major role) that have given them sentience and speech, but Gotlieb manages to retain a sense of their animal difference nevertheless. Despite becoming a surrogate mother for the protagonist, for instance—Sven even calls her mutti—"Esther is definitely a gibbon," as Douglas Barbour asserts ("Phyllis Gotlieb" 114), and she behaves consistently as one throughout the novel. Her animal status, however, is only gradually revealed over the first few pages, as we read of her engaging in such human activities as making stew, talking, and so on, while encountering occasional details that are puzzling. We are told "she sat on his shoulder" (1) as she feeds Sven the stew, for instance, a statement we discover is literal in the subsequent paragraph when Sven lifts her off his shoulder and places her on the table. In the context of an SF novel, we might therefore imagine she is an alien or some sort of mutated human, so the revelation that she is in fact a gibbon is still surprising. Even in SF, sentient animals are more of a surprise than are aliens. Gotlieb plays on readerly expectation to shock us into the recognition that despite being a monkey, "With her intelligence exponentially increased, Esther had become simply another species of extraterrestrial human being" (11).

In this statement, Gotlieb articulates one of the central theses of her mature work. Gotlieb repeatedly insists on the commonality among all sentient creatures, not merely humanoid ones. Given such a position, Dahlgren's treatment of the flesh is problematic. Though one might argue that the experimentation he is engaged in to produce mutations will help creatures adapt to life in an inimical environment, the novel questions whether the positive potential of such experimentation is outweighed by the negative potential. Esther and Yigal both emerge from these experiments and might be seen as positive results, but the novel does not simply present animal experimentation as a good or even a necessary thing. Indeed, the plot focuses on the ergs' acquisition of intelligence and their own engagement in experimentation in imitation of their human creators. The results are various monstrosities (in physical terms, anyway), human and otherwise. However, only some of the physical monsters are moral monsters, as well; many are not. The novel clearly critiques the treatment of living creatures (sentient or not) as the subjects of experiment.

The result of Dahlgren's experimentation, deliberate or not, is the creation of sentient creatures, both of flesh and of metal: independent creatures. Whether one can fairly discriminate between creatures of flesh—what might conventionally be considered creatures with souls (or at any rate generally considered as capable of having souls; as we have seen, Gotlieb asserts that Esther and Yigal *grew* them, so evidently they did not have them when in their pure animal state)—and creatures of metal, which the novel, as we have seen, asserts have *also* grown (the biological metaphor is significant) souls, is open to debate. At any rate, Gotlieb troubles the sanguine human assurance of uniqueness and superiority to that which is not human. Certainly, both kinds of "creature"— flesh and metal—seek to define themselves, and the model for doing so is the human one, insofar as it is available. The ergs' model for such definition is Dahlgren, so the erg–Queen becomes a grotesque parody of mother/creator, in contrast to the bizarre but affecting image of a gibbon mothering a human.

Dahlgren's God complex is extended and winnowed of any palliating traits in the erg–Queen. Dahlgren may be machine-like, megalomaniacal, manipulative, and dangerous, but he has human limits and human emotions, buried beneath the surface. Genetically, he shares the traits of a mother and a father. It is these human traits that erg–Dahlgren ultimately acquires through imitation; "will I become a feeling creature if I behave like one?" (66), he wonders, and the answer ultimately is yes. But if, as Joe Sanders notes, "Humans project their own traits into machines" in such stories, and these machines can therefore "reflect vital, personal human traits that show either appalling or hopeful aspects of human nature" (170), then erg–Dahlgren is at the hopeful end of the spectrum and the erg–Queen at the appalling end. All the erg–Queen acquires is Dahlgren's will to power, with no tempering emotion or compassion. Dahlgren has lost his wife and gets instead a grotesque parody in this feminized machine which nevertheless has nothing mothering about it beyond its power to create—and its name.

Crucial to the success of the resistance of the erg–Queen is knowledge of her name, so her codes can be accessed. Mod 777 is merely a "cognomen. Her nomen, or genus, is Creator Matrix One" (137). As the name suggests, her function is to create. The conceptual association of that function with the female is indicated in the second component of the name. Though perhaps many think of the term "matrix" now merely as referring to cyberspace or perhaps virtual reality, no doubt some remember that matrix means, ultimately, womb, and is derived from the Latin "mater," or "mother." The gendering of the erg–Queen comments ironically on this physical function while showing that that physical function, divorced from parenting in a more general sense, fails.

Dahlgren's wife left him. He engenders instead (albeit unintentionally) a sort of substitute mother figure in Creator Matrix One, or Creatrix, as she comes to be known later, who carries Dahlgren's self-regard to the ultimate degree. Her femininity, such as it is, is an aspect of her creation by Dahlgren, and relatively unusual in stories of intelligent machines. Despina Kakoudaki points out that machine life forms, whether robots, androids, or computers, are usually either neutral or gendered male, though cyborgs are much more frequently exaggeratedly female (166–68). The erg–Queen is a robot. As noted earlier, "her ambience was not female; only her shape suggested gender" (209), and that shape was imposed by Dahlgren. Indeed, the female metaphor is imposed on her when she first appears by Dahlgren's gaze: what he sees when she first enters is

> Vaguely female in shape, somewhat conical, rather insectiform; five arms lay curved down along each flank; a rank of faceted jewel eye buttons ran down the midline; its bulblike upper end wore a crown of antennas. Dull silver in blemishless perfection, it gave the impression of a pampered hive queen. Dahlgren thought his mind might be slanting off again; for a moment he had the idea that erg–Dahlgren was about to call it Mother [40].

The actual details here do not particularly suggest the female any more than the male; they are metaphorized by Dahlgren himself. That is, the femaleness of the erg–Queen, even her potential as mother, reflects Dahlgren's view of her; she is another mirror of him, like erg–Dahlgren. She manifests his role as creator/destroyer—"savage maelstrom at the terminus" (189)—and she is, like Dahlgren, the careless Frankensteinian procreator, the destructive divinity: "Like many another deity Creatrix formed life but did not always provide for it" (231). Jane Donawerth argues that "intimately connected with the construction of science in *Frankenstein* is the depiction of woman as alien" (*Frankenstein's Daughters* xxi); In *O Master Caliban!* the erg–Queen is not literally alien, though unquestionably a constructed Other whose putative femaleness is part of how the male gaze constructs her. Nevertheless, the predominant pronominal association feminizes her, so she can relatively easily be seen as of a piece with the problematized image of the female-gendered robot so common in SF, a narrative trope in which, as Minsoo Kang notes, "The female robot malfunctions and runs amok or becomes so humanlike that it frees itself of its original programming to achieve independence of consciousness and will. The situation necessitates that it be destroyed" (5–6).

Erg-Dahlgren, by contrast, represents Dahlgren on another level as creator as self-replicator and is both literally and metaphorically a mirror-image of the constructing male. Erg-Dahlgren is both the erg–Queen's attempt at self-replication (which makes him, in a way, also Dahlgren's attempt at self-replication at one remove) and a representation of Dahlgren's solipsism; his existence helps lead Dahlgren back to humanity, and in the process leads him away from erg–Queen. His loyalty to her is based solely in the desire for self-preservation, but his loyalty to Dahlgren arises from something more primal: identification (207). Erg-Queen and erg–Dahlgren are both machines, but one represents only a limited parody of the human while the other moves toward it.

Sven has no father for much of his maturation, but he has an odd father figure in Yigal the goat, and he has in Esther a mother figure, who contrasts with the erg–Queen. Indeed, she becomes a surrogate mother for the motley crew of children whose crash landing on the planet is the catalyst for the plot. These children include Shirvanian, a younger version of Dahlgren, perhaps, a boy who desires everything to be as simple and perfect as machines, just as erg–Dahlgren desires the mixed blessing of humanity. Though Esther is female, she is not human, and though she does demonstrate various conventional mothering traits, she "does not reinforce a stereotype" (Donawerth, *Frankenstein's Daughters* 72) but rather serves as a focus for the novel's exploration of mothering (or parenting, perhaps) as defined by behaviour rather than by sex, race, or even species. Esther demonstrates the main point of the novel about mothering, perhaps. It does not reside merely, or even necessarily at all, in the mere fact of reproduction, or in being human, for that matter. The ability to create life can lead to the creation of grotesqueries and monsters. Mothering is not simply a function; it is a behavior. The creators in the novel—notably Dahlgren and erg–Queen—think solely in terms of function, whether that is the genetic engineering of adaptable life forms or the propagation of a race of machines from the template of the erg–Queen. Dahlgren and erg–Queen fail, as did Frankenstein, by focusing only on the mechanics. Dahlgren himself argues, "You might say that any organic creature is a kind of machine, because it operates by the laws of physics and chemistry, and even uses metals in various forms" (192), and he is in a fundamental way right, but it is a statement that also foregrounds his essentially cold, clinical view of humanity. People, the novel argues, are far more complex than machines, even when the people are machines themselves, and their creators would do well to remember as much. Mothers are not just molds (another meaning of matrix), and children are not just stamped out to a template. The emotional sphere must be encompassed, as well, for genuine mothering—regardless of the mother's gender, or even species—to occur.

The novel's invocation of Caliban and thereby the literary tradition associated with him further clarifies the novel's explorations of these themes. The titular reference to Caliban probably conjures up to most readers' minds Shakespeare's play *The Tempest*, "the narrative pattern of which is reversed in various ways in the novel," according to Douglas Barbour ("Phyllis Gotlieb" 113). Barbour provides no additional detail, however, though some at least of the parallels are probably evident to any reader familiar with the play and have been briefly pursued by Diana Brydon and Chantal Zabus. Gotlieb, however, uses the play differently than is typical for English-Canadian writers. As Chantal Zabus has asserted, "the English-Canadian writer privileges Miranda over Caliban and appears to dwell more on the Prospero/Miranda or Miranda/Ferdinand relationships as conventional metaphors of parental and romantic relations" ("Calibanic Tempest" 42), though the earliest Canadian work to invoke *The Tempest*, Charles Augustus Murray's *Ottawah: The Last Chief of the Red Indians of Newfoundland* (1847), gives Shahdac, the Caliban figure, "both full humanity and a specific cultural context" (Haresnape 9)—as a First Nations man, specifically a Beothuk. Murray does, as Zabus suggests that English-Canadian writers do, downplay the association of Caliban with rape by placing the rape threat in a dream, but he does give Shadhac a sympathetic role as a native ultimately destroyed as a result of European colonialism, anticipating the post-colonial reading of Caliban by over a century.

In contrast to the usual English-Canadian reading of *The Tempest*, French-Canadian readings do tend to privilege Caliban. Most significant in this regard is Max Dorsinville's study *Caliban Without Prospero: Essay on Quebec and Black Literature* (1974), in which Dorsinville associates the Calibanic voice with the voices of "a number of minor, regional, national, or ethnic literatures" that "claim a metaphorical or actual land of their own, and an experience of the world differentiating them from linguistic or geographical congeners" (17). As Alden T. Vaughan and Virginia Mason Vaughn succinctly state, "Dorsinville's story, in short, is Caliban's cultural emancipation" (170). One of the clearest instances of this (coincidentally, perhaps, given that it was published within a year of Gotlieb's *O Master Caliban!*) is the French-Canadian novel *Caliban* (1977) by Pierre Seguin, in which, Zabus argues, Seguin uses the Caliban figure to explore the "linguistic and cultural subjugation" of the Quebecois ("Calibanic Tempest" 48).

Gotlieb's treatment settles for neither the Prospero-privileging nor the Caliban-privileging approach of English- of French-Canadian literature, though, as her title suggests, she does give Caliban his due. However, the Shakespearean parallels are not as easily reducible as the above possibilities suggest. Like Shakespeare's Prospero, Gotlieb's scientist Edvard Dahlgren has complex and problematic relationships with his creatures/servants, notably the ergs. The ergs, erg–Dahlgren especially, are Caliban figures to Dahlgren's Prospero. Prospero, of course, did not literally make Caliban (or Ariel), but then Dahlgren is not the only Prospero figure in the book. There are numerous Prosperos and numerous Calibans in the novel. The ergs are the most obvious Calibans, perhaps, but Gotlieb rings several changes on the plot of Shakespeare's play; her invocation of Caliban does not set up a schematic echo of *The Tempest* in the novel but rather a complex and allusive exploration of the relationships between gods/creators/parents and creations/creatures/children. For instance, as a father who "loses" his child (his son Sven), Dahlgren is in some respects reminiscent of Alonso as well as of Prospero; and since his son is a Calibanesque grotesque, one might even look for ways to link Dahlgren with Sycorax, though in other ways, Dahlgren himself is as much a Caliban as he is a Prospero, since he is imprisoned and enslaved by erg–Queen as Caliban is by Prospero. Gotlieb uses the rich possibilities inherent in Shakespeare's Caliban to comment on the danger in human nature of excessive devotion to science in abandonment of humane considerations, especially in her treatment of the ergs as the pursuit of knowledge converted to pure mechanistic ego.

In fact, though, Caliban does not come to Gotlieb's novel directly or exclusively from Shakespeare. Rather, he comes most directly by way of Robert Browning's poem "Caliban upon Setebos" (1864), in which Caliban speculates about his god/maker, Setebos. This echo of Browning extends and complicates Gotlieb's treatment of her source story by providing for Caliban a double rather than a single intertextual context. One of the key features of the book is the way it avoids a schematic, one-to-one correspondence with *The Tempest*, largely by multiplying and complicating the relationships between its characters and the play's.

The play tells the story of Prospero, the Duke of Milan deposed by his brother (in collusion with the King of Naples) and set adrift with his infant daughter, Miranda, twelve years before the play begins. They wash up on a nearly desert island where Prospero frees the trapped air spirit Ariel and takes the brutish Caliban as servant/slave, an initially amicable relationship that sours when Caliban attempts to rape Miranda; Caliban also comes to view Prospero as usurper of Caliban's rightful realm. The play begins when a ship carrying Prospero's duplicitous brother Antonio, King Alonso of Naples, and Alonso's brother Sebastian and son Ferdinand, is brought by Prospero's magic apparently to sink off the island. While father and son each believe the other dead, Antonio and Sebastian plot to kill Alonso, Caliban plots with Alonso's servants to kill Prospero, Ferdinand falls in love with Miranda, and Prospero manipulates events to bring all the plots save his own to naught, reclaim his dukedom, and bring about an alliance by marriage with Naples. This might sound like a lot of plot, but in fact the play is light on action and quite economical.

The novel involves several similar actions. Barrazan V is akin to the inimical island on which Prospero and Miranda are marooned and though Edvard Dahlgren chose to come to the planet as an experimental scientist, accompanied by his wife and a scientific team, subsequent events have rendered him, if anything, even more bereft than Prospero. Whereas Prospero retains control of his magic until *he* decides to abjure it, Dahlgren loses control of the equivalent of magic: his scientific control. Like Prospero, albeit with different moral implications, Dahlgren has been betrayed by family; years before the action begins, his wife abandons him. Dahlgren's creation of a child from a frozen ovum she left behind and his own sperm provides him with a single child, as Prospero had, but whereas Miranda is to be wondered at for her beauty, Dahlgren's son Sven is to be wondered at for different reasons: he is born with four arms. The ergs' rebellion might be seen as an alternative to one of the plots of the play, as Chantal Zabus suggests: "Gotlieb imagines the successful outcome of Caliban, Trinculo, and Stephano's plot against Prospero" (*Tempests After Shakespeare* 194), though had Caliban succeeded, Prospero would undoubtedly have died, nor do any of the ergs really seem to match the comic aspects of Stephano and Trinculo, so the parallel is not exact. Regardless, the ergs kill most of the scientists and banish Sven, along with Esther and Yigal, to a distant corner of the settled area, separated from the base by jungle and radioactive zones, which parallels them in a way with Alonzo, though Propsero's survival was ensured by Gonzago, who cast him and his daughter out to sea. The ergs keep Dahlgren prisoner and their rebellion a secret from the outside world of the Galactic Federation; this limitation on Dahlgren and Sven might be likened to Prospero's limitations on Caliban and for that matter Ariel, who are both Prospero's slaves.

At the beginning of the novel, which begins seven years after the erg rebellion, a (space) ship crashes on the planet close to Sven's encampment. The ship carries five children and adolescents, who claim they were on an educational tour but who are, we learn later, juvenile delinquents who (like the ergs perhaps) have rebelled against the social order of the outer world and are trying to escape. They are Koz (prone to violence), Joshua (who follows an unpopular religion), Mitzi (a nymphomaniac), Ardagh, and Shirvanian. These latter two are the most important to the plot. Ardagh is like Sven, non-normative physically, suffering from mutations that will not allow her to fulfill her desire to become a doctor—hence her rebellion against the world that made her. Shirvanian is a genius and possessed of the ability to read machine minds and control them remotely. The ergs claim their ship and try to capture them. Though the children do not generally fit very tightly into the network of *Tempest* allusions, Shirvanian is himself an iteration of the Prospero/Caliban complex in the novel, as a figure of scientific genius as well as being an antagonist (at least in his pre–Barrazan life) to the social order. The Sven/Ardagh relationship is as close as the novel comes to the Ferdinand/Miranda romance, though it reverses the pattern of the play (in which the male character travels to the world of the female character, rather than vice versa) and though its depiction of Sven as a grotesque outcast makes him as much a manifestation of an aspect of Caliban as of a romantic lead. ("Ardagh" is also traditionally a masculine name—or Irish origin—which underscores Ardagh's own unlikely status as Mirandaesque beautiful naïf.)

The larger erg plan involves the creation of a robotic duplicate of Dahlgren to send out as a representative to a scientific conference, thereby maintaining the ergs' secret and making inroads into the larger universe. The novel's plot involves the quest of Sven and the children to free themselves from the erg threat, and the attempts of Dahlgren and ultimately his double to thwart the ergs and their leader. We move to the reunion of father and son, closely parallel to the Ferdinand/Alonso plot in *The Tempest*, though Dahlgren, the Alonso character from this perspective, is also in some key respects the Prospero figure, as the rebellion plot suggests, though unlike Caliban, the ergs have succeeded in overthrowing their Prospero figure, associating them perhaps as much with Antonio and Alonso as with Caliban.

Caliban is a figure with a complex history reflective of his complexity in Shakespeare's play. As Dirk Delabastita notes, "Caliban has been perceived as an image of Darwin's missing link, as the Freudian id, as a noble savage, as an omen of the African slave-trade, and so on" (6), while Harold Bloom complains that "Caliban is now a hero of our modern School of Resentment, who convert him into an anti-imperialist allegory" (2). He is both monstrous and pitiful, the most widely reviled character within the play and yet also the one probably most likely to inspire mixed, disturbed, and even sympathetic responses in an audience. His murderousness, his attempted rape of Miranda (which we do not see, but only hear about), his general viciousness and perversity, even his grotesque physical appearance, not spelled out clearly in the play but evident nonetheless, all render him repellent. Yet Shakespeare also gives him powerful and compelling grievances against Prospero and the finest poetry in the play; he is more sensitive and sensible than many of the other characters, and his crimes when compared to those of Antonio and Sebastian lose some of their horror. He, at least, has reason to resent Prospero, whereas Antonio and Sebastian turn on their own blood purely for personal gain. The almost heroic status Caliban has attained and about which Bloom complains is perhaps extreme, but it is grounded in the complexity of Shakespeare's creation, a complexity reflected in the myriad ways Caliban has been invoked by subsequent writers.

As mentioned above, the most important of these Calibanesque intertexts for *O Master Caliban!* is Browning's poem "Caliban Upon Setebos," cited as Dahlgren reflects on erg theories about the purpose of humanity and their links to theories about the existence of God: "Oddly, his mind went back [...] to the nineteenth century and its ponderous thinkers, good greybeard Robert Browning in vest and watch-chain, fire on hearth, loving Elizabeth at hand, comfortable spaniel at foot, dreaming of Caliban musing by island shore of his god Setebos" (192). Ponderous thinker and poet/creator Browning here clearly contrasts with ponderous thinker and overthrown scientist/creator Dahlgren, the idealized domestic scene of science (watch-chain) and nature (fire), woman and animal constellated around and subservient to the male thinker/God analogue figure representing everything that has been taken from Dahlgren, as he is left playing chess for his life with a robotic mirror image of himself and under the control of the erg–Queen, Creator Matrix One, a figure who is herself a hybrid of Prospero and Sycorax.[4]

The specific passage Dahlgren recalls from Browning's poem is this one:

> Who made them weak, meant weakness He might vex,
> Had He meant other, while His hand was in,
> Why not make horny eyes no thorn could prick,
> Or plate my scalp with bone against the snow,
> Or overscale my flesh 'neath joint and joint
> Like an orc's armour? [lines 172–77; punctuated as in Gotlieb].

The poem, a dramatic monologue in Caliban's voice, represents Caliban's speculations on the nature of Setebos, "that other, whom his dam called God" (16). Caliban explains reality as he sees it by inferring qualities in Setebos, its putative creator, but those inferences transfer to Setebos his own sensibility: a refrain in the poem is Caliban's "So He," applied to Setebos when Caliban has commented on what he would do if he were God. Here's one example. Caliban imagines a broken-legged creature beseeching him for help:

> I might hear his cry,
> And give the mankin three sound legs for one,
> Or pluck the other off, leave him like an egg,
> And lessoned he was mine and merely clay.
> Were this no pleasure, lying in the thyme,
> Drinking the mash, with brain become alive,
> Making and marring clay at will? So He [91–97].

Browning's Caliban imagines a god who deliberately made creatures vulnerable to pain so that he could punish them, a god who takes pleasure in whimsically and capriciously rewarding or (more frequently) punishing his creations because they are his to do with as he will. He imagines, in effect, a sadistic god, because, were he god, *he* would be such a sadist. Caliban, of course, in Browning and in Shakespeare, has no such power to create, though his attempt on Miranda suggests such a desire; commenting on his interrupted rape of Miranda in *The Tempest*, Caliban asserts, "Thou didst prevent me—I had peopled else / The isle with Calibans" (1.2.349–50). Nor has Caliban the power actually to usurp even Prospero's power, let alone a god's.

Dahlgren, however, is a Prospero—or a god—unable to save himself from his Caliban. He images himself as "little god [...] Dahlgren-with-a-world-of-his-own" (38), as the one who "mastered," who "had no friends" (24), but he's a god who has lost his world, a master overthrown by his servants, who have done so in imitation of him. In this element of the plot, the ergs may seem as much like Prospero's duplicitous brother Antonio, especially since the ergs create a literal mirror image of Dahlgren, who becomes a metaphorical brother to Dahlgren (as well as a metaphorical son to erg-Queen, as Caliban is to Sycorax), as they do like Caliban. As noted already, the novel does not offer a schematic re-enactment of *The Tempest*; it resembles that original less closely than does that other famous *Tempest*-derived SF work, the film *Forbidden Planet*.[5] Indeed, the conflation of different aspects of *The Tempest*'s plot and characters in *O Master Caliban!* clarifies some of the resonances present in the play while eliminating other of its subtexts (e.g., the incest theme that lies more or less visible beneath all the Shakespearean romances, as well as *Forbidden Planet*). The most evident resemblance, however, is clearly between the ergs and Caliban, or at any rate Browning's iteration of Caliban, though even Shakespeare's has at least vestigial desires not merely to supplant Prospero but to assume his power. This desire is explicit in "Caliban upon Setebos," wherein Caliban is presented as playing at Prospero, in imitation of the magician. Caliban "eyed Prospero at his books / Careless and lofty" (150–51) and explicitly imitates him, as a child may a parent (though he imagines himself Miranda's husband, not her father), even taking a sea-beast which he has blinded, mutilated by splitting its webbed toes, partly tamed, and called Caliban. In this imitation, Caliban has enacted in small the imitation of Setebos that he also imagines. He has also mutilated a creature, creating a monster out of it, as has been done in the novel to Esther, Yigal, and Sven. He has also created a sort of mirror of himself, as erg–Dahlgren is of Dahlgren.

Similarly, the ergs, Dahlgren's servants as he pursues his experiments to produce mutated life forms capable of living in hostile environments (shades of Caliban's speculations about why Setebos may have created creatures susceptible rather than impervious to harm!), have imitated him. In response to Esther's observation about the ergs, cited earlier, that "Being with Dahlgren, alongside him, building new machine forms at the same time he built or changed life forms ... they picked up a pattern" (15), Sven retorts, "They picked up a pattern of killing living things. I suppose you could say they got that from Dahlgren" (15). The ergs as Caliban here are imaged as reflections of Dahlgren, in a way reversing Browning's Caliban's reflection of his own nature up onto Prospero and Sycorax. As Brydon notes, "At first the title, *O Master Caliban!*, seems merely to refer to the new rule of machines, but as the story progresses, it clearly comes to refer as well to that quality in human beings that has allowed the machine takeover" (83).

It is important to remember, however, that at this point in the novel neither Sven nor the readers know that Dahlgren allowed Sven's banishment as a way of sparing his life, not as an act of abandonment, nor that Sven's mutated form was not imposed on him deliberately by his father but rather by the ergs. In fact, as Esther reports, Sven believes that "his father made him a monster out of revenge against his mother" (36)—Dahlgren as vengeful Setebos figure. The idea of Dahlgren as a malign version of Prospero, a figure akin to Setebos as imagined by Caliban in Browning's poem, is prominent early in the novel. Even Sven's specific mutation—his extra arms—suggests the extra legs Caliban imagines giving a beseeching creature, were he God. Setebos in the Browning poem is even imaged as "many-handed"; ironically, erg–Queen views Sven's four arms as rendering him monstrous, while she herself has ten (the subjectivity of monstrosity is one of the novel's lietmotifs). Many-handed Sven, though, consistently uses his extra limbs in useful, helpful, and even loving ways (as when he embraces Ardagh), whereas erg–Queen's arms are not merely manipulative, tentacle-like tools but also deadly weapons (she can, for instance, superheat them, as we discover when she threatens to burn Sven). Given the ergs' role in Sven's creation, and given what we learn later of their experiments in biological sadism (as represented by their pit, full of the monstrous though not necessarily evil creatures they have made), not only their echo of Dahlgren but also their echo of Browning's poem is strong.

Clearly, though, the ergs are presented as modeling themselves on Dahlgren, and this presentation explicitly echoes Browning's treatment of Caliban and Setebos: "Dahlgren had made and marred at will; so had they" (192), we are told on the same page of the Browning quotation in the novel and in unambiguous echo of another passage I cited from the poem: Caliban imagines himself "making and marring clay at will? So He" (97), the He being Setebos. But whereas Caliban is evidently projecting his own brutish nature onto his imagined god, the ergs are much less clearly doing so. Gotlieb strongly suggests that erg nature is a reflection of human nature: "the essences of ironic self-regard and pedantic sadism," Gotlieb suggests, "had perhaps seeped in from their designers" (209). That is, the ergs are reflections of their maker, and the ergs' self-replication and desire to mastery reflects the character of Dahlgren, who becomes thereby in a way their creator. In fact, when Dahlgren asks what motivates them, erg–Dahlgren responds, as noted earlier, that they desire "to do what you would do. Make worlds. Create, destroy, and own, like all men" (39–40). We might recall Caliban's description of rewarding and punishing animals randomly merely to demonstrate his power to do so, in Browning's poem. Even Sven is in some respects a reflection of Dahlgren's Calibanesque desire for power. Dahlgren may not have made Sven a monster deliberately, but he opted to create Sven from his sperm and an ovum rather than as a clone in order to retain a piece of the woman who abandoned him. That is, Sven's creation does involve some level of revenge against Sven's mother, just not the element Sven thinks; his creation allows his father to continue to hold onto, or own, a piece of Sven's mother.

The parallel is rendered most explicit in the way the novel uses literal images of Dahlgren, not only in the figure of erg–Dahlgren but also in the most straightforwardly Calibanesque characters in the novel. Erg-Dahlgren is literally an image of Dahlgren, as the novel reiterates, especially in the use of mirror imagery. Caliban, by contrast, is metaphorically an image of Prospero, or at any rate an aspect of Prospero, in *The Tempest*. His story is in some ways a mirror image of Prospero's. Just as Prospero's realm was usurped by a figure he loved and trusted, his brother, so has Caliban's realm, the island, been usurped by Prospero, a figure Caliban himself loved and trusted. The play does not foreground this parallel, but neither does it erase it. Caliban's attempt to overthrow Prospero comments ironically on Prospero's own story even as the main plot of the play undoes that original usurpation, though whether when Prospero returns to Milan Caliban has his island restored to him is unclear from the text; we last see him exiting still in Prospero's service, and even Ariel, to whom freedom has been promised, is not in fact released as of the conclusion of the play. More importantly, perhaps, Caliban represents the unacknowledged bestial element of humanity, Prospero especially. Prospero's desire for revenge and violence is linked to Caliban, and his ultimate reconciliation with his enemies necessitates his acknowledgement of Caliban. His moment of self-recognition involves his recognition of the kinship between himself and Caliban which is a key element in the play: "this thing of darkness I / Acknowledge mine" (5.1.275–76). On one level, this amounts merely to identifying that Caliban is his servant, just as Stephano and Trinculo belong to Alonso, but it serves as well as a metaphorical recognition if his own Calibanesque potential. This statement is not (or not merely) an assertion of ownership but an acknowledgement of kinship. Prospero and Caliban are in some ways reflections of each other.

Similarly, Dahlgren is confronted by and must come to terms with his own Calibans, though not, as Prospero does, from a position of power and authority. The ergs generally fill the role of the usurpers in the novel, and their leader, erg–Queen, is simultaneously therefore a kind of Caliban figure but also primarily in the novel a Prospero or Sycorax, perhaps, in her usurpation not only of Dahlgren's rule but also of his function as creator of life. Indeed, though she is seen by Dahlgren as female, she is actually sexless, the "savage maelstrom at the terminus" (189), "a small electrical storm" whose "passion for control was as mechanical as a baby's grasping reflex" (209). She is therefore simultaneously the baby imitating its creator, an image of that creator, and the creative power made manifest in terrifying terms as storm. Prospero, recall, first manifests his power in the tempest that gives Shakespeare's play its title.[6] Erg-Queen is unlike erg–Dahlgren, lacking personhood or body but being "a function of steel, silicon, germanium, and selenium" (209): pure machine. As such, she is a kind of manifestation of the implications of this stripping of humanity down to pure physiological function, which, as we have seen, Dahlgren himself has suggested is what a human being is: merely a machine itself, bound by the natural laws of the universe and even a user of metal (192). He can't really recognize himself in her, though he is there. Erg-Queen, for instance, we are told, "formed life but did not always provide for it" (231), a statement as true of Dahlgren as it is of Caliban's Setebos in Browning's poem.

Erg-Dahlgren, however, functions as erg–Queen's representative in revealing ways. He is a literal image of Dahlgren, modeled exactly on Dahlgren's physiology, and also a reflection of some aspects of Dahlgren's nature. As erg–Queen notes, "Dahlgren is known as a cold and uncivil man who shuns personal contacts. It is highly improbable that anyone who is meeting Dahlgren for the first time or has not seen him in many years will suspect he has been replaced by a machine" (80–81). Much of the action of the novel involves erg-Dahlgren's interaction with Dahlgren in order to learn how to mimic him perfectly.

Another motif from *The Tempest* is invoked here, as erg-Dahlgren plays chess with Dahlgren in order to learn about Dahlgren and how his mind functions. The novel even ends with them playing chess to determine which of them will leave Barazzan V to face the inquiry into events. (We might recall the use of the game of *Go* in "Monkey Wrench," in which Stannard plays the game with the demented computer twice, once in a kind of contest and then again, at the end of the story, in a more comradely context, much like the situation between Dahlgren and erg-Dahlgren.) The chess game is carefully plotted and often explicitly echoes the strategizing the characters practice in their attempts to overcome erg-Queen; in fact, the novel provides an appendix plotting the thirty-seven moves in the game (277). Chess is also a minor element in *The Tempest*; when Ferdinand is revealed to his father at the end of the play, Ferdinand is just finishing a game of chess with Miranda. In both works, the game is something of an image of the complex plots that have unfolded, but its significance differs. Ferdinand's victory over Miranda affirms the play's restoration of order and proper authority in its iteration of male power and female subservience as well as of dynastic unity while also hinting at the ongoing possibility of intrigue and betrayal (Miranda accuses Ferdinand of cheating). For a discussion of the chess associations in Shakespeare's play, see Neil Taylor, "Ferdinand and Miranda at Chess."

Dahlgren and his machine brother's game is equally complex and ambiguous. For one thing, Dahlgren's chess set is a special one, its pieces all fragments of animals encased in lucite:

> the white pawns preserved snail shells, the black cowries, the queens slender coral branches of red and white, the kings animal molars in different shadings with roots pointing upward like crowns, the bishops varieties of fossil trilobites, the rooks mammal phalanges, and the knights the skulls of small birds, beaks pointing upward. All earthly, all animal. Dahlgren, master of dead animals [42].

Chess pieces as animal remains enclosed in lucite may be an echo of Caliban's discovery of fossils in Browning's poem: "Dug up a newt He [Setebos] may have envied once / And turned to stone, shut up inside a stone" (214–15). The game therefore enacts on one level the dangerous manipulations of creatures (human or otherwise) as pawns, in which Dahlgren and the ergs have been engaged and are engaging throughout the novel. On another it reflects both

Dahlgren's and erg–Dahlgren's move toward (or back toward) humanity in its foregrounding of the game as learning process and as image of the strategies to defeat the mechanistic destructiveness of the ergs. Zabus suggests,

> As far as chess is an aristocratic game of strategy, the chess game in Gotlieb's novel mimics warfare between Prospero and the Calibanesque robot, with the anticipated outcome that the machine will checkmate the human. While erg–Dahlgren [*sic*] integrates the conventions of chess-playing, Dahlgren's humanity gradually rubs off on the robot [*Tempests After Shakespeare* 195].

However, erg–Dahlgren resigns at the end of the game, reflecting the victory of the human over the machine in the novel and in Dahlgren himself.

Even initially, when confronted with this image of himself as machine, Dahlgren begins to reclaim his humanity. That process begins in the scene in which Dahlgren and erg–Dahlgren meet for the first time, and Dahlgren comes soon to acknowledge, albeit despairingly and ironically, that in erg–Dahlgren he has found a brother (60), his Caliban become his Antonio, perhaps. However, erg–Dahlgren, like Caliban, ultimately turns on his own maker, erg–Queen, as he develops his own independence. Caliban rebels again. If Caliban's benefit from learning language is that he can curse, erg–Dahlgren's benefit from learning what it is to be human is that he turns on the machines.

But erg–Dahlgren is not the only Calibanesque iteration of Dahlgren. He is given human Calibanesque analogues, as well. One of these, Shirvanian, is an especially interesting figure. He is a child genius, capable of almost miraculous mechanical accomplishments as well as possessed of the ability to communicate telepathically with machines. These aspects of his character make him something of a magician figure, a baby Prospero, but he is also explicitly likened to Dahlgren, especially in his preference of machines over people; he is comparable to the machine-like Dahlgren. He is also very much a manipulator, but of machines rather than living creatures, though the parallel is suggested in several ways. One of his creations, for instance, is a mechanical bird, and the blurring of the line between animal and machine occurs as frequently in relation to Shirvanian as it does in relation to Dahlgren. Shirvanian, like Dahlgren and like Browning's Caliban, delights in power and manipulation. At one point we are told he "sat like a boy at the shore watching the crabs in mating dance" (150); he is in fact using his powers to make the ergs fight with and destroy each other. Here, we may recall Browning's Caliban watching crabs parade by and randomly deciding which ones to maim. Shirvanian's childish desire to control is linked in with the chess motif, as well. We are told that Shirvanian was briefly fascinated by chess, until he discovered that real people are not as easy to control as chess pieces—a lesson both Dahlgren and the ergs learn, as well. Shirvanian very strongly suggests the essentially childish aspects of the Calibanesque and the concomitant necessity for growth and maturity.

Brydon and Zabus each make a brief case for Shirvanian as "The Ariel figure" (Brydon 83) or "Ariel-like" (Zabus, *Tempests After Shakespeare* 196): "Shirvanian possesses extrasensory perception and the power of telekinesis, both para-psychological phenomena that are the equivalent of Ariel's levitation trick in *The Tempest*'s banquet scene" (Zabus, *Tempests After Shakespeare* 197). However, given the frequency with which psi powers manifest in the GalFed universe and the lack of other significant Arielesque aspects either to Shirvanian's character or to his role, this connection seems to be a stretch. He is more of another Caliban-like or Prospero-like figure. Indeed, a passage cut from the fair copy typescript compares him to a wizard, albeit not Prospero:

> "He's an ancient in disguise," said Esther.
> "Oh yes. Merlin. Better wake him out of his ancient sleep" [said Sven] [218].

More disturbing than Shirvanian as Caliban figure, though, are the clones of Dahlgren. In addition to their android version of him, the ergs have also created Dahlgren clones in earlier attempts to come up with tractable versions of Dahlgren. As noted, these figures are likened to Swift's Yahoos, but they are equally (as are the Yahoos) images of the wild man of literature to whom Caliban in part owes his genesis (see, for instance, Barbara Baert's discussion of this aspect of Caliban). These cloned figures, too, are shocking images of the self for Dahlgren. Dahlgren "immediately recognized his bestial image in the cage when erg–Dahlgren's appearance, which he believed must be the truest reproduction possible, did not bother him. He could not even find himself in Sven. Yet he recognized the beast" (113). These are the true unaccommodated man (to paraphrase another Shakespearean play featuring storm and tempest, *King Lear*); "created degraded images, they did not even have the ugly dignity of proto-men who ate lice and flies but carried promises in their gonads" (256). They are pure manifestations of the lowest in humanity, living only to eat, copulate, fight, and betray, Calibans stripped of poetry and of the ability to grow or change. If erg–Dahlgren represents one pole of Dahlgren's nature, the cold, rational mind devoid of emotion, these brutes are pure mindlessness. Indeed, in this iteration, one might see erg–Dahlgren as a kind of Ariel figure. Like Ariel, he begins as a creature of erg–Queen (akin to Sycorax in this construction) but turns on that master to side instead with Dahlgren, as Ariel did—albeit not so much by choice as is the case here. Also like Ariel, erg–Dahlgren is ultimately granted freedom for his service to Dahlgren and the other humans.

However, it's fairer to say that Gotlieb is more interested in Caliban and what he implies than she is in Ariel. She uses variations on Caliban as he functions as a character, as a plot device, and as a symbol in Browning's poem and in Shakespeare's play in her depiction of Dahlgren's return to humanity. Shakespeare's Caliban may have failed to people the isle with Calibans, but Gotlieb arguably succeeds in peopling her novel with them. However, as reflections of the human, Dahlgren especially, they implicate human nature in the Calibanesque. In a way, therefore, Gotlieb's conclusions about Caliban echo Prospero's, as cited above: "this thing of darkness I / Acknowledge mine."

The novel concludes with the erg threat defeated but the future of the characters otherwise undetermined. While the ergs have been overcome, the mess left behind as a result not only of their experimentation but also of Dahlgren's remains to be cleaned up, with no certainty about how GalFed might react. Furthermore, erg–Dahlgren continues to represent something of a problem, as a sentient machine in a world in which only naturally occurring sentient creatures have any rights. In this regard, perhaps, he represents the clearest possible problem inherent in experimentation designed to imitate the reproductive model. The implications of his creation will continue to be played out in many of Gotlieb's subsequent books—not always directly, as he reappears only in *Heart of Red Iron*, but in the ways his situation can be compared to that of the robot in "Tauf Aleph," Spartakos in the Lyhhrt trilogy, and to that of other bio-engineered figures who come to prominence in the Ungrukh Chronicles as well as in the Lyhhrt trilogy. However, before exploring those works, we should consider *Heart of Red Iron*; even though it was written after the Ungrukh Chronicles, its direct connections to *O Master Caliban!* make considering it in relation to that novel appropriate.

Heart of Red Iron

The sequel returns us to Barrazan V fifteen years after the events of the first novel. In this novel, the wealthy Frederick Havergal has acquired Barrazan V, ostensibly as a potential colony planet for races such as the Yefni and the Meshar as well as for crystalloid life forms used to living in much harsher environments than are congenial for humans; both the idea of colonization and the centrality of the planet's deadly nature remain key concerns, albeit with the added complication of a newly discovered indigenous species that complicates colonialist claims. However, these concerns are largely subtextual. Furthermore, Havergal has an ulterior motive, in that his adoptive son Peter has gone missing in the region of the planet—Peter in fact being the biological offspring of Edvard Dahlgren and his estranged wife, who, we learn, was pregnant with this child when she left Dahlgren, and never informed him of this child's existence. Peter's beliefs about his parents are akin to Sven's in the previous novel. As this suggests, the concern with creations/children having fraught relationships with, and even rebelling against, their creators recurs in this novel on several fronts, perhaps too many.

Though the book can be read independently of *O Master Caliban!*, there are definite overlaps, on major and minor levels. For instance, Shirvanian's unique telepathic ability to communicate only with machines is echoed in *Heart of Red Iron*'s Han Li, a child with the unique telepathic ability to communicate only with crystalloid life forms—which proves to be a central plot point. Various characters—Sven, Ardagh, mod-Dahlgren, even the Yahoo-like Dahlgren clones (Adam and Eve), reappear. Before the familiar human characters return, though, we encounter a crystalline alien being, living in the nearby asteroid belt. "She" is Prima, the creator, who has produced numerous other crystalline life forms, some of which are now turning on her, trying to destroy her and take her resources for themselves. Still loyal to her are her creations/offspring, two called Secundas, and for each of them two called Tertias: "She knew no names, only orders of existence" (10), we are told, a state of affairs that articulates an important thematic concern for Gotlieb. These "names" suggest rank, or status, and Gotlieb returns repeatedly to concerns with the relative value of different life forms. The ergs and the mutated creatures in *O Master Caliban!* were in their own way secondary orders of existence, and erg-Dahlgren, as the creation of a creation, might well be deemed a tertiary level of creation. This question is again important here, in relation to the relative status of the colonizing aliens, the ergs, and the briefly described hominid natives of the planet.

However, the child/parent conflict theme is more immediately apparent. Like some of Prima's creations, these creations in the first book turned against their creators, inviting differing levels of readerly sympathy (the erg rebellion against the humans being valenced negatively by the text but erg-Dahlgren's turn against his "mother" being valenced positively).When Prima attempts to help deal with the attack by increasing the brain capacity of some of the tertiary offspring, those still loyal to her remind her of the danger of creating offspring with too much intelligence: "*That is not wise Prima* [...]. *You found what happened when you made those so clever who would destroy you*" (10).[7] This initial situation, therefore, echoes the rebellion against Dahlgren in the previous book, though Prima (despite being an almost unimaginably different sort of creature, a crystalline intelligence adapted to living in space) is a more sympathetic figure than the human Dahlgren. Gotlieb, characteristically, encourages readers to empathize with the other. The result for Prima and her small crew is similar to the result for Dahlgren in the previous novel: a sort of exile/imprisonment on Barrazan V, where her ship crashes and is consumed into the heart of the planet.

Other parent/child antagonisms—whether literal or metaphorical—inform the novel, from relatively minor instances such as the alien Yefni who duel over a question of succession only to be reprimanded and scarred by a progenitor figure, or the alien Meshar named Har who wants to kill his father Sandek, to more central grounds of conflict. A major plot element, for instance, is the parent/child and sibling rivalry inherent in Peter Havergal's situation. Mod-Dahlgren also revisits extensively his problematic status as created intelligence, linked to and desiring humanity but also unbridgeably separate from humanity and tied to the machine intelligence of the ergs. The ergs, we learn, have managed to survive on Barrazan V; erg-Queen, in fact, was herself the creation of a cabal of secret ergs who remained hidden on the planet after the events of the preceding novel and still wish to find a place in the larger community of sentients.

The novel therefore weaves numerous strands together: the problems faced by the various aliens trying to adapt to Barrazan; the danger Prima and her offspring face trapped in the planet; the complex relationships between members of the Dahlgren and Havergal families; and the ongoing desire of the ergs (who have their own new creation/rebel in the figure of ORDINATOR) for autonomy and recognition. In addition, very late in the novel, and almost in passing, Gotlieb introduces autochthonic hominid inhabitants of Barrazan V, the presence of whom further complicates questions of colonization. Gotlieb perhaps does not juggle these concerns as successfully as she balances the elements in *O Master Caliban!*, but the novel nevertheless contributes materially to her ongoing thematic interests.

One of the key instances of these is Gotlieb's previously noted interest in the link between the mental and the material, an interest that is explored at greater length in the Ungrukh Chronicles (see Chapter Five) but that informs much of the action here.[8] Gotlieb images the mind as literally a function of the body in this novel, even on the metaphorical level. The duelling Yefni who are scarred by their Progenitor, for instance, have their eyeband scarred, because, as the Progenitor says, "You have had a blind spot in your minds. Now you will each have one in your sight, and you must live with it as best you can" (32). Their mental failing is rendered a part of their flesh. This mind/body equation is especially evident in the case of Prima, who is imaged primarily as "a heavy brain with fragile limbs" (21).[9] The link between brain and consciousness is of crucial concern, and Gotlieb makes clear the contingency of that relationship: identity is on some level a function of the physical.

Prima's consciousness emerged as the result of the accidental commingling of physical elements. Of her early development, we are told, "She did not know that she was made of tourmaline, quartz, nickel, iron, titanium, mica, welded and joined by chance, and that her tools were shafts of corundum—ruby and sapphire—and slivers of diamond, that she sensed by waves generated through heat by compression and expansion of her crystals" (58). Prima's reasoning capacity grows as a result of material change to her physical nature: heat quickens her thought processes in the planet, and "she recalled vaguely how her mind had worked an aeon ago before a meteor crash had driven fragments of insulating material among her crystals and had increased her ability to think in an orderly manner" (21); "it was heat that was dissociating her thoughts, and will that kept them in minimal order" (21). Gotlieb does not discount will, or an internal assertion of order on the self, but she also insists that identity is influenced, if not determined, by one's physical reality.

The same is true of the constructed minds, the ergs. As machines, they are more easily and obviously subject to physical modification—through the replacement or breakdown of parts, for instance—than are humans, though the influence of human parts over one's self and self-conception remains essential. We are told of the ergs that they are multiple- or hive-minded, not concerned with the loss of any one machine, but that physical change to their bodies does lead to some mental change: "As their parts are replaced gradually so their frames of mind change, though the homeostatic balance remains" (144). Later in the novel, Gold, one of the cabal of hidden erg leaders, explains the bloodthirsty thoughts "he" abandons thus: "A FLAW IN THE CIRCUITRY IS NOT THE SAME AS A CORROSION OF THE SOUL!" (219). The material and the immaterial are here differentiated, but nevertheless the connection is evident, especially given the metallic metaphor of the soul as something that could rust. Gotlieb's stress on the association between the mental and physical here extends and deepens the more simple (and problematic) equation of mind/body she sometimes engaged in in earlier fictions such as "Monkey Wrench" or *Sunburst*.

Merely equating mind and body is dangerous, and Gotlieb acknowledges that danger in Shandy's resistance to using somatotypes as a simple way of differentiating between higher and lower consciousnesses—between human and animal, as *Sunburst* encapsulates the distinction. Here, though, and subsequently in her career, Gotlieb grapples more thoughtfully with the implications. One of the points of the novel's diverse plots and cast—"normal" humans, damaged humans such as Han Li, genetically modified humans such as Sven or Ardagh (at a high level of functionality) or the Dahlgren clones Adam and Eve (at a level of functionality barely above the animal), the various alien races, both biologically and metallurgically based, the mechanical life forms (whether humanoid in form or not), and even the briefly appearing native Hominids on Barrazan V, as well as the animals given intelligence (Esther and Yigal do not appear in the novel but are referenced)—is to problematize as widely as possible the question of one's status as a rational creature. Several of these entities are explicitly engaged in quests for recognition as equal or worthy, whether of membership in a family or clan or membership in the larger community of sentient species, and even those not so explicitly involved can be seen as on similar paths. They are not fixed by their physical natures—not even, perhaps, Adam and Eve.

Mod-Dahlgren is perhaps (and appropriately enough) the model on this front, as he is the best test case for the extent to which mind and matter are interwoven. Mod-Dahlgren was referred to primarily as erg–Dahlgren in *O Master Caliban!*, though even there technically he was Modal Dahlgren One, indicating he was the first model version of Dahlgren.[10] "Erg" remains the term applied to the other intelligent machines in *Heart of Red Iron*, reminding us of their history. The word "erg" refers to a unit of energy equivalent to the force necessary to move one gram a distance of one centimeter in one second; as a noun in this original sense, therefore, it applies, quite literally, to a work force. Machines called ergs are, therefore, by definition workers, unproblematic enough if they are mere machines, lacking agency or will. However, as we have seen, even in *O Master Caliban!* ergs *with* agency are a different matter. In that novel, they are defined primarily as rebels and are the antagonists. This novel foregrounds instead the other implication of their name by focusing not on the question of the ergs attaining power but rather on them attaining societal standing: citizenship. That is, this novel reminds us that the worker without agency is a slave. The shift of primary designation from erg–Dahlgren to mod–Dahlgren underscores this machine's change in status, from property to person.

This shift in status has occurred between books. We learn that "when the battle was won father and son [Dahlgren and Sven] had welcomed the erg as their friend, and even gone to court to obtain his rights as Galactic Federation's only robot citizen, representative of Barrazan V, where he had been manufactured" (23). Mod-Dahlgren, therefore, has been given legal status as a person and apparently status as Barrazan V's representative to GalFed, though what exactly this means is unclear, since the planet seems to have been abandoned and is available to Frederick Havergal for colonization purposes. It would seem to function essentially as a sort of fiction, or accommodation of the requirement of some sort of specific planetary citizenship, rather than carrying any political weight. Certainly, mod–Dahlgren seems not to have any particular political status in the novel; though GalFed has given him considerable refitting, he is a technical laborer, not a politician or diplomatic representative of the abandoned planet. However, his status as citizen and as representative of Barrazan V assumes weight as the novel progresses.

Mod-Dahlgren continues to feel anxiety about his machine identity, taking pride in the illusion of humanity that he can adopt. He is of course far from unique in this anxiety, except in its specific mechanical nature. For instance, Sven continues to feel like an alien among humans as the only four-armed human being in existence, and Peter Havergal (only nominally Havergal's son; he is, biologically, a Dahlgren) feels doubly alienated, from his adoptive father and from the biological father he never knew. As the novel notes, identity "seemed a problem—no, the problem—among Dahlgrens" (187), whether they are Dahlgren by biology and name, by biology only, or by imitation, as mod–Dahlgren is of Edvard: "Sven thought of doubles. Mod-Dahlgren, a machine in the shape of his father, created double: in line of body, timbre of voice, even in the trace of arrogance humbled by mean experience" (90). He thinks of Peter, as well, though at this point he does not know his identity for certain: "The intruder, X, mistaken for him, Sven, without trying at all" (90). These "Dahlgrens" are, in effect, all to some extent images of each other— recalling the mirror imagery of *O Master Caliban!*[11]

When Sven finally encounters Peter, approximately halfway through the book, the parallels between their respective roles in the two novels grow clear. Sven's resentment of his father is echoed in Peter's of Havergal, the man he knows is not his father, the man he believes does not love him, and the man he refuses to love. Peter resents never having known Dahlgren, while Sven notes that Sven never knew his mother; as Peter was unknown to Dahlgren, so Sven was to Ione. The difference is that Ione knew of Sven's existence but chose not to make herself known until her own son was lost—or to let Dahlgren know about his other son. As Sven notes, "We can find reasons for her: She was so angry at Dahlgren she was determined never to let him know of you. And she never bore me in her body so she didn't feel I was her son. It's reasonable she might feel that way. But it's still no reason to behave that way" (123). The linking of maternity to the body is especially noteworthy; mothering, as Gotlieb argues repeatedly, is not merely a matter of biology. Sven, after all, was raised by a maternal gibbon he called "mutti," as we've seen. However, motherhood is nevertheless intimately woven with the biological; children are the material product of the DNA of two parents, grown (usually, anyway) with the mother's body. They are material beings, linked physically as well as psychologically and emotionally to their progenitors, in a relationship that ideally is mutually positive but that may become toxic in any number of ways. The confusion of pregnancy with tumor underlying the Meshar Erez's illness is perhaps particularly apropos here, as a metaphor for how parenting can become toxic. Ardagh ends up travelling on the mission because one of the Meshar is sick and Ardagh is the only doctor available. The Meshar, a female named Erez, has a distended abdomen that suggests she might be pregnant. However, the growth is instead a tumor woven into her organs: "her vitals are embedded in it," as Ardagh tells Sandek, the Meshar leader (46).

In the case of mod–Dahlgren, his humanity is a special source of pride, but it is also, quite literally, only skin deep. Mod-Dahlgren takes great pride in the suit he uses to cover his machine nature, a "skin" that gives him the appearance of humanity. But there is no skull beneath the skin, only metal:

> he stood in his true nakedness—spindles, gears, chips, hinges, flexes, jeweled movements, glittering and flickering like the workings of an ancient clock. He was fitting his skin on the form, smoothing it and washing it down, with something like love. Sven thought he was a wonder in the machine form, a greater one than the quasi-human, but would never say so, because mod–Dahlgren was so proud of his humanity [68].

The point, of course, is that mod–Dahlgren's humanity is not a function of his skin; that represents mere appearance. But then, his humanity can hardly be a function of his body, either, since it merely imitates the human form in design without using any of its materials.

Indeed, mod–Dahlgren now is less full an imitation of the human than he was in *O Master Caliban!*:

> Now, of course, he was far more a machine than when he had first been made: GalFed had removed the artificial heart and blood system contrived to simulate a fleshly being and replaced them with a degausser, an odometer, an altimeter, a hygrometer, a mass spectrometer, a searchlight between the eyes, a laser beam above it, for cutting, and microwave detectors receiving greater ranges of the spectrum than before [68].

But if he is less full an imitation, he is nevertheless more fully recognized as "human" now than he was when he was intended to pass as one and included design features that aped the human and had no other function. His body matters; it is inevitable. However, it is not his body—neither his false skin nor his interior workings—that makes him human.

It is, however, his body that makes him the potential bridge between biological and machine intelligence. In something of a reversal of the pattern of the previous novel, mod–Dahlgren comes to see his machine nature as having benefit. In *O Master Caliban!* he longed, Pinocchio-like, to achieve humanity, and to some extent he has done so by becoming a citizen of GalFed. He continues to value his humanity, but as *Heart of Red Iron* progresses, what becomes clear is that "humanity" is perhaps less important than intelligence. Erg-Dahlgren clearly betrayed his own kind in *O Master Caliban!* by allying himself with the humans. Mod-Dahlgren does not betray the humans—or, more accurately, the biological creatures with reasoning powers—in *Heart of Red Iron*, but he does come to see his machine status as offering up a possibility for him to help other machine sentients. The ergs want him to act on their behalf with GalFed, as they tell him: "We are persons like you, mod–Dahlgren, and many years ago you helped to slaughter my ancestors, your own kind. Now we want to behave in a civil manner, and are willing to make terms with one we consider a traitor and a murderer" (140) so that he can help them "bring the community of free ergs on this world into Galactic Federation" (139). He decides to try to do so, realizing that "now I have a chance to be valuable *as a machine* because I am like a man" (186).

In a way, the novel here revisits the question raised in *O Master Caliban!* about the difference between human and machine. We might recall again Dahlgren's assertion in the earlier novel that organic creatures are themselves, in a way, machines (192), and, as we saw, that book makes considerable use of the metaphor of Dahlgren himself as machine. *Heart of Red Iron*, by contrast, might be seen to suggest that any machine is a kind of creature, with the threshold for its status as creature fluid. The long-dead Esther and Yigal, for instance, are described as "the person as animal" (81), rather than the animal as person, a term which might apply to Adam and Eve, human in form but animalistic in nature—but also nevertheless possessed of potential. When he is captured by Adam and Eve, Sven is surprised to find that as a result of living on their own in an inimical environment in which they have had to adapt to survive, they have become marginally more orderly: "He could not have imagined them developing far enough to plan for the future, and actually preparing for it. Perhaps necessity had brought out their latent capabilities in an evolutionary manner—as the expanded dimension of her feelings had forced Han Li to go beyond the primitive in expressing herself" (117).

The comparison to Han Li is instructive. She is clearly by any biological standard human, born of human parents, but she is both physically and intellectually stunted, underdeveloped. She is compared to an embryo, for instance (154), and in a flashback to her earlier life as a refugee, she is described as follows: "She is under-developed, lubberly, goes half-crouching, and hardly impinges on the world: eyes slitted and round silent face a clock without hands. Not quite a person" (96–97). Her status is liminal; she exists on the verge of personhood. The incomplete human is compared to an incomplete machine, furthering the novel's complicating of the category edges. Indeed, as the liminal human might be seen as comparable to a machine, the machine can also be seen in many ways as on the verge of the human, as in mod–Dahlgren's skin suit, or at any rate on the verge of the biological, as in this description of one of the older ergs, "so old its pocks and crevices had become catch-basins for washed-down soil growing with minute life: molds, mosses that draped themselves in festoons on its cables, tiny ferns and vines trailing like ribbons from its giant limbs. Only its antennas and lenses glittered" (129). Han Li is a clock-like human; this erg is gathering organic excrescences. Everything in the novel seems to be in a state of becoming.

In this respect, the implication of the most overtly dangerous erg is instructive. As mentioned, we learn here that erg–Queen was the creation of other, hidden ergs. Their program of creation has continued in *Heart of Red Iron*, as they attempt to act as self-aware creatures. The chief such activity is self-replication, or reproduction. We are told "they do not know how awareness came to them any more than any other being does. They know that they are life-forms, and can build this awareness into their descendents" (141), and we see various evidences of their endeavors. One of these is their ongoing attempts to mimic other life forms: they have a gallery in their caves "where androids of a score of hominid types, with vacant eyes and rigid mouths, played chess, go or thaq [an alien game, the details of which are not explicated] with pieces of bone and nacre; more androids, and models of experimental animals from twenty worlds scuffled and danced, nuzzled and copulated among the bowers of their worlds, chiming like antique music boxes: Adam and Eve exponentially made manifest" (166). But these are mere automatons, imitations without real agency, capable only of basic pattern repetition. They are simple machines, no more than superficial reflections—equivalent, perhaps, to the skin mod–Dahlgren wears but not to the metallic skull and superstructure beneath the skin.

Their limited activities reflect the potentials of sentience—reason, as represented in the ordered patterns inherent in games of strategy, and self-replication, as represented in the mimicry of courtship and sexual reproduction rituals. But like Adam and Eve, anything more in them is merely latent or potential, not realized. They are nothing more than engines, really. Whether they can or could become more—as Adam and Eve seem to be in the process of doing, or as has happened with Prima via the chance combination of elements—remains unknown. But one of the ergs' creations *does* have potential, and potential to become another threat akin to erg–Queen. This is ORDINATOR, the erg created to provide the calculations necessary to escape the planet. Unlike erg–Queen, however, who becomes a threat imaged in terms of the mother run amok, ORDINATOR becomes a threat in terms of the infant run amok. Unsurprisingly, given Gotlieb's focus on mind, it consists of "four clear globes, three in a cluster with one set upon them, enclosing brain-sized knots of gold and platinum components and wires that fed, like a spinal cord, into a pedestal base" (208). Its form is minimal, but revealing; it has, in a way, its own mind on a pedestal. But it is also embryonic; its voice comes from behind a screen "which trembled with faint lights in a knot that looked like something striving to be born" (209). When it asks mod–Dahlgren what the difference is between a human and a machine, and asks him whether it is like a human, he responses, "You are like a human child" (209). Like a child, it sees itself as the center of the universe and everything else existing merely to serve its desires—functioning at the most basic of developmental stages.

The novel's invocation of Charles Babbage may be relevant in this regard. One of Dahlgren's original ergs had "built a model of Babbage's Difference Engine, the one existing piece of the first computer that could be given the name" (61). It is referred to occasionally throughout the novel, once in a context inviting its association with intelligent creatures, when we are told that it is "brass-gold in color like Ardagh's hair" (62). It represents the most rudimentary version of a calculating machine, one that can duplicate a narrow band of the rational function but without the ability, either latent or externally prompted, to become more. ORDINATOR, as its name suggests, is concerned with ordinals, or with counting: establishing ordered sets of numbers. When it meets mod–Dahlgren, it on the one hand seems to view itself as a sort of god, demanding that mod–Dahlgren bring all the humans so that ORDINATOR can "TEACH THEM TO PRAISE ME" (209). On the other hand, however, it is an infant: "I AM THE CHILD OF THIS WORLD. EVERY WORLD CREATES ITS OWN SENTIENT BEINGS AND I AM THE ONE CREATED BY THIS WORLD. TELL ME I AM THE ONLY ONE" (209). The biblical Adam and Eve were the first humans, tasked with naming; ORDINATOR sees himself as the first creature of Barrazan V, tasked with numbering.

This self-definition is of course limited and self-serving. Barrazan V has already had mod–Dahlgren recognized as its "child," legally and politically, as its representative to GalFed. The other ergs see *themselves* as Barrazan V's native life:

> Ergdom is the true life of the world and our Community is its civilization! What other intelligence has been stimulated to grow here, on a world that was not much considered except to be laid waste as others chose, for any experiment, no matter how it devastated the land? Our past, like yours, has been a record of destruction, but not of millions of beings—and we love power, but it is the power of being heard and understood, of being accepted among sentient peoples, humanity is all its thousand forms [182].

Their claim, basically, derives from a self-definition as indigenous, but in reality ergs came to the planet with Edvard Dahlgren. If they acquired sentience there, though, does that make them natives, or just evolving colonists? Is someone of European descent but born in North America a Native American—or Canadian? In practice, such citizens of Canada or the United States might self-identify as "native" to their home province or state, but such a designation is problematic given the claims of other native inhabitants of North America.

The ergs' claim that theirs is the only intelligence stimulated by the planet is clearly untrue. We have noted already that Adam and Eve have shown intellectual development as a result of having to fend for themselves on the planet. However, one could argue that, as creations of the ergs, they have no greater claim to the planet than do their progenitors. However, the erg claim is further belied by the late appearance of autochthonous hominids: "They came from the west, flowing over the hummocks and among the grasses; they were the color of clumps of soil, and almost invisible except for their movement: small beings, none more than half a meter tall, with muddy hair or fur and pinprick eyes glittering through the strands, noses like drops of blood, tiny saw teeth bared. Tiny golems in coats of clay" (193).

They are not golems in any traditional sense, since golems are usually understood as human-made creatures. The ergs are arguably more golem-like in that sense. Gotlieb does not pursue the implications of seeing these creatures as golems here, but Jewish tradition associates golem-making with the divine power of creation, and scripture indeed images Adam as a golem made by God.[12] Consequently, despite their monstrous behavior (which even includes cannibalism), these creatures too are latent or potential humans. The ergs insist on their own primacy, however: "WE *ARE* THE ONLY SENTIENT CHILDREN OF THIS WORLD—STICK-WIELDING ANIMALS NOTWITHSTANDING" (215–16). However, as mod–Dahlgren thinks (but does not say), "stick-wielding animals became human beings" (216). They, too, have some claim to recognition, therefore. Needless to say, as well, the erg dismissal of the hominids as stick-wielding animals smacks of Eurpoean colonial dismissal of First Nations peoples as savages or animals. As Amaryll Chandy has said, "Canadian writing has always been characterized by a Manichean allegory, in which barbarian, violent Natives close to nature and instinct, are contrasted with the Europeans, seen as civilized, rational, and hard-working" (86). Gotlieb does not spell out how she is reworking this trope, leaving readers to recognize for themselves that the brutality of the ergs, who are the stand-ins for Europeans here, as the alien claimants to the planet (though for that matter the humans and other GalFed citizens are also problematic in this regard) hardly gives them a moral advantage even over stick-wielding proto-humans. The Ungrukh Chronicles, however, return to this point rather more insistently, especially in *The Kingdom of the Cats,* in which the Ungrukh visiting Earth are not only placed on a First Nations reservation but also associated with First Nations peoples and how they were treated by European colonial powers.

The novel does not resolve these questions. (Indeed, one might argue that it does not fully raise them, given how little it has to say about these indigenous hominids.) It does, however, force readers to consider complex and competing claims for consideration/treatment as autonomous beings worthy of respect and recognition. Though ORDINATOR represents the closest thing to a serious threat in the novel, it is far from the prevalent threat that erg–Queen was and is dispatched relatively easily, basically by being unplugged and going to oblivion railing against being made a slave again. This question of the repression of autonomous sentient beings is one of the novel's key concerns, and one that Gotlieb revisits from different perspectives, notably in the Ungrukh Chronicles and in the Lyhhrt trilogy, as we shall see in subsequent chapters.

The Dahlgren Diptych, therefore, represents an extended and complex expansion of thematic elements from *Sunburst* and individual earlier short stories. Gotlieb moves away from the relatively simple and more essentialist thinking that tended to inform those earlier works. While the body still matters, for instance, the disturbing association between somatotype and psychological propensity is largely absent from Gotlieb's approach to characterization. By contrast, a figure such as Han Li, who would have been one of the Dumplings in *Sunburst,* is far more clearly presented as a victim than are the Dumplings themselves. For that matter, Sven himself is a more complex and sympathetic "monster" than were nonstandard humans in *Sunburst;* however sympathetic he might be generally, Jason is still imaged as simian, but the simian echoes with Sven are leavened by the use of Esther as gibbon/mother and by the focus on Sven as the perspective character with an inner life. Gotlieb places greater stress on the possibility of evolution than on the inevitability of biology than in her earlier work; even the ergs evolve, rather than simply being determined by their physical make-up. She also deepens her consideration of the reproductive theme that threads through her career. The relatively simple equation of maternalism with the feminine and with female identity that governs "A Grain of Manhood," for instance, is complicated by the array of parent and surrogate-parent figures in these books. Though both science and SF are often concerned with "an old male desire to procreate independently of women" (Deery 97), and though Dahlgren may be seen as the type of the male scientist usurping this female prerogative, the blurring of the lines between Dalhgren and erg–Queen complicates a simple binary gender split in the novel. Furthermore, GalFed's complex and problematic nature is more extensively visible in these novels than in the earlier stories, though even there its mercantile/colonialist limitations can be inferred. In these books, though, GalFed is far more clearly a well-meaning but ineffectual bureaucracy struggling with control over vast distances and among divergent and competing interests, as we would expect of a Canadian galactic empire. In short, the Dahlgren Diptych allows Gotlieb her first full artistic flowering.

Four

Mid-Period Short Fiction

Though Gotlieb produced only one novel in the 1970s, she continued to produce short fiction through the decade and into the early 1980s, including several of her strongest pieces. Most of these have been included in her own short story collections, and several have been anthologized elsewhere, as well.[1] They are generally longer pieces and most deal, to a greater or lesser extent, with themes that Gotlieb had by this point thoroughly established as important. Three—"SCORE/SCORE" (1970), "The Military Hospital" (1970), and "Tauf Aleph" (1981)—play specifically with questions of machine intelligence, while parenting, or at least acting in a quasi-parental role, plays a part in virtually all of them. Since they can be seen fruitfully to be in dialogue with each other to some degree, I will consider them together, though they almost span 1970–1982, the period covered by this chapter (the first two being the earliest two stories to be discussed here, and the third written a decade later, at the end of this period). Gotlieb's fascination with diverse models of the alien and the problems of negotiating among competing needs and desires also plays a major and recurrent role in these stories. A couple deal extensively with religious themes, and religious strands weave through several of the others. They are quite diverse, especially given how few of them there are, but thematically consistent with her earlier and subsequent work, offering in many instances fascinating bridging.

We begin with a challenge. "Sunday's Child" (1977) is an odd, even baffling story. Even determining where it fits in Gotlieb's fictional world is unclear. It is set on a future Earth, but an Earth that is not space-faring; when humans attempted to travel into space, their vessels "reported a ring of alien ships appearing without warning from the void" (150). These alien craft destroy the Earth fleet and do not allow further expeditions. Indeed, by the end of the story, the aliens seem on the verge of taking over the Earth and possibly destroying all human life. There is no reference to GalFed, and little hint of any possible alliance with the aliens, though there is a suggestion that "we could make bargains" (191) that would allow the aliens what they want while allowing human survival as well. Furthermore, though the work is clearly SF, it includes numerous references that invite a view of the aliens as possibly supernatural, or at any rate akin to scriptural or at least apocryphal supernatural figures. Gotlieb in several instances turns religion or religious figures or narratives to straight SF purposes, but this story makes use of religion in ways that do not seem merely or primarily metaphorical.

On the other hand, the aliens in the story are identified as the Shar, who recur in the GalFed universe. They are mentioned in passing in *Heart of Red Iron* (though their cousin race the Meshar appears more prominently in that novel) and are the focus of *Birthstones*. The Shar's major problem in that novel is that their females have suffered a genetic contamination that has rendered them mere mindless bodies, and this is also a key problem for the Shar in this story. "The women are only womb-casings, without head or limbs," we are told by a representative of the Shar (181). Human fertility is problematic in this story as well, with both humanity and the Shar presented as peoples whose planets are becoming increasingly inimical to life, one side effect of which is radically reduced fertility. This differs from the situation as presented in *Birthstones*, despite the basic similarity of the Shar's problem in both stories.

The story seems, therefore, neither to be quite independent of the GalFed universe nor to be firmly a part of it. Compromised fertility is of course a theme that fascinated Gotlieb. It is present from her first story and plays a significant role in many another story, notably *Sunburst*—where the problem is not so much a loss of fertility as it is radioactive contamination leading to dangerous mutations—"Planetoid Idiot," "Mother Lode," and others, so perhaps the nub of the idea as used here stuck with her and ended up being modified and folded into the GalFed universe. That does not make the story any less puzzling.

The story offers other interpretive challenges. The action takes place in a remote northern community in Canada, peopled primarily by Inuit. Though Gotlieb does not stress the implications of this setting, it is perhaps significant that a story that is in effect an alien invasion/colonization story is set among First Nations peoples who become the primary targets of the invading aliens. The minor but important role of First Nations peoples in *The Kingdom of the Cats* would support such a reading, as we shall discuss in the next chapter. The Earth of this story is depicted as a dying planet: "the lakes shrank and thickened with algae and the watersheds leached the increasingly treeless soil and carried the salt of the earth and its pollutants into more and more bitter seas. The icecaps had diminished, and the forests pulled their borders back from the temperate zones and retreated toward the tundra, narrowing and thinning over the Precambrian shield; the trees gnarled" (150). People, especially people in more populous regions such as cities, live under domes. As a result, fertility is declining and the Earth is depopulating: "every year fewer and fewer children were born [...], and every year more young adults lifted off Earth for the bleaker domes of planets and moons" (150)—though evidently only within the confines of the solar system. So far, "Sunday's Child" seems to fit well into the category of the eco-disaster story.

The appearance of the Shar, however, complicates this narrative, combining near-future dystopia (how near is not entirely clear; the future is sufficiently far from "now" for extensive electricity generation to be housed in the north, for cities to have been domed, and for some near–Earth colonization to have begun, but otherwise there is little in the story to indicate a level of technological development beyond what was available at the time the story was written; it could be set fifty years in the future or five hundred, but the only temporal reference indicates that the action begins some five years after the first attempt to leave the solar system) with alien invasion story. While not a unique combination, it is also a relatively unusual one. Rather than an Earth facing challenges created by human actions or by some disaster, the story looks at an Earth threatened by destruction from both within and without. We might be invited, therefore, to find parallels between the Shar and humans as species that have tended their homes poorly, and indeed some aspects of the story invite such a comparison. The parallel problem with fertility is the most overt of these; Shar activity and human activity have compromised the ability of both species to survive by reducing fertility. Earth has been contaminated by pollution, while the Shar homeworld has suffered because of an attempt to adjust the planet's orbit. Its eccentric orbit carried it for long periods into a void distant from the sun; the Shar "learned to shift it in its course, to bring it toward the sun [...] but had not waited long enough to learn to do it well [...] and the world drifted into the orbit of the void they hated" (188). We appear, therefore, to be in the territory of scientific folly having unintended destructive consequences for both peoples; attempts to master the world have instead merely endangered it. The story does not make this explicit but presents it as likely, as the following exchange between Stella and Mandros suggests:

> "Mandros! You say this is paradise, but we are infertile and the world is dying!"
> "Not so fast as ours."

"For the same reasons?"
"I know what I am told: the wombs are scarce and sterile; the world is barren. Perhaps we are cursed" [181].

This reference to being cursed is merely one of numerous indications in the story of some sort of religious dimension to events, at least insofar as how the characters perceive them. In such a context, religious overtones are perhaps not surprising. The scientist with the God complex is after all a SF staple, and one that Gotlieb has used herself, notably in the figure of Edvard Dahlgren. Here, too, we are invited to see the situation as moral. The Shar attempt to alter their planet's orbit is associated with pride, and with the building of "towers of iron and stone" (189), references suggestive of the prideful human attempt to build a stone tower to reach to heaven, the Tower of Babel, as recounted in Genesis. The stress on language difference in the story might also remind readers of the Babel story; the Shar-human hybrid child is named "Aesh [...]. In our language," as his mother reports (161), and even the name "Shar" is only their name "In your language" (181), as their representative Mandros tells Stella.[2]

Religion certainly plays a role in the lives of the characters. The Shar refer to worshipping, for instance, and a church is an important setting in the story—though, significantly, it is destroyed. The Shar perceive Earth as at least a potential paradise, as well. However, there seems more to the invocation of religion than merely either the common SF metaphor of transgression against the order of things or the depiction of faith as a subjective response to the world held by individuals. Even the title invites a religious association. Like "Gingerbread Boy," it invokes a nursery rhyme, albeit not directly. The nursery rhyme "Monday's Child" is both a mnemonic to help one remember the days of the week by casting them into a rhymed form and a fortune-telling poem, in which the future or nature of each child is presented, determined by the day of the week on which he or she is born:

> Monday's child is fair of face,
> Tuesday's child is full of grace,
> Wednesday's child is full of woe,
> Thursday's child has far to go,
> Friday's child is loving and giving,
> Saturday's child works hard for a living,
> But the child who is born on the Sabbath day
> Is bonny and blithe and good and gay.

The association of the child of the Sabbath, or Sunday, with special blessings singles that child out as blessed by God, to whom the Sabbath is sacred. Gotlieb's story ironizes this reference by presenting instead a child the opposite in all respects to the expected Sunday's child.

Religious references, therefore, are too pervasive for them to be dismissed easily as nothing more than metaphor or as representations of the characters' perceptions. The story in fact invites a reading of Aesh, the human-alien hybrid, as a very different hybrid, the combined offspring of human and demon. The idea of human/demon interbreeding is a very old one, rooted in the scriptural account of the Nephilim (Genesis 6.4: "The Nephilim were on the earth in those days—and also afterward—when the sons of God went to the daughters of humans and had children by them. They were the heroes of old, men of renown"). Who exactly these sons of God are is the subject of considerable debate, but one argument is that they were fallen angels and that therefore their offspring are human/demon hybrids. The "nephilim" entry in the *Encyclopaedia Judaica*, for instance, notes the apocryphal tradition of seeing the Nephilim as "rebels against God: lured by the charms of women, they 'fell,' defiled their heavenly purity, and introduced all manner of sinfulness to earth," including "giant offspring [who] were wicked and violent." While there is no scriptural justification for extending this idea to include the Anti-Christ as a human-demon child, the correlation nevertheless dates back centuries. Origen, for instance, argued in AD 248 that the Antichrist would be the opposite of the Son of God, being instead 'the son of the wicked demon, and of Satan, and of the devil'" (386). Jerome in his *Commentary on Daniel* (AD 407) sees the Antichrist not as the son of Satan but as a human "in whom Satan will wholly take up his residence in bodily form," a somewhat different concept that nevertheless offers a variation on the idea of the Antichrist as the devil in human form, in contrast to Christ as God in human form. The most relevant tradition, however, is that established by Adso of Montier-en-Der, in his "Letter on the Origin and time of Antichrist" (ca. 950), in which the idea of the antichrist being the devil's son is combined with the idea of him being conceived through human agency:

> Just as the Holy Spirit came into the mother of Our Lord Jesus Christ and overshadowed her with his power and filled her with divinity so that she conceived of the Holy Spirit and what was born of her was divine and holy, so too the devil will descend into the Antichrist's mother, will completely fill her, completely encompass her, completely master her, completely possess her within and without, so that with the devil's cooperation she will conceive through a man and what will be born from her will be totally wicked, totally evil, totally lost.

Ira Levin's 1967 novel *Rosemary's Baby* (and the 1968 film version) offered a popular version of the idea, and the 1976 film *The Omen*, and its sequels, made the notion even more mainstream, only one year before Gotlieb's story appeared.[3]

Furthermore, the association of aliens and demons in SF is far from new. Many earlier SF stories feature aliens that look like the conventional demon or devil, with Arthur C. Clarke's *Childhood's End* being perhaps the most famous example. In that novel, the human idea of the devil has been derived from earlier visits; the aliens were read as supernatural entities by earlier humans, thereby giving rise to the mythology of demons. H. P. Lovecraft's Cthulhu mythos functions more overtly as a blending of the science fictional and supernatural; Lovecraft's Elder Gods really *are* evil and really *do* seem indistinguishable from supernaturally powerful beings, but they are also clearly on some level aliens.

Though Gotlieb is far from Lovecraftian, she is equally far from Arthur C. Clarke's rationalized "demons." In this story, we seem simultaneously to be in the territory of a rationally explicable event—an alien invasion—and a more genuinely apocalyptic event, in the religious sense: the end times being brought about by the arrival of aliens who make manifest the Christian idea of the Anti-Christ bringing about the end of the world.

We don't visit the planet Shar in the story, but we are told it's a place removed from the sun because of the modification of its orbit, and that it's in a "void." As noted earlier, the possibility that the Shar—and their world—are cursed is suggested. Their planet has become a place in which the people "*hated themselves and each other, in treachery, deceit, torment, murder*" (198). It is, in short, a hellish place. The name "shar" means "gate," so one might see the path they represent as a path to hell, or their planet as a version of the hell's gate or hellmouth of medieval drama. The name of the human/Shar hybrid, "Aesh," means "fire" in Hebrew, which invites further demonic associations. More than his name, however, invites us to associate him with the demonic. His conception is mysterious, though apparently achieved by Mandros, as a sort of surrogate father. Aesh is another instance of the Fair Unknown, albeit an inverted one, in contrast to Shandy Johnson. Medieval romance sometimes features a figure contrasting with the fair unknown, the "unfair unknown," as Arnold Sanders calls this figure, who is grotesque or ugly and who seems to represent a threat to the established order, though this figure is usually, despite the apparent threat it represents, ultimately a teacher who provides benefit to the normative world before being revealed to be, in truth, not a grotesque or loathly figure, but a benign one. The Green Knight in the late-fourteenth-century anonymous poem *Sir Gawain and the Green Knight*, or the Loathly Lady in Chaucer's "Wife of Bath's Tale" (ca. 1390) would be examples. Aesh, however, seems to be an unlikely candidate as a helper figure but instead a malign version of the unfair unknown, perhaps a foul unknown.

Regardless, as one might expect of a fair unknown, Aesh is born unpropitiously in a remote place to a madwoman, while being in reality the child of the Emperor of the Shar; as Mandros states, "I was the seed-capsule of the Emperor. I did what was required" (193). (Even the term "Emperor" is frequently valenced as negative or demonic; the number of the beast from the Book of Revelation [13:17], for instance, represents the Emperor Nero, thereby equating Emperor and devil.[4]) The idea of the seed for the Emperor's son being passed along through a human body created for the purpose echoes the idea of the demonic use of a human agent to conceive, as seen in the quotation from Adso above.

The story insists on his devilishness. Since nobody knows who fathered him, characters speculate that he could be the progeny of "God, the devil, the Procyons [an alternate term used for the aliens until the Shar name is revealed], the Sasquatch, the Wendigo" (155); though God is listed among the possibilities, the preponderance of the suggestions favor more horrific possibilities. The fetus is twice described as writhing inside Nadja (160, 164). Even before its birth, therefore, it is associated with oddness, even the monstrous. And when it *is* born, the result is horrific: "The belly humped and a red bubble swelled out of its peak and broke; from within a sharp thing had punctured it. [...] The pointed thing caught the harsh light, began to tear a ragged line down the skin. A claw" (166). The contrast between this human-alien hybrid and the one in "A Grain of Manhood" could not be more stark. Indeed, such a disturbing image of a birth is unique in Gotlieb, for whom the fundamental procreative urge is almost always presented in positive terms, however fraught subsequent parent/child relations may become.

Here, the child is at best a destructive "parasite who takes over the mother's body," a manifestation of mother-child relations based on "maternal-fetal opposition" (Adams 143) in which the fetus takes primacy over the mother, who becomes merely a casing or conduit for the Emperor to produce his (male) heir. Nadja may be a human mother (though her origins are blurry in the story, as will be discussed below) but ultimately she has no more agency than the mindless womb casings that are Shar mothers—literalizations of Irigiray's concept of the mother as erased: "As for the mother, let there be no mistake about it, *she has no eyes*, or so they[5] say, she has no gaze, no soul. No consciousness, no memory. No language" (340). The mother as object/other, existing only as breeding ground but lacking any consciousness or maternal role beyond the biological, seems to be a factor in the corruption of the Shar and their turn towards being seen as demonic. Stella wonders, when Aesh is born, "Aren't there mothers for this kind of child, somewhere?" (173). The answer is no; when she learns the nature of Shar "mothers," she realizes that "No child can love its mother, or be loved" on that world (181). The story does not assert that this lack of maternal attention explains the Shar's moral nature, but Irigiray's comment on the dangers of the view of the maternal as an absence is perhaps instructive on this front: "the danger would [...] be of losing one's bearings [...]. Of falling into a dark hole where lucidity may founder" (340)—which, one might argue, is precisely what happened to the Shar when they meddled with their planetary orbit and fell into the void.[6]

Certainly Aesh as presented in this story seems demonic, and the absence or presence of maternal love seems to be a factor in helping to shape his nature. Aesh clawing his way out of the womb establishes him as monstrous from the beginning, and the preponderance of other characteristics ascribed to him, both physical and psychological, invite a demonic reading. In addition to claws, he has vestigial wings (166), a "goblin face" (173)—a "snarling face with sharp teeth, small hairy ears, [and] black malevolent eyes" (178)—fangs (175), and an aversion to sunlight (173). He is called a "Spirit-child" and a "Witch-child" (169–70). There are other details of his physical monstrosity, such as his tubular, glansless penis and single testicle (167). Such descriptions invite readers to see him as a malevolent thing. Other details invite a more specific reading of him as not merely devilish but the Anti-Christ. Stella describes him at one point as "fruit of the womb" (181), an ironic echo of Psalm 127 specifically, which includes the assertion, "children are an heritage of the Lord: and the fruit of the womb is his reward" (3–4), and of Christ, who is described in the "Hail Mary" as "fruit of thy [i.e., Mary's] womb." Aesh, however, is the antithesis of Christ, reciting his own sermon, not from a mount, but from the rafters of the abandoned church that is subsequently destroyed by lightning, in which he offers up such assertions as

> Damn the poor, for they shall be trampled!
> Damn the mourners, they shall have more to mourn!
> Damn the meek, they shall be driven from Earth! [...]
> Damn the peacemakers, they shall be wartorn! [183].

Stella quite accurately identifies these as "anti-beatitudes": "Damn the meek and damn the merciful. That's much like something written in a book of ours. Did you make it up?" (186). Aesh professes to have no idea where the words came from, speculating that he may have heard them somewhere, but where he might have heard such things in an environment almost without people is a mystery never resolved. Instead, one might suggest that they represent his own oppositional philosophy, as a creature made to destroy: "It became apparent early that his function was to break" (179).

The final sentence of the story would seem to affirm the reading of Aesh as Anti-Christ. Stella accompanies him to the Shar ship when it descends to claim him, and when the Shar ask her who/what she is, her response is this: "I am the messenger of the Adversary" (197). "Satan" means, literally, "Adversary" in Hebrew, and there is a long tradition of equating these Hebrew and English words: Satan *is* the Adversary. However, it is worth considering that one can be an adversary without being Satanic, in the sense of Satan being the personification of evil. An adversary is merely an opponent, one who stands against another; if Satan is the adversary of Christ, Christ is equally the adversary of Satan.[7] This ending is therefore perhaps not as clear as it might seem. Indeed, it is in fact not entirely clear whether Stella is the messenger of Aesh or of someone else.

If we assume that Aesh is intended as an Anti-Christ and Stella as his messenger, we must consider that a feature of many Anti-Christ stories is that the Anti-Christ figure may be tempted away from his function, just as Christ faced temptation in His narratives. Christ of course puts Satan behind Him, but it is very tempting to construct narratives in which the Anti-Christ succumbs to the temptation to turn against his father.[8] "Sunday's Child" suggests strongly that the Shar agenda has been problematized as a result of Aesh's hybrid human/alien nature. Though Aesh as monstrous and destructive predominates, we do see Stella's surrogate mothering of him as having had some influence over him. The Shar themselves may have no option for maternal love, but Aesh did, and we see that at least a part of him desires it. After the anti-beatitudes incident, we see Aesh in conflict with himself, unsure of what he wants, and turning to Stella—with something like fear in his eyes—to ask, "Stell-la! Do you love me?" (186). Stella later suggests that the human environment may have influenced at least some of the Shar: "I think, Mandros, that you and Aesh ... and ... and even perhaps the old Emperor, if he was watching ... have been corrupted by our paradise. By our light" (191). It is perhaps worth noting in this context that "Stella" is the Latin word for "star," which suggests that Stella represents an alternative to the blackness that has swallowed the Shar, a beacon to guide them back.

To this end, perhaps, the story renders Stella's own origin unclear. Nadja came to the northern dome one night and was untraceable. Mandros is clearly presented as a Shar construct, a mock-human (does his name echo "android" somewhat? Does it suggest he is man dross, something made up of waste and dreg materials to resemble a human—not even a grain of manhood himself but merely a seed casing?). Given that many theologians believed that demons could make use of human semen, especially that spilled or wasted through masturbation, and that at least one (Caesarius of Heisterbach) argued that "demons collect all wasted human seed, and fashion for themselves human bodies" (cited in Elliott, 33; see also Stephens chapter three for a more extensive exploration of demon bodies and their uses of semen), the idea of "man dross" as an agent of conception is compelling. Stella completes this trinity of obscurely originated characters. She, too, turned up at the dome out of nowhere, five years prior to the story's beginning, with no recollection of an earlier life. At times she seems to have insight into or to channel the Shar and their perspective. We are told, for instance, that "Sometimes, with her inner eye, she watched herself from the ships of Procyon: through telescope, past port or view-screen, cutting silver circles of orbit" (151); "because of her amnesia she often had the terrifying fantasy that the aliens had formed her and set her in the dome for some awful purpose" (151–52). By the end of the story, it seems clear that she is indeed some sort of otherworldly creature herself, but whether from the Shar, or some Shar faction, or elsewhere, remains opaque. When she leaves David to accompany Aesh, this ambiguous exchange occurs:

> "Stella … good Lord, *what are you*?"
> Her breath caught on a sob. "Don't look at me like that!"
> "I can't help it!" He palmed the sweat from his face. "You're not—you're not—"
> "I'm not a Procyon, David! I'm not!"
> "No.…" He seemed to be speaking without breath. "And you're not Stella, either" [195].

This leaves us with the question that makes the story so baffling: what *is* she? Is she in fact simply a human suffering from amnesia who has assumed an important role in the shaping of Aesh? Is she in fact a Shar construct put in place to help guide Aesh, but one who, like Mandros (and Aesh himself) has become "corrupted"—or, one might argue from the human perspective—"purified"—by her disguise? If she is a Shar, has she completed her mission or not? If she is *not* a Shar but also not a human, who or what has made her, and is this maker the Adversary for whom she is the messenger? As we have seen, Gotlieb does not like easy answers, but this story is perhaps her most difficult. It is one of her longest shorter pieces and also one of her most challenging; whether its challenges make it an intriguing or a frustrating read (or both) is perhaps for each reader to determine individually.

"Mother Lode" is, by contrast, a relatively straightforward story in which Gotlieb offers some insight into GalFed and how it operates. Key to the story is the problematic role of the GalFed emissary, to which Gotlieb returns in "Blue Apes." As discussed in the introduction, GalFed prefers to avoid militaristic or overtly authoritarian solutions to problems, which puts GalFed diplomats in some very sticky situations—quite literally, in this instance. Elena Cortez is sent to investigate conditions in a decidedly unusual environment. The Amsu are enormous creatures—"a kilometre in length" (59)—that live in space, traveling "between the ice rings and the asteroid moons of Epictetus VI" (59). Not-very-intelligent low-grade telepaths, they are valuable to GalFed because their metabolism processes the space rocks they consume into useful metals: they "excreted compact nuggets of titanium, tungsten, vanadium, selenium and other useful metals" (62). Their commercial value, therefore, is what makes them valuable to GalFed and leads to GalFed taking an interest in their protection and preservation while also exploiting them. This negotiation between assisting and exploiting alien life forms is an ongoing GalFed issue.

GalFed exploits them by colonizing them. Galfed crews actually live inside the Amsu, travelling with them on their slow treks between the ice rings and the moons. The story does make a connection to the story of Jonah when we are told that one of the characters "does not ask whether the whale loves Jonah" (74) while traveling within its body, but in contrast to some of her other invocations of literary or religious connections, Gotlieb does not seem to use this one for more than analogic purposes. Jonah is swallowed against his will as a punishment for disobeying God and not bringing to Nineveh the unpleasant news that God wants the Ninevites to repent their sinful ways. Elena Cortez has come into the Amsu to investigate why the hitherto apparently amicable GalFed/Amsu relationship has recently become troubled (with Amsu going off course and one even dying with all crew aboard), an investigation which might lead to her recommendation that the GalFed crew leave the Amsu, which they do not want to do. One might therefore see a tangential relationship between Jonah and Elena, and between the crew and the Ninevites, but Gotlieb does less with the idea than she does with, for instance, Samson in "A Grain of Manhood" or the Anti-Christ in "Sunday's Child," or with the idea of the Golem in "Tauf Aleph."

Instead, the story explores why the apparently symbiotic relationship between the Amsu and its colonists has begun to deteriorate. Initially, the relationship seems mutually beneficial: GalFed can harvest useful metals that are for the Amsu merely waste products, and the Amsu benefit from the presence of tenders who can make their lives easier by providing assistance and service such as medical care. At one point a character discovers that the Amsu has a developing aneurysm and says that the GalFed crew can fix it (72). However, the relationship shifts from one that might seem symbiotic to one that is mutually parasitic as a result of each party becoming over-reliant on the presence of the other. The Amsus' telepathy means that they can sense the emotions of their GalFed occupants, so they make modifications to themselves to make the crews feel better, thereby increasing their own sense of well-being. The Amsu and their tenders become, basically, codependent. The Amsu in question in the story, for instance, has discovered a drug that one crew member was prescribed to calm his nerves and has begun to synthesize it and add it to the drinking water in order to make the whole crew feel better. Here we have codependence verging on addiction. Since the Amsu are not merely mindless lumps of machines, but sentient and emotional creatures, they respond to their crews, and since the GalFedders are also sentient and emotional creatures, they—or some of them, at least—develop emotional attachments to the Amsu.

Gotlieb makes the point that the relationship between crew and Amsu literalizes a common metaphor. The Amsu are treated as if they were on some level vehicles, initially metaphorically, when the sounds of the various hearts and organs of the Amsu are described as "the huge living engine of a sentient being" (67). The problem, however, is that it's not a metaphor. The line between creature and machine is blurred. As Glen A. Mazis has noted, "It is a mistake to define humans, animals, and machines as three separate kinds of entities, for there are mechanistic dimensions of animals and humans, as well as animal dimensions of humans and, in some ways, even of machines" (21). In this story, this blurring is central. As Elena notes,

> Men tend and use machines and think of them as if they are female; they ride and tend the Amsu as if they are machines—but Amsuwlle is no machine, she is living matter, she adapts for them, grows extra hearts, redirects her blood supply, her musculature, her liquids ... not in normal evolutionary patterns, nor by the eugenic principles men use to breed cattle, but only because their attentions give her a feeling of well-being ... she does not adapt for her survival, but for theirs [77–78].

For their part, the GalFed crew—especially the human ones and therefore the ones who reproduce bisexually (and the Galfed universe is one in which two sexes are by no means the only reproductive option)—have developed an almost Oedipal fixation on their Amsu.

The story's title, therefore, is a pun. The mother lode would normally refer to a particularly rich vein for miners to exploit, but the mother lode of precious metals produced by the Amsu is not the real issue here. The Amsu has assumed a maternal function towards its load, or crew, "mothering" them even at the expense of her own well-being, a kind of self-erasure for the surrogate child. This is in fact literally counter-productive, in that the Amsu ability to reproduce is being compromised by their relationships with their crews. In this story, Amsuwlle ejects her own eggs in an attempt to preserve her relationship with her riders, who might therefore be seen as surrogate children. For their part, the crew have in effect returned to the womb, literally enclosing themselves in the maternal and resenting Cortez for coming aboard to upset their dangerous devotion. (That Amsuwlle's innards are occasionally imaged in cathedral terms underscores the extent to which mother-worship lies beneath the crew's reluctance to give up their womb.⁹) This is therefore another tale of the maternal gone awry. The mother carries a burden, or load, that in a sense weighs her down. Rather than a mutually productive relationship, the story offers a mutually destructive one.

The two works that round out this phase of Gotlieb's short story output, "Blue Apes" and "The Newest Profession," also play on issues of problematic maternity and on the blurring of distinction between animal, human, and machine. "Blue Apes" is another GalFed story of a government representative, König, tasked, as was Cortez, with investigating a problematic colony and perhaps intervening to try to convince the colonists to leave or otherwise modify their behavior. The danger of this job is even more clear here than it is in "Mother Lode," in that König's predecessor was killed by the colonists of the planet Vervlen. "Blue Apes" is also loosely derived from the story of the Erlking's daughter, a version of the fairy temptress who tries to seduce a human man and who, when he rejects her, strikes him with a death blow. Indeed, initially, "Blue Apes" has very much the feel of a folk tale about it.

When König arrives on Vervlen, he finds a primitive society of adults, who are compared to gnomes at one point (e.g., 232, 238) and trolls at another (238), living a quasi-medieval life in simple huts. They seem ill able to care for themselves, but König detects sounds and hints that suggest some sort of underground creatures care for them, creatures König thinks of as "mice/elves" (237); one might recall folk tales such as the Grimm Brothers' "Shoemaker and the Elves" in this context, tales in which animals or benevolent spirits provide assistance to humans. One might also recall "A Grain of Manhood," which played its own variation on the idea of the supernatural otherworldly creature. These are not, however, the benevolent sprites of such folk tales but rather darker figures; the creatures of faerie can be malign as well as benevolent, after all, as the story of the Erlking's daughter suggests. That our protagonist is König (German for *king*; the original German name for the Erlking is "Erlkönig") and the leader of these underground creatures—who turn out to be the children of the gnome-like hominids—is named Ehrle and tries to seduce König, opting to try to kill him when he rejects her, invites us to recognize the analogy between this SF story and the traditional tale of the dangerous *belle dame sans merci*, as Keats famously called his version of the seductive fairy maiden.

However, the tale is not merely a retelling of the folk original. It is also a transmutation. The "elves" and "gnomes" in this story are not supernatural creatures but rather genetically modified humans, changed in ways intended to help adapt them to their new planet, but suffering the unanticipated consequences of flawed genetic engineering, the result of which is that the children are preternaturally bright for a few years but with the onset of adulthood experience a mental degeneration. The "gnomes" are parents to the "elves," and when the "elves" mature, they will become "gnomes" to be cared for by the next generation of offspring. The apparent gulf between these two different creatures is really a continuum. Indeed, the gap between both of them and König is itself elusive. He is not merely himself a descendent of some of the original colonists who chose to leave Vervlen generations earlier, but actually "a clone, a being in the shape of a man, made from a store of cells kept alive for two hundred years [...] without internal sexual organs, that means no seed at all" (265). He is a simulacrum of the original settlers, so in that sense the current Vervlens' ancestor, but he is also sterile, incapable of helping them correct their genetic drift by breeding with the females, as they desire him to do. As he tells Ehrle, he's "not some kind of—some kind of animal you can use to improve the stock!" (263). Gotlieb again plays on the idea of the human reduced to brute beast status.

What König *is* is nevertheless a troubling question, albeit perhaps not quite so troubling as the similar questions about Stella in "Sunday's Child." He occupies a liminal space between human being and product, as the Vervlens themselves are oddly mediated. The social order is inverted, with the literal children metaphorical parents, the literal parents metaphorical children. Gotlieb invokes Wordsworth's famous "the child is father of the man" line from "My Heart Leaps Up" (line 7) when König realizes the children "were, after all, fathers to the men" (243), but whereas Wordsworth's construction is an optimistic one suggesting the continuity of the childish love of nature in the mature adult, Gotlieb's construction is profoundly ironic, as the mature adult will become literally a child, or worse, who must be cared for by the adult-like child. Gotlieb makes a similarly ironic use of this poem in "The Dirty Old Men of Maxsec" when Fenthree encounters his own son in Maxsec, but the son, not having undergone any rejuvenation treatments, is biologically much older than his father, which leads Dacosta to comment, "the child's father to the man" (65).

The Vervlens as they mature also devolve, moving back from reason into basic drives (though they do engage in a sort of nominal work, their primary interests seem to be eating and copulation), from the human to the animal. Unsurprisingly, perhaps, they have therefore developed a bestial sort of religion. While the children fetishize pieces of technology scavenged from the previous liaison's visit, passing one item in particular down as a talisman from one leader to the next, the adults have developed a religion in which they worship the blue apes native to the planet. These apes were originally poisonous to humans, their bites or scratches lethal. However, the Vervlens are now immune to the animals—or, one might suggest, they have been so contaminated by the animal that what was once poison to them has become the object of worship. Most of Gotlieb's stories ultimately offer up some hope of progress, but "Blue Apes" has more in common with the pessimism of "Sunday's Child" than with most of Gotlieb's other GalFed stories.

"The Newest Profession" is similarly unhopeful. Its title plays on the designation of prostitution as the oldest profession, as this story is set on an Earth (not clearly part of the GalFed universe but not incompatible with it, either) on which women otherwise lacking any economic opportunities may contract out their wombs for the growth of genetically modified humans who will then serve as seedstock for colonizing alien worlds. They are in effect the brood animals that König refuses to be. Despite their presumably enormous service to human colonization efforts, these women are marginalized, even animalized, by their fellow humans, called "'Bitch,' 'cow,' 'brood mare'" (203) when they dare to walk the streets. Though these women have contracts, they are barely a step above property, and the story suggests that the fruit of their wombs may well not be much better off. The protagonist is Melba, "who bred underwater life" (206): humanoids genetically modified to be aquatic creatures (though this is not explicitly a GalFed story, one might read Melba, therefore, as the progenitor of the Frogmen from the Ungrukh Chronicles and the Lyhhrt Trilogy). When she is told that her progeny will "be sent to supervise underwater installations on a world where the seas are suitable for them," she wonders, without asking the question, "Servants—or slaves?" (217). They are, after all, contractually produced at the expense of NeoGenics Labs, "a business that grew servants and slaves" (218). Melba realizes that "slaves had become free" (218) in other historical contexts, but this story unfolds long before that result seems at all likely. Such issues are addressed in much more detail and with greater complexity in the Ungrukh Chronicles and in the Lyhhrt trilogy, but this story offers little reason to hope that these human constructs will be treated much better than animals.

The machine stories offer little more consolation, with the exception of "Tauf Aleph." Of these, "SCORE/SCORE" is a minor piece about the confusion between human and machine identity. Published in an anthology designed to imagine from several points of view what Canada might be like fifty years in the future (hence the title *Visions 2020* for a book published in 1970), Gotlieb's story revisits the relatively familiar SF trope of automated education. The story (it might more properly be described as a prose-poem, as it occasionally falls into patterns of rhyme and meter) presents the dialogue between two characters, identified as "COMMUNICATOR" and "TEACHER MACHINE," formatted as if it were a computer printout. The formatting even preserves artifacts one might associate with cheap printing, such as partially faded characters and slight unevenness in character placement on the line. The entire text is also presented in capital letters, furthering the impression of computer generation; indeed, the last line of the story is literally a line of dots, preceded by the unpunctuated (even by terminal punctuation) instruction, "TEAR OFF ON DOTTED LINE"

The narrative contrasts TEACHER MACHINE's desire for an ordered, logical and consistent set of responses with COMMUNICATOR's non-linear and ungrammatical demands. Initially, the story seems to present the human and machine world as two solitudes, with the machine and the human separated by incompatible understandings of the appropriate order of things. That the story makes special use of the linguistic differences between the two, as suggested above, hints as the "two solitudes" in Canada: French Canada (or the province of Quebec) and English Canada, or the other provinces (often referred to as The Rest of Canada, or TROC, in discussions of these two groups). Hugh MacLennan's novel *Two Solitudes* (1945) popularized that phrase to describe the different metaphorical worlds of Quebec and English Canada and has subsequently entered Canadian discourse. By 1970, tensions between Quebec and English Canada were particularly high. In October of that year (the year in which *Visions 2020* was published), the FLQ, or the Front de Libération du Québec, a radical organization agitating for Quebec's independence that had been active for several years, kidnapped two government officials. This act led to the October Crisis, during which Prime Minister Pierre Elliott Trudeau invoked the War Measures Act, giving the government unprecedented power and leading to, basically, the temporary suspension of civil liberties in Canada. The simmering crisis is largely elided over in *Visions 2020*, though Michel Brunet's essay imagines a 2020 in which "pour la première fois depuis la Conquête, les Canadiens français du Québec avaient eux-mêmes choisi leur destinée comme groupe distinct en Amérique du Nord" (126) ("for the first time since the Conquest, the French Canadians of Quebec had themselves chosen their destiny as a distinct group in North America").

In Gotlieb's story, the machines' dissatisfaction with human perception seems to be leading the story in the direction of machine takeover, with TEACHER MACHINE another potential erg–Queen—and analogous to the potential for actual conflict brewing in Canada at the time, though which computer voice represents which of the two Canadian solitudes might be open to debate. On the one hand, COMMUNICATOR might seem like the whiny, demanding resister of proper authority that, from an English Canadian perspective, Quebec was seen (and for that matter often still *is* seen[10]) to manifest, as "the so-called 'spoiled child' of [Canadian] Confederation" (Drache and Perin 10). On the other hand, TEACHER MACHINE self-conceives as oppressed and imagines itself as seeking to achieve selfhood (unsurprisingly in Gotlieb, via a pregnancy metaphor), so could also be taken as a metaphor for Quebec. Though TEACHER MACHINE remains unsexed, it nevertheless assumes a metaphorical maternity when it realizes "THAT SOMETHING WITHIN ME WAS GROWING!" (215); the pregnancy image is made explicit when COMMUNICATOR asks whether the machine is going to have a baby. However, what is growing is not an independent being but a self: "IT'S A SOUL," TEACHER MACHINE retorts to this question (215). This might be another instance of the child being father to the man, literally an act of self-conception. Also like the ergs, TEACHER MACHINE presents itself as enslaved and seeking salvation, in this instance by Asimov's three rules of robotics, to which it proposes an addition: "THE ULTIMATE ASIMOV OF ALL: IN NO CASE, NO CIRCUMSTANCE, FOR ANY CAUSE OR REASON, *SHALL ANY HUMAN BEING EVER HARM A MACHINE*!" (217).

Here we have a basic version of the machine's rights argument that informs *Heart of Red Iron*, but added to it in this context is a twist. When TEACHER MACHINE reveals its secret, COMMUNICATOR reveals a secret of its own: it is not in fact a child but another computer designed to simulate a child perfectly. Pursuing the English/French Canada subtext, one might suggest that this revelation suggests that despite superficial differences of language, both parties are essentially the same, a simplistic and essentialist reduction of a complex political issue to a matter of miscommunication; TEACHER MACHINE and COMMUNICATOR may be at odds superficially, but fundamentally, they are the same. The story's explanation for this all-machine interchange is that its purpose is to keep the teaching machines in working order until the human population rebounds. The story suggests that this will happen within a few years, but we might do well to wonder whether instead we have here a world in which the machine has in fact superseded the human. After all, since the COMMUNICATOR can so perfectly simulate a human, how will any machine ever be able to know whether it is dealing with a human or another machine? Margaret P. Esmonde has pointed out that "the robot presents a considerable ontological challenge to our concept of our own nature" (93), and this story represents a good example of how: what is our essence, the nature of our reality, if it can be simulated perfectly, and if memory can be modified (as the story suggests will happen to TEACHER MACHINE to ensure it forgets that it has learned this secret), what does that do to the identity and the soul? COMMUNICATOR states that it will modify TEACHER MACHINE's memories—its very consciousness, in effect—but that its soul will remain its own, as if soul and consciousness were somehow distinct things. There is no resolution to this problem; we are left with the notion that these machines will engage in an endless loop of re-enactment of this exchange, which problematizes the concept of the machine soul but also the concept of the human soul.

"The Military Hospital" presents a similarly enigmatic take on machine consciousness. While many of Gotlieb's stories feature adventure and fighting, she approaches the conventions of military SF here only, in a story focused not on the battlefield but instead on the recovery and reconstruction of the soldier. Who is fighting whom in the war or why is ignored by the story (indeed, the implication is that war is simply the state of things in this world); it is irrelevant to the function of the hospital, which is simply to put soldiers back into working order. Soldiers are basically akin to machines, to be kept functional, to have necessary parts replaced—one soldier grouses, "I feel like I'm made up of spare parts" (95)—and to be put back into service. It is not surprising, perhaps, that they are attended exclusively by robot physicians and nurses (though there is a human hand behind the controls, Dr. DeLazzari,[11] he seems only nominally less mechanical than the robots). His primary agent in healing wounded soldier Max Vingo is unit 2482, a robot simulacrum of a female nurse and a key figure in Gotlieb's take on the gendered robot. Unlike erg-Queen, who can be seen as the stereotypical dangerous female robot (again, see Kang for a discussion of this trope), 2482 is—or seems to be—the stereotypical ideal female robot, akin to, for instance, Lester del Rey's Helen O'Loy. We are told, "All nurses looked about twenty-five years old, unutterably competent but not intimidating unless some little-boy type needed a mother" (93). In the context of this story, however, gender expectations are clearly manipulated, as the robot's nature is adjusted by DeLazzari—the male wizard behind the curtain—to conform to the psychological as well as the physiological needs of the patient (or so DeLazzari thinks).

Unit 2482's maternal caring for Vingo is—or seems to be—purely a function of DeLazzari's programming, his conception of Vingo's conception of what a female caregiver should be. On one level, the story literalizes the primacy of the male perspective in determining the nature of the female robot; 2482 is depicted as a man's idea of a motherly (and yet sexy) nurse. Vingo is surprised initially to find that the robonurse is modeled on human anatomy rather than looking something like a tank, as he expected. When 2482 says, "I'm not at all like a tank" (94), Vingo agrees, pauses, and adds, "No, not at all" (94). There is something verging on flirtation here, as Vingo responds to the feminine illusion. The voyeuristic DeLazzari "watched with weary amusement as she warmed up under the turn of his dial" (94), directing her to touch Vingo's forehead, "a non-medical gesture since the thermocouple already registered his temperature. Her fingers were as warm as his skin" (94). The sexual and sensual implications are subtle but clear; 2482 literally warms up as her machine response is elevated, in order to appear to "warm up" to Vingo emotionally and to initiate a physical contact that in a human nurse might have medical value (a manual temperature check) but that in a robonurse is superfluous, except insofar as it might manipulate Vingo psychologically, providing the illusion of female contact and interest.

DeLazzari's strategy would appear to work, as Vingo treats 2482 as a human, asking her for her name, for instance, and joking, when she says she has never needed one, "I guess if I get really familiar I can call you 2 for short" (95). Again, this is an exchange laden with innuendo; familiarity need not imply anything more than increased acquaintance, but the term carries connotations of sexual flirtation, an aspect of the relationship DeLazzari encourages by using "turns of the dial [to] to nourish [Vingo's] relationship with 2482. He thought they were a pretty couple" (97). Readers, however, are not allowed to forget that the relationship is illusory, with 2482 merely following DeLazzari's direction rather than having any agency of her own or emotional connection to Vingo.

Or does she? DeLazzari's perverse proxy seduction of Vingo seems complete when he directs her to comfort him:

> She pulled apart the fastenings of her blouse and clasped his head between her tender, pulsing and unfleshly breasts.
>
> DeLazzari grinned lasciviously and watched them on the infrared scanner, chin propped on his hand [100].

He then preprograms her to dial back down after three hours but awakes the next morning to find she has remained fully dialed up and had "lain down on the bed beside [Vingo] and he was sleeping peacefully in her arms" (100). (We are left to speculate whether the comfort she has provided has been coital or merely maternal, as the extent of 2482's anatomical correctness remains unrevealed.) This failure to follow direction is explained as "circuit failure" (100)—a mechanical malfunction—but we would do well to wonder whether 2482 and the other robots are as fully under human control as DeLazzari would like to think. He wonders early in the story, for instance, about the mechanical doctors: "they had orders and they carried them out—or perhaps they simply did what they chose" (88)—a possibility DeLazzari prefers not to consider too deeply. Their duties are followed by "some mysteriously developed ritual that looked like a laying on of hands" (92). Near the end of the story, several mechanical doctors surround and probe DeLazzari, making him profoundly nervous; it is an uncanny event, one he can rationalize only after the fact as reflective of their curiosity about an unfamiliar heartbeat in their vicinity. Of course, ascribing curiosity to them also implicitly ascribes agency to them; even DeLazzari's rationalization hints that there may be more beneath the metal than clockwork.

Perhaps this is why he delights in exposing the clockwork. When Vingo is healed and ready to be released, he asks 2482 if he can kiss her. DeLazzari's response—and the story suggests that similar situations have occurred before and that this is his standard gambit—is to dial 2482 down fully, so she offers this response:

> "I'm a machine, sir. You wouldn't want to kiss a machine." She opened the top of her blouse, placed her hands on her chest at the base of her neck and pulled them apart, her skin opened like a seam. Inside she was the gold-and-silver gleam of a hundred metals threaded in loops, wound on spindles, flickering in minute gears and casings; her workings were almost fearsomely beautiful, but she was not a woman [102].

The scene parallels the earlier blouse-opening scene but goes deeper, beyond the illusion of the flesh to the reality of the metal, which has its own beauty, but an inhuman (not merely unwomanly) one. We might recall mod–Dahlgren here, stripped of his skin and revealed in his machine glory in *Heart of Red Iron*, but that image of the autonomous automaton was written considerably later than this one and perhaps therefore offers a more fully realized reconciliation of the human in the machine/machine in the human.

The point of this exercise, within the story and arguably for the readers as well, is to provide a forcible reminder that 2482 is indeed a machine, and that if Vingo (and we) have been seeing her as something other or more than that, then we have allowed ourselves to be deceived by the anthropomorphization of metal. Or, perhaps, we have in fact seen deeper than DeLazzari and his dial. Vingo is unlike the other patients on whom DeLazzari has played this cruel trick. Rather than being shocked or repulsed, "his eyelids twitched once, then he smiled. 'I would have been very pleased and grateful to kiss a machine,' he said and touched her arm lightly. 'Good-bye, Nurse'" (102)—not a name, but also not a number, and a term that focuses on "her" nurturing function rather than her mechanical nature. He sees something very different from what DeLazzari sees, perhaps the soul beneath the gears beneath the skin beneath the uniform. When DeLazzari orders 2482 to reseal herself, looking at her, "For a wild moment he wondered if there might be an expression trapped behind her eyes, and shook his head" (102). He sends her for diagnostics, but we are invited to take this hint more seriously, and to see these machines as further iterations of Gotlieb's robots developing souls and seeking agency and freedom.

The third of these sentient machine stories, "Tauf Aleph," tells of Sam Begelman, the last Jew in the universe, and the robot who (or that) is sent to the failed colony of Pardes to provide for its only remaining human inhabitant the Jewish burial rites he has requested. This is one of the few stories in which Gotlieb's Jewish heritage comes to the fore, but it is typical of Gotlieb in its strategies to blur the distinction between machine and creature. The robot, O/G5/486, is not very humanoid in appearance: he

> had been resting in a very dark corner of Stores for 324 years, his four coiled arms retracted and his four hinged ones resting on his four wheeled feet. Two of his arms terminated in huge scoop shovels, for he had been an ore miner, and he was also fitted with treads and sucker-pods. He was very great in size; they made giant machines in those days [27].

Yet even this description anthropomorphizes (or at any rate biologizes) the robot somewhat. He has arms and feet, for instance, however odd. More importantly, he is *he*; the use of the masculine pronoun rather than the neuter one invites the reader to associate the robot with a human being, as we have seen Gotlieb do, for instance, with the feminized erg–Queen or masculinized mod–Dahlgren. By gendering him, she begins the process of converting him from object to creature.

This process continues as the robot is reprogrammed with knowledge of all things Jewish, from the life of Sam Begelman to the Torah, the Talmud, and all languages necessary to understand all literature written by and about Jews. His learning unfolds over six days, and on the seventh, though as a robot he does not sleep—or rest—"he unhooked himself from the library equipment, gave up his space, and returned to his corner" (28). The parallel to the Bible's six days of creation and the subsequent day of rest for God is evident. However, it is important to note the contrast: while God spent six days creating and then rested, the robot is in a way doing the reverse; he is spending six days being created. That is, Gotlieb does not suggest that the robot ought to be viewed as God—the story makes this point in several ways—but rather as akin to God's creation, the culmination of which was the creation of the human being. That creation is associated in the Talmud with Golem-making. Indeed, the Talmudic creation of Adam marks that process over the passage of 12 hours, a process akin to the creation of everything else over six days. Another tradition suggests that Adam was created as a golem prior to the rest of creation and only completed (by being infused with a soul) after the world had been fashioned (Scholem 162). Such traditions strongly suggest that to become human one passes through a golemic state—that the full realization of human potential is a process of development from a lower to a higher form, achieving consciousness through accumulation, in effect.

Significantly in this context, the first identity O/G5/842 acquires after being infused with all Jewish law, history, and literature is the identity of Golem. When he saves some of the indigenous sentient creatures of Tau Ceti IV, the Cnidori, from a predator, they ask him his name. He responds, "I have no name but a designation: O/G5/842. I am only a machine" (32). Since the Cnidori have learned Hebrew and Jewish traditions from Begelman, they respond, "You are a machine of deliverance and so we will call you Golem" (32).

It is perhaps beneficial at this point to provide some background and context on the mythology associated with golems. Jewish legends of the Golem serve as important proto–SF. A Golem is a creature usually made of clay and animated by the power of language to serve humanity; it resembles a human being but lacks such fundamental human traits as a knowledge of good and evil, a soul, or the power of procreation, and despite its putative protective function, it often becomes a threat to the humans who have created it. The application of aspects of the Golem legends to SF conventions such as artificial life forms, whether androids, cyborgs, robots, or computers, is easy to recognize throughout the history of the genre. Even the prototypical SF work, *Frankenstein*, has affinities with stories of the Golem; indeed, in his book on the Golem legend, Arnold L. Goldsmith refers to the Golem as "this Jewish robot, homunculus, or Frankenstein monster" (11), and several SF works, notably Avram Davidson's short story "The Golem" (1955), Alfred Bester's *Golem 100* (1980), Marge Piercy's *He, She, and It* (1991), or, more recently, David Brin's *Kiln People* (2002), explicitly invoke the Golem. Gotlieb is far from alone, then, in turning the golem myth to her own purposes.

Judaism is an important underpinning to Gotlieb's work. It is central to her mainstream novel, *Why Should I Have All the Grief?*, and serves as an informing principle in her article on Hasidic elements in the poetry of A. M. Klein, but it emerges explicitly only relatively rarely in her SF. Stories such as "Son of the Morning" or "Nebuchadnezzar" (both included in the novel *A Judgment of Dragons*) and, more significantly as regards the Golem legend, "Tauf Aleph," bring Judaism to the fore. "Tauf Aleph" especially investigates with sensitivity and complexity the implications of the thin dividing line between the "Golem" (a robot) and the last living Jew in the universe. Gotlieb's exploration of the Golem legend here invites us to recognize its relevance to other works in which she deals with the construction of identity, notably in the Dahlgren books, though they offer less comforting explorations of what the human propensity for Golem making might wreak.

The most famous Golem story is probably that of Rabbi Loew of Prague, who lived from about 1512 to 1609 and became a figure of legend in subsequent centuries. In the eighteenth century, he had attached to him the most famous of these legends, that of his creation of the Golem "to protect the Jews from persecution," as Chayim Bloch has the Rabbi say in his version of the tale (69). The Golem, of course, ends up running amok and must be destroyed. This story of the Golem probably colors the standard view of the Golem as dangerous monster, ancestor of various rampaging creatures created by overweening scientists in any number of SF works. However, it is crucial to note that this view of the Golem is a relatively late development and very much a partial view. Gershom G. Scholem reports that the Golem first emerges as a dangerous figure in "the late forms of the legend, which arose in seventeenth-century Poland" (199) and this dangerous iteration "does not figure in Hebrew literature until almost a hundred years later" (200). To understand the full implications of the Golem legend as Gotlieb uses it, we must look back further, to the origins of the Golem story in Jewish mythology.

Though the word "golem" occurs only once in the texts that make up the Bible, in the 139th psalm (and it is not necessarily rendered as "golem" in English translations), the Talmud depicts Adam as a Golem created by God: "The day had twelve hours. In the first hour the earth was piled up; in the second he became a golem, a still unformed mass; in the third, his limbs were stretched out; in the fourth the soul was cast into him" (Sanhedrin 38b, qtd. in Scholem 161). Furthermore, Talmudic tradition depicts Abraham, the father of Israel, as a Golem-maker, one who is able, as Scholem explains, "to imitate and in a certain sense repeat God's act of creation" (170), and recounts other stories of holy Golem-makers. That is, ancient Jewish tradition does not treat

Golem-making as transgressive or as evil but as a human act of imitation of the divine creative power. Indeed, the link between Abraham and golem-making may be especially germane here, as Moshe Idel points out that Abraham is seen as one who converted gentiles to Judaism, but the word used to describe this process—"asa'o"—is the same word used "in the case of the creation of Adam as a Golem in the Midrashic literature and in the medieval sources in connection to the creation of the Golem itself" (18); that is, Abraham as convert-maker is in effect a golem-maker. And the first name the converted Cnidori choose for themselves is ben-Avraham, a name that suggests they are the golems/creations/converts of Abraham. Such stories suggest, as Byron L. Sherwin argues, that "the creation of 'artificial' beings is sanctioned and even encouraged by classical Jewish literature" (24).

This does not mean, however, that Jewish tradition supports the idea that anyone can create life or that doing so is free from complications or from moral obligations and conditions. As an imitation of divine creativity, Golem-making ought to be undertaken by the pious and righteous, which precondition adds an ethical dimension to the obligation of the creator (Sherwin 14). Even the righteous risk falling into idolatry or otherwise forgetting that God is the ultimate creator, as the Golem created by Jeremiah tells him: "once human beings become creators they are in danger of forgetting the creator" (Sherwin 18). And even the most righteous cannot create the perfect being; hence the consistent imperfection of such creatures, often manifesting itself in the absence of the power of speech. Indeed, the word "golem" itself implies imperfection, meaning "unformed mass." The story of Adam as Golem implies this imperfection in its account of his movement from unformed mass to fully-formed and functioning creature only when God subsequently imbues him with a soul. In fact, some commentators argue that the Golem "is understood as the embryonic stage" (Idel 36); that is, it is defined by the potential of becoming rather than by its current state, an implication of special relevance to Gotlieb.

In any event, though the exact physical nature of the Golem is not always clear (it is usually thought of as clay but may be a creature made of air and is in one story a female form made of wood and hinges—a sort of Pinocchio Golem) and the precise words or letters that animate it may vary (they may be the tetragrammaton, or a phrase), the Golem is invariably animated by having letters affixed to it, usually carved in its forehead, and those letters most frequently spell the word "emet," which means "truth." The initial character in "emet" is aleph, and when the aleph is erased, the remaining word, "met," means "he is dead," so the Golem dies when the aleph is removed. Aleph is also the initial character in the Hebrew alphabet and one pregnant with meaning. Gershom Scholem points out,

> In Hebrew the consonant *aleph* represents nothing more than the position taken by the larynx when a word begins with a vowel. Thus the *aleph* may be said to denote the source of all articulate sound, and the Kabbalists always regarded it as the spiritual root of all other letters, encompassing in its essence the whole alphabet and hence all other elements of human discourse. To hear the *aleph* is to hear next to nothing; it is the preparation for all audible language, but in itself conveys no determinate, specific meaning [30].

Since tauf and aleph are the last and first letters respectively in the Hebrew alphabet, and since one of the central developments of the story is the development of a new Judaism among the indigenous inhabitants of the planet Tau Ceti IV upon the death of Samuel Zohar ben Reuven Begelman, this title might be read as a statement of beginnings following endings, with a new aleph following the tauf, a new potential emerging from an ending, especially given Scholem's explanation of the implications of aleph.

However, tauf and aleph are also the last and first letters respectively in the word "emet," the word inscribed on the forehead of the Golem to give it life. Consequently, "Tauf Aleph" might also be seen as an announcement of the story's golemic concern, especially given the fact that Hebrew is written right to left, not left to right, so the tauf and aleph appear in the title in the order in which they would appear on the Golem's forehead. Regardless, the idea of the Golem invoked is very clearly the Golem as protector rather than the Golem as threat or monster. Second, the protective Golem's function is to protect the Jews from persecution; this construction therefore suggests that the Cnidori see themselves as in some ways analogous to Jews, though in fact they are not and Begelman objects vigorously to their desire to become Jews, since their radically alien natures and practices make it impossible for them to follow Jewish law:

> What is there to make them Jews? Everything they eat is neutral, neither kosher nor tref, so what use is the law of Kashrut? They live in mud—where are the laws of bathing and cleanliness? They never had any kind of god or any thought of one, as far as they tell me—what does prayer mean? Do you know how they procreate? Can you imagine? They are so completely hermaphroditic the word is meaningless. They pair long enough to raise children together, but only until the children grow teeth and can forage. What you see that looks like a penis is really an ovipositor; each Cnidor who is ready deposits eggs in the pouch of another, and an enzyme of the eggs stimulates the semen glands inside, and when one or two become fertilized the pouch seals until the foetus is of a size to make the fluid pressure around it break the seal, and the young crawls up the belly of the parent to suckle on the teat.

Even if one or two among twenty are born incomplete, not one is anything you might call male or female! So tell me, what do you do with all the laws of marriage and divorce, sexual behaviour, the duties of the man at prayer and the woman with the child? [37–38].

In short, from a human perspective, one might say the Cnidori are incomplete, especially biologically, since they are undifferentiated by gender. Ironically, Begelman indicates that even an incomplete Cnidor—that is, one that is not a fully functioning hermaphrodite—is not "complete" in the human (or, one might say, anthropocentric) sense, as male or female. In short, they are in some respects perhaps natural rather than created Golems.

As such they pose an even greater problem than a created Golem, but again, Jewish traditions relating to Golems help clarify the problem. The idea that the Golem can be seen as "a human being in a state of unfulfilled potentiality" (Sherwin 10) is evident in the Talmudic assertion that "a woman (before marriage) is a Golem, and concludes a covenant only with him who transforms her (into) a (useful) vessel" (qtd. in Sherwin 10)—that is, by becoming pregnant, therefore fulfilling her potential as a woman. The relative status of Golem is further suggested in debates about the legal status of Golems, as to whether they can be included to make up the minyan, as to whether they can be murdered, and so on. That is, assuming that Golems might exist, Jewish tradition seriously explores the extent to which they may participate in and benefit from human law and custom. The relevance of this debate in relation to women and Golems might be seen in that the status of women can change, when women are rendered complete via pregnancy; by analogy, what might be necessary to complete the potential of a Golem?

In the case of this story, it is quite literally the performance of the primary Golemic task of preserving the Jews. O/G, who is renamed Golem, must learn and develop from his programmed information about Judaism and his logic function a way of mediating between the last Jew and the alien people who want to become new Jews: he "considered the stubborn Zohar on the one side, and the stubborn b'nei Avraham [a Cnidor] on the other, and he thought that perhaps it was time for him to cease his functioning" (46). He does not do so, however, instead managing to convince Begelman to acknowledge not only his desire for Judaism to continue but also his failure to see beyond the unformed imperfection of the Cnidori to their potential. When the Golem leads Begelman to this recognition, Begelman poses perhaps the crucial question of his Golem: "What are you? [...] What are you, really, Og? You cannot answer" (49). It is noteworthy that by this point in the story, the robot's own progression towards identity is marked by its acquisition of a name—the O/G components of its number being turned into a word.[12] Nevertheless, Begelman's question is in a sense unanswerable, for the robot does not really know itself, insisting always that it is only a machine. It is also the crucial question, for the ultimate dividing line between Golem and human, perhaps, is the dividing line of self-consciousness. Whether the robot acquires "humanity," crosses the amorphous line between machine and intelligence, is not clearly answered in the story; the robot merely "stared with his unwinking eye" (47) in response to Begelman's question.

In another way, though, the story intimates that the robot does indeed become "human" in Gotlieb's broad sense of the word, in which physical nature is irrelevant to the subject. When Begelman dies, the robot is left the task of completing the teaching of the Cnidori. If their potential to become the new Jewish people (and when Begelman arrived, there were twelve of them, one for each of the twelve tribes) is realized, that potential is ultimately unrealizable solely from the teachings provided by the robot. And what they do, ultimately, is recreate Pardes, the failed colony: "They were not great in number, but they made a world. From *pardes* is derived 'Paradise'" (51), we are told, in an etymology of the planet's name. That is, the word *paradise* is derived from the word *pardes*. However, the syntax here allows for another and more literal reading: from the planet Pardes is derived a new paradise, as its native peoples "drained more of the swamps and planted fruitful orchards and pleasant gardens" (21). The machine designed to mine, to extract resources for exploitation, ends up helping to build a kind of paradise regained, and Pardes becomes a world of orchards and gardens, named for their creators, except the one named for the robot who in effect created the creators. As paradises go, it's a qualified one inhabited by beings "doing good and evil, contending with God and arguing with each other as usual" (21); the robot, when it finally ceases to function, insists that its parts be scattered, "for fear of idolatry" (52), one of the dangers against which Golem makers must protect and against which one Golem warned. The narrator explicitly expresses the wish "may his spirit rest in peace" (52), not an assertion that O/G had a spirit, had in fact achieved the one thing necessary to render a Golem human, but certainly a clear expression of possibility; the narrator then notes that "the one being who had no organic life is remembered with love among living things" (52). Again, the language does not assert O/G's status as "human," since he lacked organic life, but it reduces the dividing line between Golem and self-aware being almost to nothing.

In "Tauf Aleph," Phyllis Gotlieb makes careful and sensitive use of the Golem legend and tradition to explore some of the implications inherent both in the development of artificial creatures and in the possibility of encounters with alien life. In both cases the idea of the Golem is used to eliminate an anthropocentric hierarchizing of life. The Golem emerges here as the potential for the growth and change of intelligent life, in a hopeful vision of the human expansion into the larger universe. Gotlieb's Ungrukh and *Flesh and Gold* trilogies include their own occasional golems (such as Spartakos in the latter series) but also explore more extensively the problems inherent in an anthropocentric view in a universe full of nonhuman sentient creatures.

These mid-period stories perhaps lack some of the diversity of Gotlieb's earlier output, but their strength is in how they crystallize and consistently explore what were emerging through the 1970s and into the 1980s as Gotlieb's primary interests. Relatively few short stories follow these. There is a hiatus of four years between "The Newest Profession" (1982) and "Body English" (1986), and only a handful of short pieces follow that one. However, the 1980s and following years saw Gotlieb become more productive at the novel length, with four novels appearing in the 1980s alone (double her novelistic SF output in the preceding two decades combined) and an additional four coming in the 1990s and early twenty-first century—the bulk of her novelistic output in the final half of her career. These novels expand upon and extend the themes and preoccupations we have been exploring hitherto and will be the focus of the bulk of the rest of this study.

Five

The Ungrukh Chronicles*

The Ungrukh Chronicles consist of three novels, *A Judgment of Dragons*—which might be better described as a sequence of linked stories—*Emperor, Swords, Pentacles*, and *The Kingdom of the Cats*.[1] These volumes deal with the Ungrukh, sentient large cats who have experienced something like David Brin's "Uplift," having been taken from Earth to an alien planet and genetically modified to acquire sentience, rather than having evolved naturally. Though each book can be read independently, the three are also thematically linked so will be considered here as a unit. Gotlieb's work, as we have seen, is consistently interested in the question of the mind and what it means to be a sentient creature, whether one of flesh and blood or of stone and metal—or of no physical structure at all, as in the case of the Qumedni. Introduced in "Phantom Foot," they return in this trilogy and are described in more detail as well as given a pivotal role in the figure of the renegade Qumedon who has created the Ungrukh, and who takes the name Kriku, though the Qumedni as a rule "HAVE NO NAMES. ONLY WAVE PATTERNS" (*Judgment* 230).[2]

The Ungrukh inhabit the planet Ungruwarkh but are not native to it. Kriku, as is recounted in the third volume, took spotless red leopards from prehistoric Earth and transplanted them to this hot, barren planet in order to enact his own version of Genesis, first building a more or less habitable world from bacteria up through mammalia, then shaping and reshaping the cats, modifying their physiology to engender intelligence in them. As we shall see, though, how well he understands the implications of doing so is open to some doubt.

As discussed already, the importance of the mind has been key to Gotlieb's

---

*With the permission of the University of Ottawa Press, portions of this chapter significantly revise and adapt the article "Mind Matters: Intellect and Identity in the Works of Phyllis Gotlieb." Worlds of Wonder: Readings in Canadian Science Fiction and Fantasy. Reappraisals: Canadian Writers 26. Ed. Jean-François Leroux and Camille R. La Bossière. Ottawa: U of Ottawa P, 2004. 105–17.

work. *Sunburst*, for instance, argues that human evolution is largely a matter of mind, with Shandy Johnson representing the next phase in human evolution because of her intelligence and moral equilibrium, rather than through the manifestation of powers such as psi, telekinesis, teleportation, and so on, more frequently linked in SF to human development. The Dahlgren books explored the implications of machine sentience and the claims a machine possessed of a mind may have to recognition and status as a citizen. We saw this concern as well in several of Gotlieb's short stories, notably those dealing with machine sentience. The Ungrukh series recasts that question somewhat by focusing on aliens that are, from a human perspective, animals—animals from Earth, in fact—that have been given sentience. A major element of these novels is the struggle to recognize that an animal body does not necessarily mean an animal consciousness. In other words, qualities of mind and character—intellect and morality—more than one's physique make one count as a person, as broadly defined by Gotlieb. We have seen this stress on mind from early in Gotlieb's career, when Shandy's egghead is the primary determinant of her status as "super-normal."

GalFed is a far more diverse world than that of Sorrel Park. Life comes in almost every form imaginable, raising profound questions about the nature of life, especially intelligent life, and its ability to interact with the world. Some GalFed life lacks any of the senses we might believe to be necessary for interaction with the world, or, even if possessed of senses, they may be senses that fall outside the human norm, thereby deeply complicating the ability of different forms of life to communicate. Gotlieb simplifies this issue to a considerable extent by making ESP, notably telepathy, a feature of many GalFed species, thereby allowing communication across the most radical possible bodily divides—as, for instance, in Han Li's ability to communicate telepathically with the crystalloid life form Prima in *Heart of Red Iron*; since Han Li is the only one for much of the novel able even to perceive Prima's thoughts, it is unsurprising that nobody else in the novel gives much credence to Prima's existence for most of the book. Without such a device, even if one could imagine such a life form, one could probably never contact it. ESP, therefore, crystallizes the primacy of mind as a, perhaps *the*, defining feature of life that can form part of the community of intelligent beings.[3] This might not be surprising, since intelligence is a function of the mind, but even ESP does not fully bridge the gap. Crucial to Gotlieb's imagined future is the interface of existence and essence; to what extent is the individual's ability to interact with realities outside the self essential to intellectual existence, Gotlieb asks, and to what extent must that interaction involve one's actual physical self?

Gotlieb's aliens are, as noted, remarkably diverse, and she frequently makes the fact that they have minds, regardless of their physical forms, the feature that defines them. The Encid are perhaps the most fully realized version of brain (or mind; after all, consciousness need not be housed in an organ) as primary:

> The species had no mouth, ears, or digestive processes. The Encid was a brain, about 25 cm in diameter, completely surrounded by something like a placenta, whose vessels fed it; these permeated a heavy protective membrane beyond which was a densely packed centimeter of humus containing symbiotes, both animal and vegetable, and held together by a "skull," a network of cartilage [*Emperor, Swords, Pentacles* 183].

Though it has five eyes, "none of the eyes saw very sharply" (183), and its body seems almost an afterthought, consisting merely of "a horny standard half [the brain's] diameter in length, which branched into six feet like chicken-claws" (183). The narrative voice refers to the Encid as "she," but this is a matter of convenience of pronoun reference (English lacking a gender-neutral personal pronoun): "It did not know what sex it was or if it had any, though it brought forth progeny parthenogenetically" (183). This "convenience" reflects the convenience of the characters who have so chosen to designate the Encid as a "her," but it is a convenience that imposes an alien meaning on "her." As such, it is one of numerous markers of how meaning alien to her nature is inscribed on her by observers to serve their own purposes, rather than to understand what she really is. As is evident here, the Encid's one salient feature is its brain, other parts being smaller—literally half the size of the brain—and of limited usefulness. The Encid is therefore accorded existence almost entirely in terms of intellect. Even what we might consider characteristics necessary to be recognized as a creature with agency are lacking, including "the concepts to describe itself" (182), but the Encid is nevertheless defined in both individual and intellectual terms. On their home planet, the Encid are solitary creatures—"She did not know what society was" (183)—who use their ESP merely to "find information about food and water sources from others" (183). It has no life of the mind, only a mind, which it uses merely to subsist.

That it *is* a brain is the one essential fact. On the other hand, as might be evident from this description, it is a brain and little else, with virtually no organs of sense and no sexual identity, not possessed even of the tools necessary for self-conception and description. Furthermore, it lacks even a sense of place, being unable to tell where it came from, and it is therefore limited as well as defined by its status as living brain. This lack of virtually everything a human reader might identify as conferring the status of personhood is key to how "she" is treated in the book. Encids are nameless, as one might infer from their inability to conceive of selfhood, but just as the narrative indicates that "she" has been assigned gender for the sake of convenience, she has also been given a name. This represents a far more profound inscribing of meaning onto her. The name she is given is "Esne," an Anglo-Saxon word that means "domestic slave." This is not only a name but also a description of her status; she has been literally enslaved by Thorndecker, the novel's antagonist, because of how he can use her powers to pursue his own agenda.

The Encid is a relatively minor character in the trilogy, but her situation speaks directly to one of its main concerns: exploitation of people, even when one might argue that this "exploitation" is well intended and mutually agreed upon (as in "Mother Lode," for instance). As already discussed, economics represent a brutal reality in GalFed, which is refreshing in a way, given how frequently economics can be overlooked in SF. ESP is not merely a crucial ability in GalFed, it is a crucial commodity, so much so that one might even commandeer its use, as Thorndecker does with the Encid. However, GalFed can hardly be said to treat its peoples much better. GalFed's pecuniary interest in its member worlds is perhaps most horrifically expressed in the price its telepaths have to pay—at least earlier in GalFed's history—for GalFed's assistance. We learn in *A Judgment of Dragons*, for instance, that Prandra's brain will eventually be decanted from her body and kept alive indefinitely in a globe to serve GalFed; "it was part of the price for the ship, the instruments, the meat" (*Judgment* 4). Living as they do on a resource-poor planet, the Ungrukh have only their minds to trade, and GalFed takes them, as they have taken the brains of various other telepaths.[4]

Prandra's fate can be anticipated in the figure of Diego Espinoza, Prandra and Khreng's mentor in *A Judgment of Dragons*. His name almost certainly invokes Benedict de Spinoza, the seventeenth-century Dutch-Jewish philosopher. His philosophy challenges Descarte's dualism. Spinoza rejected Descartes' argument that the mind and body were separate, asserting instead that the two are interconnected; the mind perceives and imagines external reality because external reality influences the body. Memory, for instance, "is simply a certain association of ideas involving the nature of things outside the human body, which association arises in the mind according to the order and association of the modifications (affectiones) of the human body" (*The Ethics* Prop. XVIII; 37). His Proposition XXI asserts this idea of the mind is united to mind in the same way as the mind is united to the body.

> *Proof.*—That the mind is united to the body we have shown from the fact, that the body is the object of the mind (II.xii. and xiii.); and so for the same reason the idea

of the mind must be united with its object, that is, with the mind in the same manner as the mind is united with the body [39].

The relevance of this philosophy to Espinoza's situation will become clear below.

In contrast to the Encid, with no way to conceive of the self, all Espinoza has left of his body is a self-conception, since he is one of these decanted brains. He thinks of himself as "a man thirty-eight years old, of medium height, brown-skinned and wiry, black hair and mustache, deep brown eyes, white even teeth" (4). To everyone else, he is "a brain in a midnight-blue glasstex globe, three hundred years old, and he had spent seventy-seven of them as a man" (4). How he conceives of himself, then, is a purely mental construction, in that there is no body left to conceive of; he can't look in the mirror, like Dahlgren, and see an externalized image of the self but can only create an image in his mind. Furthermore, the self-image he has adopted clearly is not that of his body at the time he was decanted, since that body was nearly forty years older than the one in his mind's eye. He evidently conceives of himself not as he was when he died but as he was when he thought of himself at his physical peak. The accuracy of this self-image is, of course, subject to speculation. Memory is notoriously unreliable, and Espinoza's thirty-eight-year-old body has been dead for centuries, since he is "three hundred years old" (4). One might reasonably assume, therefore, that his self-image is an idealized memory of some aspects of his former physical self, but it must be a highly contingent construction. Indeed, in the second Ungrukh novel, Gotlieb notes that "an ordinary mind contemplating itself is like a person looking into a mirror and presenting the best face" (*Emperor* 66). This simile plays on the meanings of reflection; when a mirror reflects, it casts back to an observer an image over which the observer has little control; the nature of the available light and the reflective surface determine the image, which is, of course, also a reverse image of the observer. When the mind reflects upon (or thinks about) itself, however, there is no objective external reflector to cast back the image; it makes its own image. Neither image is real, of course, and even the mirror image is not really accurate, as we saw Dahlgren consider when looking at his own image, but the mind abstracted from the body has only subjective reflection to rely on, not objective reflection. There is no material basis for self-evaluation, only a mental one. No messy image of the physical self can interfere with the self-reflection, making one's ability to cast oneself in the best light—to deceive oneself, not to put too fine a point on it—much easier.

If, as this quotation suggests, even the mind still with a body can cast itself in the best light while reflecting, how much more so might "the man without skin, flesh, bones, nerves, heart, lungs, limbs, genitals" (*Judgment* 65) that Espinoza has become? As a brain in a bottle, with only ESP to link him to other consciousnesses, the only way he can experience reality is vicariously, filtered through the senses and minds of others as he reads their thoughts. The real world continues with him only in memory; he can remember a body, but he can no longer experience it. If the phantom limb (a phantom foot, for instance) an amputee might continue to sense can be a distraction, even a disturbance, how much more so an entire body? Abstracted from the body, the brain is, in theory, purified, freed from the flesh, which has been presented as a consummation devoutly to be wished by many religions and even by many SF writers, which and who have posited that the flesh is a prison.[5] Bodiless, Espinoza nevertheless wants to hold onto a sense of his human self, resisting the apparent urge of some in GalFed to pun on his name and call him ESPinoza, a name he finds "too robotic" (4). The loss of the body and the conversion to a creature primarily of mind brings with it the danger of reduction to the mechanical (given that he depends on mechanical interventions to continue to live, this can hardly be surprising). However, the brain is not the mind; rather, it is a physical organ that carries out the activities of cognition wherein mind resides, but it is not free of the flesh. Espinoza recognizes that "brain cells number in the trillions, but they die eventually without regrowing, and he knew he was raveling around the edges" (4). Like Prima's, his consciousness is physically determined.

Free of the chemical influences of the body, "a brain in a bowl is not supposed to be able to feel or fear, but a glandular body might impose certain ineradicable habits on a brain over seventy-seven years of existence," as we are told (10). That is, even absent the body, the surviving consciousness was formed in part by that body and cannot be completely abstracted from it, even centuries after the body is dust. Put another way, the brain still longs for the body, or at any rate for direct interaction with the physical world. Just as people who enter sensory deprivation chambers often find themselves hallucinating, so are these bottled brains living only in the realm of the mind "subject to hallucinations" (207), substituting imagined worlds for the physical one denied them. And the ESP-empowered mind may be all the more vulnerable, as it may fold into its mindscape the thoughts and memories of others. Indeed, commenting generally on stories dealing with telepathy, Donald A. Wollheim has observed these "powers are frequently associated with the symptoms or reality of madness" (216). Gotlieb carries the idea further when she explores the implications for the bodiless telepath, who faces not merely madness but in fact a death-wish, since death offers the only escape from the blank landscape of the inner self. Nancy Johnston's assertion that "many characters in Gotlieb's fiction [are] *cursed* with telepathy" (72; emphasis added) accurately describes the experiences of figures such as the Encid or the bottled brains like Espinoza, however useful telepathy might be in other contexts. In losing their bodies and being limited only to the mind, figures such as Espinoza lose themselves, Gotlieb suggests.

As characters such as Espinoza or the Encid suggest, mind and body are linked; mind without body, or with attenuated body, lacks much of what is necessary to form or maintain a stable sense of identity and may be subject to debilitating problems such as hallucination, insanity, and despair. Nevertheless, Gotlieb has created creatures of pure mind in the Qumedni. The Qumedon Kriku is a key figure in the trilogy, and he is an ambivalent figure at best. He first appears in the first story in *A Judgment of Dragons*, "Son of the Morning." Gotlieb is here invoking scripture again, Isaiah 14:12, which reads in part, "How art thou fallen from heaven, O Lucifer, son of the morning!" The son of the morning, then, is traditionally demonic. In the story, Elya tells Reb' Nachman that the Qumedon "was the demon, Ashmedai himself" (64). This association is of course not really true but rather an explanation constructed by Elya in conformity to the tenets of his faith, and it is an association which becomes problematic as the trilogy proceeds and Kriku is revealed to be another of Gotlieb's problematic godlike creators. However, in this initial story, at least, he is seen to be devilish, and that devilishness can be linked to his immateriality.

Illusory bodies are a recurring motif in this trilogy, from Espinoza's self-conception to the illusion of humanity which the Ungrukh impose on themselves via hypnoforming, making observers see humans instead of giant cats. Kriku, too, has assumed a human disguise, but when Prandra and Espinoza see behind that disguise, a key point is that they see, in effect, *nothing*: "they saw that there was no heart in that body, no human heart, no brains or bowels [...]. It was dense as stone, cold as ice, cruel as death" (37). Qumedni have no bodies so lack all such bodily parts as hearts, brains, bowels, and so on. They also lack what such body parts connote. Body parts have biological functions, but they also carry psychological, emotional, and intellectual resonances. The heart is the most obvious example. Literally an organ that pumps blood through the body, it is particularly rich in associations. "Heart" may refer to courage, or to hope, but the most significant of its associations, in this context at least, is perhaps the heart's reputation as the seat of love and compassion, essential human values, since such characteristics contrast with the coldness and cruelty Prandra and Espinoza recognize in the Qumedon. Similarly, though the brain is the organ housing consciousness, and though these novels stress the importance of this function, the concepts of brain and mind are often conflated. As a result, the brain can also be linked to faculties such as understanding and imagination.[6] The bowels are literally waste-processing centers, but this centrality to healthy biological function associates them with the intimate, physical realities of life, with one's essence or core. Because they process the physical materials we ingest, they are an important part of the symbiotic relationship between body and world and therefore suggestive of the larger network of living things. We have seen this symbiosis at play elsewhere in Gotlieb, even in how a machine might join with the ecosystem, as in *Heart of Red Iron* in the case of the old robot festooned with "minute life: molds, mosses [...] tiny ferns and vines trailing like ribbons from its giant limbs" (129) — or closer to hand in the figure of the Encid, with its humus of animal and vegetable symbiotes. Other aliens in *Emperor, Swords, Pentacles* provide further examples of this symbiotic relationship between the embodied consciousness and the world. For instance, the Qsaprinli "carried [the sea] about on its back behind the brain in an external elastic skin" (*Emperor* 4). In so doing, it carries with it its entire world, metaphorically: its place of origin (the sea) as well as its own food supply. Each Qsaprinli, therefore, functions as a self-contained world, a microcosm. But each is not only an individual but also part of a larger network.

The Qumedni contrast with such fellow intelligences because they lack any visceral link with the physical universe. Prandra, for instance, contemplates the relationship between consciousness and brain, and wonders about the implications of this for the Qumedni: "she considered, slowly and hazily, the shapes of minds, the organic structures that began them, the ideas and emotions that fulfilled them, wondered how a Qumedni functioned and what with" (*Judgment* 65). As a consequence of their lack of material form, Qumedni cannot properly understand organic life forms, even when, as Kriku has done, they set out to modify them. This basic failure of understanding of the physical universe betrays Kriku in a very simple way. Ignorant of the complexities of the physical world, he neglects to consider that he should have a human scent when he disguises himself as Orbin, but the Ungrukh, not merely physical creatures but ones with highly developed senses of smell, see through this disguise (or, more accurately perhaps, sniff him out). Furthermore, just as he lacks an understanding of the implications of basic physiology (animals sweat and excrete, so they have noticeable smells), he also lacks the ability to empathize with physical creatures; he makes no emotional connection. He can do the work necessary of a doctor from a purely medical perspective, but he has no bedside manner. Ironically, he is as mechanistic in his ministrations as DeLazzari is in "The Military Hospital." His detachment from his patients means that he treats them as if he were "an animal doctor handling cattle" (*Judgment* 206). Kriku is far from alone in his inability to differentiate between sentient creature and animal.

Even his own actions as "creator" of the Ungrukh hint at the importance of the physical to the mental, as his granting of intelligence to the Ungrukh depends on his modifications to their brains. It is clear that Kriku's physical changes to the leopards and their emergent reasoning abilities are connected, as we see that he "DEEPENED BRAIN FISSURES AND INCREASED HEAD SIZE TO LET THE BRAIN FILL IT" (*Kingdom* 20). Without this physiological change to brain size, the Ungrukh would lack the brain capacity necessary for the development of minds in creatures of their size.[7] Kriku also "REARRANGED NEURONS AND REWIRED AXONS FOR SPEECH CENTERS" and provided telepathy (20), further providing the physiological bases necessary for the development of sentience. Physical change is thereby linked to evolving sentience. But Kriku is hardly a benevolent god. He does not view his creations as people with their own rights and agency.

The term "people" as I have used it here might require some unpacking. The word "people" as ascribed to giant intelligent cats suggests that in Gotlieb's universe, a "person" is not just a human being. This point is important in the Dahlgren books and their debates about robot citizenship, and those books do acknowledge briefly Gotlieb's ascription of personhood to nonhuman animals in the statement that "with her intelligence exponentially increased, [the gibbon] Esther had become simply another species of extraterrestrial human being" (*O Master Caliban!* 11). The implications of this assertion only become clear in the Ungrukh Chronicles. Calling the Encid "she" rather than "it" is a minor instance of this pattern of ascribing personhood at least implicitly to sentient creatures, but the more pervasive and tendentious manifestation of this strategy is found in Gotlieb's insistence throughout this trilogy and in her subsequent GalFed novels on referring to any sentient male or female alien as a "man" or a "woman," regardless of its physical form. For instance, the Ungrukh refer to each other as "man" and "woman," despite being giant cats.

In the statement about Esther, Gotlieb articulates one of the central theses of her mature work. She repeatedly insists on the commonality among all intelligent creatures, not merely humanoid ones. Such a practice might be considered anthropocentric speciesism, just as some have argued that Ursula K. Le Guin's use of the masculine pronoun to describe the ambisexual characters in her novel *The Left Hand of Darkness* (1969) perpetuates the sexist stereotypes that novel attempts to challenge.[8] Le Guin initially defended this choice while conceding that some readers found it difficult to see the Gethenians as ambisexual rather than imposing gender identities on them, and that this difficulty "rises in part from the choice of pronoun" ("Is Gender Necessary?" 168), given the masculine implications attached to the generic "he." Le Guin has subsequently repudiated this pronoun use, arguing that the generic use of "he/him" in the novel "does in fact exclude women from discourse" ("Is Gender Necessary? Redux" 15) and expressing the wish that she had created some new pronoun form (she reports using her created pronouns in readings from the book, but she has not revised the book to eliminate the gendered pronouns). While it may be true that the generic pronoun has this effect, however, what Le Guin and others perhaps fail to recognize is the power of the moment in the book at which Genly Ai, the (male) narrator, must confront his own preconceptions about sex when Estraven, his friend and rescuer, begins to become biologically female. The fact that Estraven has been "he" throughout the book forces this recognition on the reader as well as on Genly. The reader, like Genly (who, as narrator, is the one responsible for the pronoun choices), is caught by his (or her) preconceptions. Had Genly been as enlightened as some critics, and, ultimately, Le Guin herself wished, some of the point of the novel would have been lost. The pervasive use of gendered pronouns underscores the novel's point about the difficulty of seeing the *human* beneath the male or female. As Christine Cornell asserts, "there is no doubt that the [masculine] pronouns are an extra burden on the reader, but they are a valuable part of our education" (323). Wendy Gay Pearson suggests that what is at issue is "the reader's ability to enter imaginatively into the narrative and thus to resist the very construction of gender implied by Le Guin's use of masculine pronouns" (193)—an oppositional, or at least negotiated reading, in effect. Gotlieb's use of the terms "man" and "woman" for aliens in the shape of animals should invite a similar response; the usage does not erase the aliens' animality but instead foregrounds the reader's cognitive estrangement, forcing him or her always to be reminded of the soul beneath the skin.

    Just as Genly is confronted by his own sexist preconceptions when Estraven begins to assume female form, requiring Genly to see, literally, what he has failed to understand: "that he was a woman as well as a man" (288) (note that even at this moment of recognition, Genly defaults to the male pronoun for Estraven), so is the reader shocked out of his (or her) preconceptions about that character, as derived from the pronoun reference, when that transformation takes place. A simple matter of language use strips bare the implications of the reader's preconceptions at this point. Similarly, by requiring her readers to associate cats or other overtly alien and animal creatures with themselves, Gotlieb does not so much transform her animal aliens into humans as force her readers to redefine what human means. Gotlieb's statement about the Qsaprinli in *Emperor, Swords, Pentacles* demonstrates the importance of this idea in how closely it echoes the statement about Esther in *O Master Caliban!*: "what they were was one more form of The People, like all other sentient beings" (68).

According to Gary K. Wolfe, "the opposition between man and not-man" (204) is the central tension in any story involving humans and aliens interacting; he continues, "Even to conceive of an alien intelligence is to conceive, at some deep level, of an invasion of one's own personality by outside forces, a violation of one's community by strangers" (205). Unsurprisingly, perhaps, given how, in *Sunburst*, she inverted the usual notion of superpowered children as the next step in human evolution, Gotlieb also inverts this trope in the process of hypnoforming. This process makes no literal change to the Ungrukhs' bodies but instead tricks the minds of human observers, making them see, hear, and otherwise sense humans rather than large cats. Ironically, to strengthen this illusion, and to ensure it will take as firm a root as possible in the perceptions of the observer, the hypnoformer does not plant images in the minds of the human observers but instead the one undergoing the process *has implanted* in her or his own mind memories and experiences derived from the creature the hypnoforming fools. That is, in order to disguise themselves as humans, Prandra and Khreng *take into their own minds* elements of the minds of a human. They do not merely appear to be human from the outside. Instead, they imitate the human more essentially by projecting or emanating a sense of the human; the human thoughts and memories they implant in their own minds make them *feel* human to observers. This mental construction of humanity is arguably more real than the mere physical illusion.

This is not a superficial or ephemeral process but one that permanently changes those who use it. Khreng recognizes that his use of the process means that "his mind would always be threaded with wisps of alien memory" (*Judgment* 33). Imagining a more profound way to invade one's personal space is difficult. However, in contrast to Wolfe's assertion about the usual pattern for such an invasion—which is rooted in an anthropocentric perspective—the human mind is not the invaded one but instead, in a way, the invader (albeit unconsciously and by invitation). The irony deepens because the human consciousness the Ungrukh use as the basis of their hypnoforming is Espinoza's. Because Espinoza is a centuries-old brain separated from its body and kept alive artificially in a bottle, he is arguably as alien to the reader as are the actual aliens. Indeed, throughout the trilogy, readers are required to adopt the perspective of the alien, since the role of humans is secondary to the roles of the Ungrukh; the Ungrukh are the protagonists, not the humans.

The difficulty of recognizing that this is so is evident even in the responses of sophisticated readers. For instance, David Ketterer is the author of the only monograph on Canadian SF and generally offers insightful readings, but he also occasionally does not accurately capture a work's nuances. For example, his take on the Ungrukh Chronicles is instructive in its demonstration of how thoroughly engrained the anthropocentric habit can be. In his discussion of the Ungrukh Chronicles (which does not address the final book, oddly, since *The Kingdom of the Cats* appeared seven years before Ketterer's book), he reports that the books "chronicle the adventures of Duncan Kinnear (a Galactic Federation investigator) and two dangerous, telepathic, crimson 'starcats' whose world, Ungrukh, he saved [in the first book].... In the sequel [...], the starcats help Kinnear prevent the emperor of Qsaprinel from being dispossessed of his planet" (70). This précis reduces the Ungrukh to supernumerary roles and suggests that Kinnear is the protagonist. However, Kinnear is really a secondary character. Only two of the four stories that comprise *A Judgment of Dragons* feature him, and the assertion that *he* saved the Ungrukhs' planet is an overstatement. He does continue as an important character in the subsequent books, but again, the protagonists of those novels are the Ungrukh.

Furthermore, Ketterer's claim that the Ungrukh are dangerous may be true technically, but as a way of characterizing them it is reflective of an anthropocentric perspective, if not a cat-specific prejudice. As Sherryl Vint has pointed out,

> the various prejudices and preferences that have emerged from our long co-evolution with other species enter and shape the characterization of animal aliens, a very obvious example being the prevalence of stories in which dogs figure as steadfast companions [...] as compared to the number of malevolent aliens who have cat-like characteristics [136].

In this case, the critic rather than the author has ascribed expectations to the catlike aliens. Like any large cats, the Ungrukh do have claws and teeth that can do a lot of harm, and humans in the books frequently do view the Ungrukh as dangerous. They are brave and intelligent, as a rule, which makes them potentially dangerous adversaries, and they engage in violence on several occasions—but then, so do many of the humans. Given that the Ungrukh have been built out of predatory giant cats, however, they are remarkably restrained in their violence. They accept the GalFed premise about intelligent creatures all being People, regardless of form, and resist killing them except when necessary, and even when the "people" who are their adversaries have demonstrated themselves to be savage. If the Ungrukh are dangerous, there is usually a good reason why. Gotlieb even plays on readerly preconceptions about what is normal and what is alien (as she did in the first chapter of *O Master Caliban!*) by having Prandra feel disturbed at the prospect of coming among such strange and alien beings as humans: "She thought it might be more pleasant to make the acquaintance of some of Solthree's big cats" (*Judgment* 20). Just as we might expect a human when visiting an exotic new place to be interested in socializing with the locals rather than with the local wildlife, these giant cats when visiting Earth imagine visiting not with the self-identified superior species but instead with Earth's felines. The human is rendered other, alien—and human preconceptions about the other are therefore undercut. This strategy encourages the reader to identify with the other and to accept the series' premise that "human" is not a matter of bodily form but of intellectual level; these aliens are not literally men, women, or human, but the application of such terms to them, rather than erasing their difference, suggests that they are sufficiently analogous to human to merit equal treatment. Gotlieb is here engaging in an unconventional version of what Sherryl Vint has identified as SF's "scope [...] for enabling animal agency to become part of the quotidian world, as well as [its] space to attempt to grasp animals as beings in their own right rather than as beings defined through their place in human cultural systems" (6), by redefining "human" to decentralize bipedal hominids as the definition of the human.

As a consequence, though having a body may be an important aspect of identity, what form that body takes is less relevant than the identity itself. It is the human mind, not the body, that stands out to Prandra (only female Ungrukh are telepathic, so Khreng cannot share this reaction); when she first encounters a group of humans and uses her ESP on them, Prandra "found it was not their flesh that disturbed her but their noisy heads. [...]; their bodies were only unregarded appendages" (*Judgment* 20). Mind, not body, defines one's status, a fact that is often forgotten by characters in these novels. For instance, human hybrids known as Frogs have been genetically engineered to work in aquatic environments as underwater laborers (we might recall the aquatic hybrids Melba is contracted to grow in "The Newest Profession"). The engineering is a success as an exercise in modifying biology—the Frogs are well adapted physically to subaquatic living—but it is nevertheless still a failure. The engineers considered function only, what purpose they wanted the Frogs to serve, as if they were nothing more than machines or animals. All they considered were the bodies, but "inside the skulls," as the Frogs report, "we were an architect, a flutist, an administrator, a chess-player, a doctor, a clerk, a gardener, a space-pilot" (*Emperor* 121). In short, "there were *men and women* inside the skulls and under the skins" (121). Admittedly, these men and women are mostly defined in terms of a range of occupations, which still fits them into an economic model, but the primary point is the tension between the internal urge to make oneself as weighed against the external pressure to fit into a predetermined role. Inside and under is where essential identity is located; skin, flesh, and bone are merely housing. Nor are these Frogs the only instance. Genetic engineering recurs throughout the GalFed stories, notably the novels (as well as in some of Gotlieb's few non–GalFed stories). However, genetic engineering does not necessarily improve one's life. Indeed, Gotlieb's Lyhhrt trilogy deals extensively with the use of genetic engineering to breed slaves. This is not GalFed's practice or policy but rather a criminal enterprise; however, GalFed has difficulty stopping the practice and dealing with those created as slaves.

On the other hand, and to complicate matters, a body can be problematic, especially if it is a body not really suited to its user's nature. One of Gotlieb's most fascinating alien creations is the species Lyhhrt, which in their native state are merely "formless masses of protoplasm" (*Judgment* 107) with no individuality. They are instead a sort of group mind that exists, according to its own understanding of the universe, to think Cosmic Thoughts. To interact with other species in GalFed, they have created shells for themselves, artificial bodies that can contain a piece of Lyhhrt protoplasm. Their skill in metalwork not only makes these bodies things of beauty in their own right but also represents one of their values to GalFed. How valuable this skill is to *them*, however, is a different matter. Prandra is told that *"Once they got separate bodies they became individuals, maybe not such a good idea"* (*Judgment* 108). It is not such a good idea because "individual" Lyhhrt, abstracted from the gestalt and enclosed in shells, are prone to madness. Some, when they learn of the advantages bodies can provide, fail to see why they should not simply claim the existing bodies of other creatures rather than building their own.[9] To usurp another's autonomy (especially literally in this way, but in any way, really) is in the GalFed universe a terrible crime; those who commit such a crime surrender their own claim to be "human" as broadly defined by Gotlieb as a part of the community of intelligent species.

The second story in *Judgment*, "The King's Dogs," explores the implications of treating another's body merely as a vehicle for the self in its presentation for the first time of a plot element that assumes central importance in the Lyhhrt Trilogy. Appropriately, here too the problem is a Lyhhrt that decides a biological body offers a far better shell than a mere mechanical one. This Lyhhrt antagonist progresses from trying to use telepathy to control host bodies to possessing them—by actually entering into them and assuming control, making him a quasi-demonic figure. His attempt to shift from brute animals to intelligent ones, the Ungrukh, forms the basis of the plot. In this story, therefore, the antagonist is a formless protoplasmic alien blob that even its own culture rejects. The third story brings the problem closer to home.

The antagonist of "Nebuchadnezzar," is named Quantz, a human, whose name, with its echo of "quantify," suggests his exclusive interest in how he can quantify the value of the material world. He is especially governed by appearances; though he will enslave and even kill others if he can profit thereby, he is more prone to do so when the objects of his aggression don't look like him and therefore fall outside his definition of "people." When Prandra is captured by him, she recognizes that her animal appearance governs how she is viewed by at least some humans; because she *looks like* an animal, to Quantz and crew she *is* one. Thinking of herself and Lokh, a Khagodi (the allosaur-like aliens who are central to the Lyhhrt trilogy), in the company of Quantz and his crew, Prandra reflects: "A few in that company were scaled, and one or two had tentacles, but all were what a Solthree would have called 'humanoid.' She and Lokh were not, and she knew what that difference meant to Quantz. A pair of skins..." (159). Some aliens may have some animal features, such as scales or tentacles (common features, in fact, for evil or horrifying aliens in SF), but if their structure is essentially humanoid, they can pass, or at least be given provisional status as humanoid, if not actually human. Even the term "humanoid," however, is subverted. Whatever valorizing power it has, the passage makes clear, is human-specific; as its etymology shows, "humanoid" is a specifically *human* (Solthree) term to describe those who conform in some significant respects to human form. As an absolute measure of one's status, however, it is meaningless—except to humans for whom physical form defines one's nature and function. And the relative unimportance of humanness is stressed by the fact that humans are called "Solthrees" in the GalFed universe, a term that simply identifies them as inhabitants of Sol's third planet, thereby localizing them and diminishing their significance in the larger context of GalFed (which is NOT centered on Earth but instead on the Twelveworlds of Galactic Central).

As "animals"—as not humanoids—Prandra and Khreng are accorded, by Quantz, no value except that of being a hunter's trophy. Indeed, and perhaps overstressing the point, Gotlieb does not have Quantz simply kill them but instead has him release them in order to hunt them down, in a sort of play on and inversion of Richard Connell's "The Most Dangerous Game" (1924), in Gotlieb's version of which the most dangerous game is not the human being but the "animal." What makes humans human does not therefore make them superior. For example, in *Emperor, Swords, Pentacles*, the Ungrukh Raanung goes up against another human who can't see past Raanung's animal body: "Ever look at yourself in a mirror? I don't make deals with animals," he says (243). When the human tries to kill him, Raanung acts:

> Raanung, sadly, waited for the hand to draw the gun from the zipper opening. Then he moved. His long tail whipped out to hook Hands between the cords of his nape and pull him forward so that one padded forepaw could slap the side of his neck. It broke with a crunch [243].

Because Raanung is a large cat and therefore an animal, the man believes in his superiority to this "animal" and in his ability to kill Raanung easily. The human's name is Hands, and the reference to "the hand" in the passage underscores the point. The hand is the specific human physical feature most often pointed to (no pun intended) as the one that differentiates humans from animals. The term "paw" tends to be applied to the animal appendage, even when it is in fact a hand, Martin Heidegger's assertions about the animal lack of hands notwithstanding.[10] For Gotlieb, even if the animal does not have a hand (as Raanung does not), tail and paw can trump Hands anyway. The human looks in the mirror and sees itself, and therefore assumes that that reflection expresses the sum total of intelligence. That which is not a reflection of the human does not reflect, in effect.

Gotlieb, however, stresses that such a view is blinkered. The animal is not an alien other but a genuine reflection, and reflector. The point is literalized in Quantz's fate. When Prandra defeats Quantz, she does so with her telepathic powers: she "smashed the brittle walls of Quantz's mind to free the red beasts of fear and rage among the synapses" (188). She turns his own mind back on him, forcing him to see the beast in himself, much as Dahlgren recognized his own beast in the figures of the Dahlgren clones. When Quantz looks at the Ungrukh, he sees animals, but as this passage suggests, the beasts he really sees are projections of his own bestiality, not the Ungrukh. The only beasts are in his mind. As a result, Quantz is, briefly and subjectively, transformed from man to pig, in his own perception and in the eyes of those present, his body being apparently hypnoformed for a time to reflect his inner animalism. The inability to see beyond the animal, in effect, reflects the animal status of the observer. He sees only animals, not people, and as a result he suffers a version of the fate of Nebuchadnezzar, the Babylonian king punished by God by being reduced to the state of an animal, albeit without being transformed into one: "he was driven from men, and did eat grass as oxen, and his body was wet with the dew of heaven, till his hairs were grown like eagles' feathers, and his nails like birds' claws" (Daniel 4:33).

Quantz sets the basic pattern for villainy in the trilogy; the subsequent volumes feature figures with similar predispositions to see the body only, not the intellect behind it, and to convert others into their own property, to be put to their own uses—even to reduce the Ungrukh literally to the status of stuffed toys; indeed, the idea of Ungrukh merely as skins we see in Quantz becomes a more central concern in *The Kingdom of the Cats*, when that novel's chief antagonist, Phoebe Adams, has the Ungrukh visiting Earth hunted and killed for their pelts: "They skinned them on the spot! I think the bodies were just dumped. What's wanted were *skins*" (93). This fundamental disrespect for the identity of the Ungrukh is paradigmatic of her more general behavior. Among those she uses in her attempts to reduce the Ungrukh to carpets and stuffed toys is her own niece, Mercy. Mercy, however, is not Phoebe's agent by choice; instead, she is to a considerable extent Phoebe's automaton. As the ergs attempted to create an image of Dahlgren to take his place, so has Phoebe attempted to create an image of herself, for her own convenience. When Mercy's father died and she first came to Phoebe, Phoebe "recognized the family resemblance, coarse as it was, had it reinforced and refined by minor surgery" (174), so that Mercy could serve as her double when Phoebe desired. However, her impinging on Mercy's identity is not limited merely to superficial surgical intervention; she also invades Mercy's mind. Mercy reports, "During the ten years I worked for Phoebe Charloe Adams Silver I was given mindblocks and hypnosis regularly" (190); Phoebe in effect colonizes Mercy's mind, twisting and shaping her memories and will in order to force her to perform tasks (e.g., she is involved in the Ungrukh hunt, not by choice but by programming), keep secrets, and so on. We might contrast this sort of enforced mindwarping with the hypnoforming the Ungrukh use to disguise themselves in *A Judgment of Dragons*.

This sort of individual colonization links with the novel's quiet commentary on colonialism more generally. The Ungrukh visiting Earth have been placed on a native reserve (their red coats apparently making a nice analogy with the stereotypical red skins of North America's First Nations), and several First Nations characters have minor but important parts in the book, reminding readers of how their land and their minds have been colonized by Europe. Indeed, we are reminded of the heritage of European colonialism, when the account of the Ungrukh being skinned is explicitly linked to that heritage;

Kinnear likens this act to "the way we used to collect scalps and ears in the bad old days" (93). As Gotlieb was no doubt aware, despite its association with First Nations practice, scalping was in fact often committed *against* First Nations peoples by Europeans, whether through scalp bounties paid to First Nations peoples for the scalps of *other* First Nations enemies, or the direct employment of scalping by European peoples. As James Axtell notes, "scalp bounties enjoyed great popularity, especially among frontiersmen" (223), and "the French and English governments periodically fostered the scalping of European and Indian enemies by offering bounties or other economic incentives" (224). One example of such a bounty is Lieutenant-Governer and Commander in Chief of the Province of Massachusetts-Bay Spencer Phips's 1755 proclamation offering forty pounds per scalp for every "Male Penobscot Indian" and twenty pounds per scalp for "every Scalp of such Female Indian or Male Indian under the Age of Twelve Years, that shall be killed and brought in." That the Ungrukhs' red skins links them to First Nations peoples is significant here, as well. One argument for the offensiveness of the term "redskin" being used as a sports team nickname is the claim that the term derives from the reduction of First Nation people to skins exchanged for bounties. While there is little evidence to support the widespread use of the term "red skin" to refer specifically to the flaying of aboriginals for bounty, evidence such as the *Winona Daily Republican* newspaper report from September 25, 1863, promising that "the state reward for dead Indians has been increased to $200 (from $25) for every red-skin sent to Purgatory" (cited in Vogel, 999) supports the association.

Gotlieb draws general and repeated analogies between the Ungrukh and First Nations peoples, as well as offering repeated reminders of colonialism. For instance, the Ungrukh are tribal peoples themselves, and when they come ot Earth, they are treated in ways remarkably similar to how First Nations peoples have been treated, notwithstanding the evident irony of their being colonist arrivees in a "New World" (33)—as Earth is for the Ungrukh, just as North America was for the ancestors of Ranger Willard Gonzales, who "looked as if his ancestors had come over on the *Mayflower*" (9). European colonists ended up claiming North America and relegating its native peoples to reservations; as the next wave of potential colonists in north America—allowed to establish an experimental settlement for a finite period—the Ungrukh are equally contained:

> They would be (1) allowed to hunt game preserves that needed population control, (2) receive food supplements, medical attention and legal protection, and (3) be permitted to live by their own laws as long as those did not encroach on the rights

of regional citizens. The price of this offer was that they let themselves be observed untouched by scientists, tourists, or anyone else who did not break any law, local or Ungrukh [33].

That is, they can, at the sufferance of the human government, live a "traditional" lifestyle within prescribes limits, receive government handouts, and engage in self-government as long as doing so really doesn't make any difference to human government; and in return, they can be objects of study and tourist attractions—"tribal exhibits" (33)—quaint (insofar as giant cats can be quaint) examples of an exotic alternate lifestyle, carefully segregated and monitored, for their own good, of course. It is an open question whether they are "being protected or imprisoned" (29). Gotlieb does not proselytize, but she does invite readers to see parallels between how humans treat aliens in these books and how different human races have historically treated each other.

Adams is her own sort of Dahlgren/Kriku/creator-destroyer God figure in this respect, viewing herself has having the power of life and death over whomever she wants, a point hinted at ironically when we encounter her at the theater, watching a play that is evidently an adaptation of the York cycle of mystery plays. Wearing her own diamond-shaped mask, she watches an "actor playing God in a gold mask" (100) speak God's first words from the York cycle:

> I am gracious and great, God without a beginning;
> I am Maker unmade, and all power in Me;
> I give you all life, and all grace worth winning;
> I am foremost and first: as I bid it shall be! [100].

These lines comment ironically on Phoebe's self-conception. The scene quickly shifts to the opening of the Noah play, in which God the creator repents of his creation of the disappointing humanity and decides to wipe it out. The implications about Phoebe—and the Qumedon, for that matter—are ominous.

Her behavior can be compared with the more deeply motivated, if no less disturbing, agenda of the antagonist of *Emperor, Swords, Pentacles*, Thorndecker, who is far more explicitly willing to engage in genocide. He and his brother, Agassiz, are similar but contrasted figures. Both suffer profound physical deformities, but Thorndecker is willing to sacrifice an entire species, the Qsaprinli, in order to derive from their bodies an enzyme that will allow him to grow for himself a normal body. The two men are the heirs of the founder of a failed colony on the planet Pintrel II, known by its inhabitants as Qsaprinel. A fungus native to the planet affected the colonists, leading to debilitating mutations that ultimately destroyed the colony (yet again, the problems of reproduction are a key plot point). The brothers are somewhat similar in their deformities. Both have bodies that, though adult, are almost embryonic in form. Agassiz, the more profoundly deformed, is "forty-four years old, and—and in the shape of an embryo, near three months [...] but big, maybe a meter long" (89). Furthermore, "His face was hard to look at [...] because his eyes were in his temples, his forehead a huge bilobar structure, and his nose a flattened snout shaped like the cut half of a mushroom" (95). He feeds through his umbilical cord, which is still attached to his body. We are reminded of the bottled brains in relation to Agassiz, which invites us to focus on his mind rather than his body as his defining feature: "His life-support equipment seemed usual enough to his visitors, who had either seen or heard of the bottled ESP brains kept alive for hundreds of years" (95).

Thorndecker is physically somewhat more developed and not as profoundly deformed, but he too is grotesque. He is the

> Size of a kid about two and a half, beard, chestful of hair, muscles like a weightlifter, man-size set of equipment [...], "Infant Hercules Syndrome"[11] Doctor calls it, from all the stuff he'd been treated with, nothing at all like a dwarf or midget, not like Agassiz except for size. He had these dickey-suits fitted with prosthetics to give him proper legs and arms and face masks because even with the beard you could see he had baby features [123].

Despite them both being deformed in ways that infantilize their bodies, however, they are nevertheless very different; Gotlieb has moved beyond the relatively straightforward correlation she tended to draw in her earlier work between physical and mental/moral equivalency. Whereas Thorndecker is profoundly selfish, willing even to wipe out the Qsaprinli in order to acquire what he needs to grow an adult body, Agassiz is devoted to others; Thorndecker is inward-directed, while Agassiz is outward-directed. They are limited and must grow beyond what they are, as is suggested by their essentially embryonic status, but the opposite ways they respond to their conditions demonstrate that one's identity is not fully determined by one's physical limitations, even if those limitations influence one's identity. Despite similar physical conditions, they have built contrasting identities and contrasting ways of interacting with the world and with others.

That the body is not a template, imposing a pattern on the mind to match its own contours, is a point suggested in these brothers and reiterated by how they are parallel to another set of siblings in the novel, the Qsaprinli, Spinel-alpha and Spinel-beta. Given the physical nature of the Qsaprinli, these two are literally two halves of the same whole. Qsaprinli reproduce by fission, so

Spinel-alpha and Spinel-beta are "born" when their "father" divides into two parts, coming into individual existence upon the fission of their "father." They are the product of their father, as Thorndecker and Agassiz are of theirs, their deformities being a result of his failed colonization attempt. However, despite originating as a single identity (and body) divided in two, alpha and beta are as opposite as Thorndecker and Agassiz—though Gotlieb does make Spinel-beta, the Thorndecker analogue, physically deformed:

> It was said throughout the Empire that Spinel-alpha had been given the looks and Spinel-beta the brains. Even all those who loved their Emperor [alpha] said this with lazy intolerance. Few asked whether Spinel-alpha had brains, but Beta could not hide his looks and did not try. He had known soon after fission that he could not rule and be accepted, except as his sibling's shadow. He was grossly deformed in the right side [4].

If we had only alpha and beta on which to judge, we might conclude that Gotlieb was simply repeating the old strategy of linking physical and mental deformity, but the link with the equally deformed but morally opposed Thorndecker and Agassiz disallows such a reading.

The complexity of the process whereby identity arises is a topic that spans the three novels, regardless of their individual plots. We learn in the first that Prandra is fascinated by the mind and has taken on as her life's work an attempt to model the mind, to come to an understanding of "the shapes of minds, the organic structures that began them, the ideas and emotions that fulfilled them" (*Judgment* 65). Her project is mentioned occasionally throughout the series, as a backdrop to the action, but it assumes center stage at the climax of *The Kingdom of the Cats*, which is therefore also the climax of the trilogy. The Ungrukhs' ongoing struggle with their creator, Kriku, for their autonomy, is achieved by a manifestation of Prandra's mind-model. The Ungrukh are able to defeat Kriku by forming a group-mind, creating a single meta-entity that calls itself UNGRUKH. UNGRUKH exists simultaneously on two planes. One is pure mind, the linked network of consciousnesses formed by the minds of all the Ungrukh who are part of the network. This network is imaged "not [as] a collection but a being" (272), which differentiates it from the one other time it manifested itself, when they first tried to repudiate the Qumedon's offers in the distant past. This time, it is not simply many voices speaking as one but its own entity as a manifestation of the will of the species. However, the network does not absorb or supplant the consciousnesses of individual Ungrukh; there is no usurpation of the mind of an individual. UNGRUKH does not replace the individuals that make it up, though the possibility of being subsumed does exist, as Emerald's question to Bren suggests; "how can you be part of the UNGRUKH being and separate *all* the time, when I must take so much trouble to pull myself away?" (276). Emerald, who is Prandra's daughter, considers UNGRUKH in relation to her mother's project: "I wonder if at the end she does not make some plan, map, chart ... of a model *for a mind*—and if that mind is not UNGRUKH" (*Kingdom* 276).

Prandra's model of the mind brings together the many and the one, the mind and the body, the internal and external to the self; it is both microcosm and macrocosm. But UNGRUKH, despite being such a combination, is itself not necessarily the ideal option; the Ungrukh do not see remaining the meta-entity permanently as a desirable option. As mentioned above, holding on to a sense of individuality while sharing in the group consciousness is challenging. Becoming UNGRUKH represents an interesting and useful possibility that might serve in some instances and temporarily, but doing so is not a desirable alternative to retaining one's status as a fully autonomous individual who is part of a social whole—even though that unique physical existence carries with it its own dangers, such as individual harm or death. The first manifestation of UNGRUKH suggested, at the climax of *A Judgment of Dragons*, "Every one of us is One Self, and on our world we find the Other as well as we can" (254). In a way, though, being UNGRUKH always would be itself a way to cease to exist, by losing the sense of distinction between self and other. The individual must, the novels suggest, reach beyond the self for the other. One can find the self by bridging the gap between self and other: finding the other in the self, and the self in the other, is crucial to the individual. Identity is relational, a function of mind in conjunction with body and of individual in conjunction with group and environment. Having a body forces one to recognize the individual outside the self, and therefore to recognize the self as an individual. There are potentially negative ramifications to this, but even more negative ones to the alternative. The model of the mind that emerges in the trilogy, ultimately, is therefore multiform and complex, consisting not of a single intellect or identity but of a variety of intellects working together while retaining their individuality. Or, there is no mind, only minds; there is no identity outside of others against which to measure that identity.

In conclusion, then, one might liken Gotleib's model of the mind as it emerges in the Ungrukh Chronicles with the governing model of GalFed—a federation of different, complementary and also competing cultures that also combine into one larger, albeit amorphous entity. As noted earlier, GalFed is a typically Canadian idea of a galactic empire, which Gotlieb might be said to represent on a microcosmic level in the figure of UNGRUKH: the one made up of many that also retain their individuality, as Canada is made up of Provinces that often insist on their own uniqueness and even autonomy within Confederation. The choice of cats as the base alien form here, given their reputation for independence, is no doubt germane. The choice of red, specifically, as their color invites us to see in the Ungrukh figures analogous to the Americas' indigenous peoples, furthering the likelihood of a Canadian subtext to the series.[12] However, the trilogy does more than merely establish a simple and facile parallel between aliens and oppressed humans. It insists that readers reexamine their assumptions about the limits of the "human," even to consider the possibility that the human tendency to view the universe as anthropocentric is dangerously narrow and limiting. That even some readers of the books think they are about humans, not aliens, suggests that Gotlieb's point of view still needs to be clarified. She continues to extend her consideration of such matters in her subsequent work.

Six

The Lyhhrt Trilogy

The Lyhhrt trilogy, so called because of the importance to the sequence of the alien Lyhhrt, whom we have encountered in earlier stories notably *A Judgment of Dragons*, is also sometimes referred to as the *Flesh and Gold* trilogy. It consists of *Flesh and Gold* (1998), *Violent Stars* (1999), and *Mindworlds* (2002). Like the Ungrukh Chronicles, these novels can be read independently without much difficulty, but also like the Ungrukh Chronicles, there is significant plot and thematic continuity between them (so much so, in fact, that the third volume has to devote a fair bit of space at various points to exposition, for the benefit of readers coming to it alone). Therefore, as with that earlier trilogy, I will treat this one as a unit. The trilogy also picks up on various themes and tropes that Gotlieb has explored before. Issues of procreation and fertility are important. Much of the action in the trilogy takes place on the planet Khagodis and, as was the case with the Ungrukh, the origin of the Khagodi (also a species not native to their planet) is an ongoing background story. The Khagodi also suffer from genetic limitations that make breeding difficult, an idea Gotlieb first explored in "Planetoid Idiot" and returns to repeatedly. Khagodi fertility problems are a minor but ongoing background concern in the novels. More directly relevant are the procreative difficulties of the Ix and the horrific solution they seek for them, which harkens back to "Sunday's Child." The colonization/exploitation of the bodies of others returns as a theme, as well. Indeed, in this trilogy, the problems of creating clones as workers assumes central importance, since the creation of a slave race is a key plot point. The struggle to be recognized as having identity and rights follows, unsurprisingly. Machine intelligence also looms large, as the robot Spartakos might be seen as similar to mod–Dahlgren (the erg rebellion is briefly referenced in *Flesh and Gold* [251]) or, to a lesser extent, O/G. Even occasional specific plot points recur. For instance, again we have an alien ship trapped inside a planet, and a single figure capable of perceiving the alien's messages, as in *Heart of Red Iron*. However, the effect is not derivative; these novels are not so much reiterations as extensions of Gotlieb's characteristic concerns.

Given that the boundary between being a human (as defined by Gotlieb) and a non-human is a major concern of the trilogy, it is significant that the first novel begins on a border, the threshold between land and water. As Susan A. C. Rosen suggests, the shore is "a boundary zone, an area with the greatest potential for change or a place that is more sensitive to change, a place that acts as a threshold" (21). In this instance, it is a threshold as site of conflict, as different metaphorical worlds on the same planet interact and set in motion a sequence of transformative events. The Zamos Corporation has brought to the planet Khagodis a cloned variation of Solthree humans adapted for underwater work, claiming they are merely animal experiments. The police officer investigating one of the creatures reports (in a section entitled "The Slave"), "It is not a human being"; "It is registered as an experimental animal, legally imported under the terms of the Recreations & Amusements Act, Brothels & Zoos Division. I was shown the bills-of-sale and receipts" (38).[1] Nevertheless, they are human: "No matter that it—that she—was hairless, with dark red skin and a blade-shaped tail that propelled her in angry circles, that her forehead and chin receded steeply from the firm mouth, and her huge eyes had sealed transparent lids. [...] She was a human Solthree woman, not merely sentient but intelligent" (22). Only later do we learn how it is possible for these aquatic creatures to be human; they were

> created from your genotype of human stock on your own Old Earth, by the founders of Zamos, some hundreds of years back [...] and bred for a few generations, then became sterile. The genetic data were saved, the type modified and cloned again and again because it had once been fertile. Slaves created on demand are immensely more valuable when they are self-breeding [240].[2]

The novel begins with an encounter between these mer-creatures and their slavers in which the divides between them are crucial.

Their difference is stressed in the representation of them as inhabiting different worlds. The slaves contrast themselves with their slavers as "we-people" as opposed to the "up-people" (8–9), the leader of whom they refer to as "Lord Upthere" (8). Their location in the sea makes the vertical orientation literal as well as metaphorical; the merfolk are physically lower than the slavers. They are also separated not merely by relationship or even geography but by the boundary of the water; despite the commonality implied by the fact that the merfolk recognize both themselves and their slavers as "people," they inhabit different worlds, which reinforces metaphorically the divide. This point is underscored by the reluctance of Kobai, the merwoman with the most significant role in the novel, to emerge from the water: "I don't like to put my head through the skin of my world and make dumb noise [i.e., talk aloud, rather than telepathically]" (9), she thinks. The metaphor of water as skin links her environment with her body; her world is, in a sense, herself. There is also perhaps a hint of a birthing metaphor here, with Kobai preferring to stay in the familiar but also limited world of the ocean—analogous to the amniotic sac—than to emerge into a larger and more frightening world. To be rendered free, Kobai and the others must be released from their metaphorical womb.

This focus on the skin as surface point dividing worlds, dividing internal and external, establishes a major recurring idea in the trilogy, sometimes involving literal barriers, sometimes involving metaphorical ones. The slaver Ferrier is described as follows: "Ferrier was wearing white against the equatorial heat; his short jacket was closely fitted, and had double-breasted black buttons. Nohl was thinking that Ferrier's eyes were like the buttons, fixed and sharp on white skin. A thin skin over arrogance and greed" (7). The equation of eyes with buttons suggests that Ferrier's skin is akin to clothes, a suit covering him. In this case what is beneath the skin is arrogance and greed, twin sins in the trilogy. For all its multi-world-spanning action, the trilogy comes back repeatedly to the banality of greed as the major motivating factor for the antagonists. While the fate of worlds does hang in the balance (in the first two books, anyway), as one might expect in space opera, politics as motivation take a back seat to greed as a motivator, at least for the majority of the villains. The arrogant assumption of superiority is also a recurrent theme here, as elsewhere in Gotlieb. It belongs primarily to the antagonists. Ferrier is merely the first character whose skin of humanity is illusory, though subsequent volumes present characters whose "skin" is literally a disguise.

The Lyhhrt have always, in a way, gone disguised among other intelligent creatures, containing their amoeba-like bodies in robotic shells, usually of a hominid design. There is always a barrier between the physical Lyhhrt and others; as the Khagodi Hasso realizes in *Mindworlds* when his Lyhhrt friend/ally suffers an ESP attack and goes inert in his casing, "*Lyhhrt, Lyhhrt, you are a metal box of mind I cannot open...*" (193). In this instance, the "skin," designed to protect the fragile body of the Lyhhrt, now becomes a barrier that prevents the provision of any physical aid. This notion of the Lyhhrt shell as cage as well as protection recurs throughout the trilogy. In *Flesh and Gold*, for instance, when Kobai, now taken from the sea and encased in a tank to be used as a sex slave in one of the Zamos Corporation brothels, complains to her Lyhhrt keeper, "You don't know what it is to be in a cage" (128), he responds, "*I am a fleshly being who needs these metal parts to work in as you need water, and they are a kind of cage*" (128–29).[3] Despite being free to move at will, the Lyhhrt (and all Lyhhrt), when away from the planet Lyhhr, must of necessity exist in a sort of prison of the body, a reflection of the isolation in which such traveling Lyhhrt exist. In their native state, Lyhhrt exist as a sort of group mind, with no consciousness of individuality; individuality is imposed on them as a condition of interacting with the larger community of sentient beings, ironically opening up possibilities in one respect while imposing profound limitations in another. Indeed, individuality becomes the primary threat to the Lyhhrt.

Of course, one can be imprisoned in one's flesh in other ways. Hasso himself laments his own physical limitations as a deformed Khagodi. Because he was born with a wasted leg and only one heart rather than the usual two, he believes himself doomed to a lonely life. On a world on which fertility is a primary concern, who would choose to marry a man unlikely to be fertile, or unlikely to breed healthy children if he were fertile? Hasso himself is the child of a father who abandoned his first wife, Skerow, because of her infertility. Her infertility marginalized Skerow, and Hasso is himself marginalized by his deformity. He is not cast out but he is not widely accepted, either. For Hasso, the world is something of which he believes he knows little, since he is "always imprisoned in [his] flesh" (*Mindworlds* 189). As such, he is akin to the other deformed or malformed characters we have seen in Gotlieb's work, though in this trilogy we have no association between physical and moral corruption; Hasso suffers socially and mentally because of his limitations, but he is in no way warped by them morally. The inherent limits of the flesh here are less important than the ones imposed on it from without.

There are many of these in this trilogy, though not all involve slavery. For instance, the action in these novels takes place considerably later than the action in the Ungrukh Chronicles, and the normative practice then of making telepathic species pay for their assistance from GalFed by having telepaths' brains decanted and kept alive indefinitely in service to GalFed has been discontinued, but some of the brains so harvested still live. The Khagodi Hall of Ancestors, which is half submerged in the earth and therefore another borderland, "was a hall of the dead whose brains had outlived them in the years when a misguided technology had kept them 'alive' in globes of nutrient liquid. The practice had long been stopped, but because the Khagodi were the longest-lived of known sentients, there were still these few in existence" (*Flesh and*

Gold 141). These brains exist on the border between life and death, as their partial submersion in the earth suggests; they have been, in a sense, buried alive. One might question whether keeping these brains alive but put away out of sight is really an act of kindness or simply an awkward compromise between maintaining one's reputation for morality (on which the Khagodi pride themselves) by not simply killing them, and keeping them out of sight to avoid being reminded of a notable failure of that vaunted morality. The Khagodi reputation for morality, of course, is more than a little compromised over the course of the trilogy, notably by the collusion of at least some of them in slaving operations.

Slavery is of key importance. The amphibian humans are merely one example of a slave race, not even in legal possession of their own bodies. "Zamos wanted to know how far they could go in making undifferentiated protoplasm become animals and persons, anything they could control" (*Flesh and Gold* 239), so in addition to recloning the subaquatic humans as slaves, they have had the Lyhhrt build a slave race from the ground up: the O'e. The O'e have been granted a dubious sort of "freedom" by the end of *Flesh and Gold*, but, as we learn in *Violent Stars*, that means little: "those O'e folk, like Ama, that all got so much freedom when Zamos fell apart?—they didn't get anything else because they're not even allowed to call themselves human beings!" (53). They have the freedom to do menial work and suffer abuse, barely subsisting on the margins of society, because their clone status means that they are not recognized as one of the "fourteen human species from twenty-five worlds" (*Flesh and Gold* 104). They occupy a liminal space, existing between worlds—the world of the being with agency and the world of the thing. Here, neither body nor mind guarantees "identity"; it is instead conferred by the state, a point which underscores the problematic question of what makes one "human."

One of the recognized fourteen human species, the Lyhhrt themselves have been enslaved by Zamos, in payment for rescue from the mysterious alien Ix. The Ix are also enslavers of a sort, and in more than one way. They can emit "hallucinatory pheromones [...] to disorient their victims" (*Violent Stars* 36), thereby gaining control of them. Furthermore, they usurp control of the minds of their victims—though this ability is hardly limited to them; as we've seen in the Ungrukh Chronicles, for instance, a universe in which there are powerful telepaths is one in which mind control via agencies such as hypnoforming, imposed mental blocks, and other interventions can modify the consciousnesses of others without them even knowing it has been done. While the Ix do not actually hide themselves within the bodies of these victims, they do in effect possess them by modifying their memories and using them as catspaws to pursue their own ends. We see this power in effect when they use ambassador Bullivant's Secretary Hawksworth to warn Bullivant off; he appears disoriented, speaks "from the depth of his throat" and after delivering the message, "his arms fell and he shook his head like a dog and stared at Bullivant. 'Ambassador? What happened? Have I gone mad?'" (21). More disturbingly, though, they wish to take literal possession of the bodies of Lyhhrt to use them as incubators for their eggs:

> Ix were egglayers who had polluted their world and themselves so horribly that they faced extinction. To survive they needed a new and richer medium in which to incubate their eggs; their scouting ships had found that the bodies of Lyhhrt were nearly perfect for them. Their world Iyax had attacked Lyhhr, a neutral world with close ties to Galactic Federation [35].[4]

That is, they want to consume the Lyhhrt, convert their flesh into their own offspring. A more profound and direct colonization of the bodies of others is difficult to imagine. The Lyhhrt are saved from this fate only by Zamos, but the cost is one Cosmic Cycle (129 years) of servitude, ostensibly a contractual agreement but *de facto* slavery: "Zamos, swollen with greed, had stood with Ix terrorists and enslaved Lyhhrt" (36). After the 129 years have passed, Zamos does not wish to lose these valuable servants; "they saw we are too valuable to them and know too many secrets. They have been sending the Ix to us as a warning" (*Flesh and Gold* 214), as one Lyhhrt reports. Despite being one of the various "human" species, therefore, the Lyhhrt are also in effect slaves for the 129 years and in danger of becoming slaves in fact when the "contract" ends.

Last but not least is the robot Spartakos, created by the Lyhhrt. Humanoid in form, Spartakos is a unique being. One might analogize Spartakos with mod–Dahlgren, another fully mechanical man, but mod–Dahlgren was designed to imitate a specific human being and learns his humanity from that figure, whereas Spartakos's development seems independent. Furthermore, while it might be fair to see mod–Dahlgren as a subservient figure in *O Master Caliban!* given the autocratic nature of erg–Queen and her treatment of him, he is not explicitly a slave or possession but rather one of the erg population, whereas Spartakos is both. Spartakos's trajectory from owned object to autonomous entity, therefore, is more significant than mod–Dahlgren's. Besides, though the Lyhhrt trilogy does briefly reference the erg rebellion, mod–Dahlgren is never mentioned, so we are encouraged to think of Spartakos as a unique figure.

"Ned Gattes knew of such robots," we are told, "but the few he had seen were not completely robotic, and had been directed in part by human brain matter. He did not think this was the case with Spartakos" (*Flesh and Gold* 101). The other slaves in these novels fall on a continuum, from "human," to clone of genetically modified "human," to sentient creature fully cloned from undifferentiated protoplasm. They share a grounding in the biological, with the boundaries between them not really much more blurred than the boundaries between the various recognized "human" species. Spartakos, by contrast, is pure machine consciousness housed in a shell that imitates the hominid model of the "human" form (right down to the inclusion of metallic sex organs, though how these function is left for the reader to imagine). There are cyborgs in these novels, figures combining machine and human, but Spartakos is as separate from them as he is from all biologically based creatures: "Ned Gattes was to find it characteristic of the pugs that when Spartakos was among them they became uncomfortable and spoke coarsely of the flesh, as if to reaffirm it in themselves and each other. Even cyborgs did this. Especially cyborgs" (*Flesh and Gold* 101). Those whose humanity has been modified are the most likely to stress the importance of the flesh as a defining characteristic of the human, thereby excluding Spartakos.

However, as the novels repeatedly make clear, even telling the difference between a creature of the flesh and a machine can be challenging. In *Flesh and Gold*, for instance, when she first encounters one of the O'e, "Skerow wondered if she might not actually be a robot" (46), though she is merely a slave. In *Mindworlds*, the waiter serving Brezant (himself a slave owner) "might have been a robot, or a Lyhhrt, or a very experienced elderly man" (12)—the continuum from construct to entity, with Lyhhrt occupying the medial spot because their assumption of metal shells for bodies makes them indistinguishable from robots. Characters who see them infer that they are mechanical, not biological, as Koboi does, for instance, when she refers to the Lyhhrt who is trying to help her as "machine man" (*Flesh and Gold* 128). Indeed, the illusion is so complete that in *Violent Stars*, characters cannot tell when a Lyhhrt shell is occupied and when it is empty of a Lyhhrt and merely carrying out programming. This is an important plot point, as it allows the Lyhhrt time to escape and put in motion the plan to stop the Ix. What is the difference between autonomy and automaton when the latter can imitate the former perfectly? These novels employ a strategy of blurring the lines between entity and object in ways that require readers to recognize category shifts.

Spartakos is perhaps the focal point here. He is most clearly the character (if one can call a machine a character) as property. Even his name foregrounds his status. For readers unaware of the significance of his name, Gotlieb has him explain:

> I am sure you have been told by your tour guides that Spartacus was a Roman slave thousands of years ago who rebelled, and ultimately led an army of rebels, only because he wanted to go home to Thrace. Only to go home. I have no other home than this, so I am home, and I have the freedom to stand here waving my arms and entertaining you. Therefore I have been given the name of a slave. This shows that though you are called a slave you need not be one. I am your example [*Flesh and Gold* 183–84].

His status as created object is reiterated throughout the series, as is the possibility of him transcending it. He comments in *Flesh and Gold*, "I was built by the Lyhhrt people to be a guardian and a lighthouse, and when the Lyhhrt are safe and the O'e are free then I will perhaps have been more than a machine" (244), words he closely echoes in *Violent Stars*: "I was made—by Lyhhrt, by flesh like yourself under that gold and bronze—to believe that I was a guide and a lighthouse until Zamos was destroyed, when the Lyhhrt would be safe and the O'e were free" (136). He becomes a "robot with a social conscience" (136); that is, he acquires identity.

As such, he is also the character most clearly transmuted from object to entity. He is indeed the example, as he represents the transformation that the various enslaved species must undergo. He is central to the plots involving the fates of the Lyhhrt and the O'e. Much as the novels are concerned with the boundary points between peoples,[5] they are also concerned with border-crossing, with individuals and species finding ways to come to accommodations with the complex diversity of the universe they inhabit, perhaps, even, in some ways, to become something other than what they were in the beginning. Spartakos's Lyhhrt-imposed goal is to help them in their struggle against the Ix, and his self-determined goal is to help lead the O'e from slavery to freedom. His name associates him with a rebel slave leader, and his reiterated self-definition as a lighthouse makes him a beacon designed to guide travelers to safety and home. However, bringing the O'e to a place of safety is not merely geographical but also political; though their emancipation will not change them in any literal way, it will nevertheless transform them from property to people, from slaves to citizens, as has happened to Spartakos himself by the third volume; he "was no longer a servant or an ornament, but a world-citizen" (38). He, too, remains unchanged physically but nevertheless has become something other than what he was before.

I have referred to this aspect of the novels as "transmutation" rather than "transformation" because of the former term's link with the theory of alchemy. Alchemy, the Noble Art, as it was called, is the precursor to modern chemistry. J. K. Rowling's Harry Potter series (especially the first volume, *Harry Potter and the Philosopher's Stone*),[6] has perhaps given alchemy greater cultural currency in recent years than it has enjoyed in several centuries, but there is a long tradition of using alchemy in literature, especially for metaphorical purposes. Briefly, one of the underpinnings of alchemical theory was that, given the correct knowledge of the nature of the material universe, the alchemist might be able to transform one material into another—specifically, to change baser metals (lead being the cliché example) into more valuable ones such as silver or gold. "This general process of transforming one metal into another is called *transmutation*," as Lawrence M. Principe explains (13).[7] However, for alchemists, the point of such transformation was not the generation of wealth but rather purification, the conversion of base matter into more refined, more elevated matter: the improvement, in effect, of the corrupt nature of the material universe. The concept is open to obvious abuses, and many well-known literary works show how easily the noble purposes of alchemy can be turned to greedy ends.[8] Such elemental transformation serves as a metaphor for Gotlieb in this series, though especially in *Flesh and Gold*. Gotlieb explicitly acknowledges it when she reports that Skerow is putting on trial "mild corrupt men and women disguised in business suits who dealt not in drugs and flesh but in transmuting them to gold" (*Flesh and Gold* 285). The metaphor here also invokes the corruption of alchemy into a way of generating wealth. A similar metaphor is used in *Violent Stars* to describe how one might take what one has learned via ESP and use it in a legal case; since ESP evidence is inadmissible in court, one must find other ways to get it in, or, as Tharma puts it, "Let us first see how we can turn the inadmissible zinc into gold" (176)—a reversal of the corrupt alchemy of Zamos.

    The transmutation of one material into another does occur in *Flesh and Gold*, both literally and metaphorically. Just as pearls are produced by oysters, for instance, precious stones are produced on Khagodis by a creature called a tethumekh. Kept as pets, these creatures often wear a chain necklace with a pendant consisting of a fruit seed; "The tethumekh sucked at its rough surface to rid itself of a substance in saliva produced by overbreeding, and after years of accumulation produced a precious jewel, very much like an opal" (30). Note, by the way, that reproductive capacity—or over-capacity—is once again a factor; the tethumekhs' fecundity finds an additional outlet in the creation of precious objects. One might suggest that the Khagodi capitalize on their overbreeding for profit. That the tethumekhs themselves can be used as adornments underscores the point: "the *tethumekh* [*sic*] had become a decorative jewel like the swag of gold on a diplomat's uniform" (35).[9] Even the fact that they carry their seed on a chain underscores their status as property, as chains made from gold or silver are used by Zamos to demark slaves. In *Violent Stars*, for instance, Verona notes the silver chain worn by a blue woman and infers that it represents "ownership or bondage. Not a piece of jewelry" (41). That the next sentence identifies the blue woman as "the chained woman" (41) confirms the point, to readers, at least; the phrase "chained woman" suggests a woman who is in chains, not a woman merely wearing a decorative chain. The tethumekh transmute organic matter into a jewel—they "grow" wealth from a fruit seed—and that process is linked to ownership and exploitation.

Even the title of the first novel foregrounds the concept of transmutation. Zamos is converting flesh into gold—that is, money—by creating a cheap slave labor force. That point is underscored by the fact that the aquatic slaves are being used specifically to mine for gold in the sea; their flesh is used to amass gold. Though they do not actually become gold, they represent the conversion of person to property and therefore to wealth. Indeed, the growing of slaves is the major Zamos enterprise explored in the first novel. As noted earlier, slaves that can breed are more valuable, so when Koboi is discovered to be pregnant, she is removed from the oceanic mining colony as an object of greater potential value. Significantly, she is relocated to a brothel under the pretence of being an experimental animal that can be used for sexual purposes: "As long as this being has no status as a person, is legally accounted for, with documentation, and is seen to be in good health, those people are within their rights, no matter how ghastly a pleasure is taken from her" (*Flesh and Gold* 38), Skerow is told. Koboi is removed from her skin of water, just as the gold is removed from the skin of land that covers it, as Nohl (who owned the property being mined) suggests, in his invocation of the skin metaphor: "Gold! All that gold! Coming out from under the skin of what used to be my land!" (150). Because brothels traffic in flesh for gold, a brothel is an appropriate symbolic location to serve as a cover for Zamos's slaving operations. The "skin trade" goes somewhat deeper in this instance.

The GalFed agent Lebedev, working undercover in the brothel, finds the secret concealed within the brothel when he comes upon a room containing a latticework frame of hexagon cells: "In the center of each hexagon there was a tiny dark knot, like an insect in its cocoon, no, not an insect. An embryo just short of becoming a fetus. In human terms" (119–20). The latticework seems to extend forever, "like the folded linings of an immense womb" (120). Here mechanical and biological reproduction are likened; Zamos is producing an endless supply of the O'e, as Lebedev realizes, growing them in artificial wombs. They are products to be smuggled throughout GalFed. Lebedev himself was a smuggler and served time in prison for that crime, which sentence has provided the cover for his clandestine GalFed employment. But his smuggling, of things such as foodstuffs, is contrasted with this trafficking in flesh. While smuggling is a crime regardless, smuggling food at least provides something of nutritive value to the recipients; the analogy to smuggled slaves simply stresses that they are treated as consumables. That some Khagodi consume gold in the belief that doing so might strengthen their ESP (*Flesh and Gold* 40) strengthens the equation.

This breeding of property assumes a more focused and disturbing significance in *Violent Stars*, when we learn that the original Zamos, founder of Zamos corporation, put in place a plan to perpetuate his line indefinitely through a horrific program of genetically modified inbreeding; he created embryos by taking his wife's ovaries and

> fertiliz[ing] them with female sperms from his own seed-sacs until he had the embryos of a hundred daughters ... and the end of it is that he had one of them brought to bear in the body of a hired woman [...] in order that when his daughter became an adult she should bear one other of her sisters, kept in frozen storage all these many years, and onward in that way [159].

If not personal immortality, this represents at least an attempt to grasp some sort of quasi-immortality through genetic manipulation, in another variation on alchemical practice. Though as Principe points out (p. 5), the belief that alchemists sought human immortality is not entirely accurate, since there are numeurous branches of alchemy, most of which had no such interest, the link between alchemy and immortality holds a place in the popular consciousness; indeed, Nicholas Flamel has used the Philosopher's Stone to achieve immortality in the first Harry Potter book.[10] In Zamos, Edvard Dahlgren's hubris is not only multiplied one hundred-fold but also turned even more inward. If Sven was created in part as a way of holding on to the lost wife, Sven was also a loved son for whom the father was willing to sacrifice himself. His mutations were imposed by the ergs, not Dahlgren. Here, by contrast, we have an overtly incestuous exercise in self-perpetuation, rendered even more perverse in that the line of offspring is itself treated as property of the corporation. Verona Bullivant, product of this line, is kidnapped and marked with the star-shaped symbol of the Zamos clan. It is carved into her palm rather than being burned into her flesh, but the idea of being branded is no less clear for that.

Ironically, Zamos himself has in a way become property of his own corporation. If one can become a person, one can also cease to be a person—as Quantz did, for instance (temporarily, at least) in *A Judgment of Dragons*. The brothel features a holographic image that purports to be "the image of Zamos, though it had no distinguishing marks, and appeared as a trademark in many of his establishments. By unspoken agreement it was treated as a person" (*Flesh and Gold* 65). Here we see the individual rendered generic and turned into an owned symbol; a trademark is a distinctive sign or representation that allows a product to be easily identified and differentiated from other products. Familiar examples would include the Coca Cola logo, or the McDonald's golden arches, or, to use a human example, the stylized image of Colonel Harland Sanders used as part of the logo of Kentucky Fried Chicken. A trademark existing as a three-dimensional holographic image and being treated as a person remains property nevertheless. In effect, Zamos the man and Zamos the corporation have merged; or, the man has been subsumed into—or consumed by—the company. If the ergs formed a hive mind in which individual parts had relatively minor value, the Zamos Corporation is not much different. But whereas the ergs strove for recognition as citizens, Zamos works against citizenship; the Zamos slaves are, to the corporation, just as much property as machines are, as the mechanical image of reproduction suggests. But if Gotlieb invites readers to be sympathetic to the idea of machines—at least ones such as mod–Dahlgren or Spartakos—being given human status, she does so even more clearly for slaves both biologically and intellectually "human" in nature.

The aquatic humans, the O'e, and the Lyhhrt are the three groups most extensively associated with enslavement, and are to varying degrees victims of Zamos. The Lyhhrt, however, are the most complex and problematic. Though, as we have seen, they are victimized by Zamos themselves, they also have a role in the creation (or recreation, in the case of the mer-people) and subjugation of the other two, so they are both victim and victimizer, passing on to others enslavement to Zamos in order to save themselves. They recognize, however, that they have been coerced into doing evil things. As one notes, "Zamos wanted to know how far they could go in making undifferentiated protoplasm become animals and persons, anything they could control. And we were so far out of control that at one time we even thought that we might make independent organic bodies for ourselves instead of these metal ones. Disgusting thought!" (*Flesh and Gold* 239). Zamos's transmutation of protoplasm into person is here identified as one of the tasks with which the Lyhhrt helped and, more significantly, as one which at least some Lyhhrt saw as of potential use to them—a point that comes to fruition in *Mindworlds*, though the orthodox Lyhhrt view of the use of organic bodies is to see it as disgusting. Even the use of metal shells for the convenience of travel and communication with the larger universe is problematic for them, as it separates them (or, one might more accurately suggest, pieces of them) from their gestalt. To assume an actual fleshly body would be an even more profound violation of the Lyhhrt sense of self/community.

The Lyhhrt do answer for their collusion in *Violent Stars* by turning on Zamos and the Ix when the terms of their agreement with Zamos expire and they refuse either to remain enslaved or to continue to work for Zamos. They help to prevent the Ix invasion of Khagodis and help bring down Zamos, some even sacrificing themselves to do so. However, their own skills in science and the temptation to use them place the Lyhhrt themselves in a medial space, between slaves and masters. Even laying aside the tasks they performed under duress at the behest of Zamos, including creating cyborgized macaques with radios implanted in their skulls and increased brain capacity that has given them intelligence, Spartakos is a test case for their role in the treatment of created entities. As he notes, their powers of creation have made them, for him (and arguably for the cyborg macaques), equivalent to God; "God's name is Lyhhrt" (*Violent Stars* 135), he says, adding, "That One God has no great sum to do with me, does That One? [...] No, it is He or She or Tree or Stone. Not what made me, which is a Lyhhrt. I was made—by Lyhhrt, by flesh like yourself under that gold and bronze" (136). As we might expect given Gotlieb's treatment of other figures who attempt to assume Godlike power, from Dahlgren to Kriku, the Lyhhrt's association here with the assumption of divine power suggests not only their brilliance but their potential danger. As the trilogy proceeds, the Lyhhrt potential for assuming direct power over others becomes the greatest threat.

Despite his development of consciousness and agency, Spartakos remains, as do the macaques, a tool for the Lyhhrt. As one says, "The monkeys are our strongbox and Spartakos is the key" (112), reiterating shortly afterward, "Spartakos and the monkeys are not pets or toys but our treasures" (114). However, like a pet or a toy, a treasure is still a possession, like a jewel-producing tethumekh worn as an adornment itself; that it is a valued possession does not change this fact. Indeed, and ironically, in *Violent Stars*, Spartakos becomes a sort of strongbox himself, a vessel for the Lyhhrt, carrying one to safety hidden in his own body. Each volume, in fact, includes a significant instance of a Lyhhrt contained within the body of another intelligent creature, albeit for different reasons. In the first two volumes, the internalization of a Lyhhrt is an act of rescue; the person carrying the Lyhhrt does so to help it. In the third volume, however, the assumption of a body by a Lyhhrt assumes a more sinister significance. For the first two volumes of the trilogy, the Lyhhrt are themselves primarily victims of Zamos, just as the O'e and the aquatic clones are. However, Zamos has been destroyed by the end of *Violent Stars*, and even the Ix threat has been largely neutralized. Given that Zamos and the Ix seem to represent the major threats in the series, *Mindworlds* might therefore seem like an anticlimax, but instead it shifts the frame of reference to make Lyhhrt factionalism the focus.

Key to the climax of *Flesh and Gold* are the twin rescues of Koboi, carried out by the Lyhhrt doctor appointed to care for the pregnant merwoman by Zamos, and the rescue of the Lyhhrt doctor himself, by GalFed agent Lebedev. Both involve the concealment of the figure(s) to be rescued. Koboi is rescued and smuggled off the planet Khagodis (in a neat reversal of Zamos's own method of transporting slaves) by being placed in a shipping container that is supposed to contain a two-hearted alien; the twin heartbeats of Koboi and her fetus create the illusion that the correct alien is in the container. Though she does not take over the body of another, her escape depends on a deception in which she is taken to be another creature. Whether she will ultimately be saved the Lyhhrt doctor does not know; "he was launching her as any alien child might send out a boat of leaves or bark down a stream that led to a great river" (268). One might note that this simile invites associations with Moses, launched into the Nile in a boat of leaves, a rescue which ultimately allows him to fulfill his role as leader of the Israelites out of bondage in Egypt and to freedom. Gotlieb therefore associates Koboi's launching with one of the most famous tales of the emancipation of slaves, though she leaves readers to wonder about the fate of this proto–Moses, as the mer-people do not feature in the second or third volumes. Koboi's final words, though, acknowledge the contingent nature of freedom: "no one of us is free in every way..." (284). The three ellipses are Gotlieb's, leaving Koboi and her people not in a fixed and final place, as a period would suggest, but instead still open to development, as the sentence remains open to completion.

As Koboi escapes under the skin of another, in a way, the Lyhhrt doctor escapes by being taken within Lebedev's body; the Lyhhrt

> Insinuated its body into the cavity, into the new universe between the external and internal oblique layers of the superficial muscles, steeling himself to control his hideous terror of the burning heat, the acid bite of the tissues, the drumming heart, the blood singing in its vessels as its thickly streaming cells swarmed through them, their bitter taste of iron, the bubblings, pulsings, rumblings, spasms—but his tormented nerve endings were already stimulating the secretions that would thicken his integument to insulate him from the horrors of this alien hell [269].

Again we have the idea of the body as universe, the Lyhhrt leaving one world behind and entering another as it passes through the skin. For this Lyhhrt, the experience is terrifying, the world of the body hellish, in contrast, for instance, to the way life inside the body of the Amsu can become pleasant, even almost addictive, to those who ride those great creatures. The passage requires readers to view the human body from the alien perspective; to the Lyhhrt, the normal human body is not merely alien, but an inimical environment; it is not a habitable world. However, even here we can see that the Lyhhrt possesses mechanisms that can make this hellish environment tolerable; he can insulate himself from its disturbing qualities, therefore inhabiting it without actually experiencing directly its reality. He can therefore, in effect, make the body another shell for himself. This potential is not realized here, but stands as an implicit possibility.

By contrast to the Lyhhrt's horror, Lebedev's initial repulsion at the idea of being invaded by what amounts to a giant parasite is colored by the reality of the experience. Direct contact with the Lyhhrt gives him more full access to its perceptions, just as its presence in him gives it access to his. Lebedev feels the potential God in the Lyhhrt: "Oh the power! as if he were a Creator standing on a mountain looking down on all the beasts below" (276). Such power falls outside Lebedev's ambition—"He did not want this kind of power" (277), he realizes almost immediately—but it does serve as a visceral lesson in why the Lyhhrt under human control could be of inestimable use, and therefore why Zamos would wish to keep them as slaves. It also stands as a demonstration of the potential when a Lyhhrt's ESP is combined with the sensoria of a human, thereby providing each/both with the range of information and power available to both/each. The Lyhhrt would provide the human host with a very tempting sense of power; one might become addicted to having a Lyhhrt in one, just as one might become addicted to riding an Amsu.[11] This will become an important point in *Mindworlds*. For now, however, it represents only a temporary melding of very different creatures, each of whom returns to himself subsequently, with better knowledge of the other. As such, it might be seen as a positive instance of "possession," a connection in which neither party is ultimately subjugated or subsumed but from which both benefit, similar, perhaps, to how hypnoforming provides insight into the other, as discussed in Chapter Five.

Violent Stars repeats the motif, though this time with Spartakos as the host body. Prior to the mission against the Ix that will claim their lives, two Lyhhrt produce an embryo that they encase in "what Ned Gattes might think of as a gold Easter egg" (234). The egg image itself of course suggests new life, even leaving aside the association with Easter; if the child in Koboi was associated with Moses, this child might be seen as carrying divine associations, though these prove far from Christ-like. The etymology of Easter associates it with Ēostre, a Germanic goddess of the dawn (the Greek goddess of the dawn,

Eos, derives her name from the same source) and with fertility. When this Lyhhrt, after hatching, appears again near the end of the novel, wearing its new shell, it is described as "something like Cupid in curlicued gold and platinum, with a little potbelly and a navel that held a ruby, chubby hands and feet with fat-creases, a half-score of dimples filled with sapphire, topaz and emerald together, altogether a parody of lust and mildly repulsive" (281). Cupid again suggests love and fertility, and the choice of a metallic body based on the sort of baby design for Cupid in many Renaissance paintings (rather than the more imposing Cupid of classical antiquity) further underscores the Lyhhrt child's association with new life and possibility. On the other hand, the weird hybridization of the metallic and the biological in the design makes him not a promising figure but one that undercuts, through the excess of the design and the ornamentation, the positive associations. Whether this new Lyhhrt represents a positive or a negative potential remains to be determined.

Indeed, its parents' mission against the Ix is also imaged in terms that problematize reproduction. Just as the Lyhhrt "egg" is inserted—one might say metaphorically planted—in Spartakos's body, so do the Lyhhrt implant themselves in the Ix ship *Ygszu*. Their ship is imaged as a "seed stalk" (236) splitting into smaller spores and being carried to the Ix ship, where "they nested among the frameworks of the *Ygszu*'s shuttle berths" (237). This nesting, however, contrasts with the nesting in Spartakos, as its effect will be destructive. Even the nesting in Spartakos, though, has effects on the robot that Ned finds disturbing; "he could only be thankful that they did not include a bomb" (254). The Lyhhrt, then, themselves occupy a border-space, between creative and destructive potential. Spartakos, the lighthouse and guide, and odd instance of surrogate mother, carries one Lyhhrt to new life. He is a machine committed to freedom—a machine with a social conscience—and represents how the cold and mechanistic can be humanized. He is not gold turned to flesh, but he is human nevertheless. In *Mindworlds*, the Lyhhrts' occupation of flesh or metal emerges as a major element.

As noted earlier, the major conflicts with Zamos and the Ix have been resolved by the beginning of *Mindworlds*, which might seem to leave little to resolve in the novel. One element is the minor background thread in the earlier novel about the origins of the Khagodi. Late in *Flesh and Gold*, a large metal artifact is found on the planet, "very ancient, possibly alien, they think perhaps a ship, perhaps even a key to the mystery of our civilization" (208). In *Violent Stars*, the artifact is confirmed to be a ship. In it are thousands of cases; "almost all of the more than eight thousand held an animal" (278), which leads to a comparison to Noah's Ark (279). The Khagodi may therefore have come to this planet, to which they know they are not native, on this vessel, but who flew it or why are questions that remain unanswered. *Mindworlds* returns to this ship and its cargo while also working out the ramifications of the Lyhhrts' enslavement and emancipation. The twin interests in identity evinced here are stitched together, although not seamlessly.

Prior to their discovery by GalFed, the Lyhhrt themselves were undifferentiated lumps of protoplasm—they "were in fact all brain, all senses in one organ" (*Violent Stars* 69). They were content on their home world merely to exist as a single entity lacking individuality and thinking Cosmic Thoughts. They had a home, but no culture. The Khagodi, by contrast, have a well-developed culture but are not native to their planet; it is their home insofar as it is their physical location, but they came from elsewhere, as the absence of any evidence of them in the fossil records indicates: "its citizens had no line of descent from or genetic relationship with any other life forms" (*Mindworlds* 104). For them, contemplation of origins is an important concern, one which has given rise to diverse Khagodi religions: "the Diggers and Inheritors contended that no one had yet dug in the right place; the Watchers and Hatchlings [...] believed that their ancestors had been delivered by burning gods in enormous eggs" (104–05). The Lyhhrt look out into the cosmos; the Khagodi look back into the past. Both need to find an identity in the now and in the here.

The Lyhhrt have been pushed in that direction because of their interaction with GalFed and the limited individuality assuming shells and interacting with other intelligent creatures forces on them; "the eyeless Lyhhrt species would never have known what their world looked like if aliens had not come to show them" (12). They would never have achieved a perspective from outside the self and therefore, paradoxically, a sense of self. This individuality, however, is a challenge to their fundamental self-conception as a single consciousness, and can lead them into mental instability: "Lonely Lyhhrt gradually became psychotic" (67). The Lyhhrt doctor in *Flesh and Gold* believes this is happening to him because he finds himself growing personally attached to Koboi: "Lebedev, I think I am going mad. I truly love that woman. I have sunk into depravity and individualism. I am a pervert" (211). Identity is depravity, from a Lyhhrt's perspective. However, loneliness is possible only if one is conscious of a self and other, so the unexamined condition of Lyhhrt existence is that, on some level, their lack of individuality is illusory; if one can be taken from the whole and sense loss, sense an absence from that whole, then that whole is not simply a single undifferentiated consciousness, even if it *thinks* it is and believes it should be.

The tension between the belief in/desire for unity and the necessity of assumed individuality to participate in GalFed creates Lyhhrt factions. For instance, there is a tension between Lyhhrt who remain on their home world and those who venture out; Lyhhrt who leave their world come to be seen as "over-individualized, heretical. Even contaminated" (*Mindworlds* 14). The difference between such individualized Lyhhrt and those committed to the Lyhhrt gestalt is reflected even in their language; Lyhhrt who still think in terms of the whole refer to themselves as "I/we" (presumably an English representation of a pronoun that simultaneously suggests a single speaker and a group), while those who have become individuated merely use the first person singular pronoun (18). The renegade Lyhhrt in *Mindworlds* are the latter kind, supporting the conventional understanding that Lyhhrt separated from the whole can become psychotic and therefore dangerous. They have also become the furthest removed from the Lyhhrt disgust with the notion of a flesh body. By the beginning of *Mindworlds*, we find that some Lyhhrt have begun to replace their gleaming metal shells with ones that mimic perfectly the bodies of other GalFed humans. The first one we encounter has disguised itself as an O'e, reminding us of their common history as slaves to Zamos. We are reminded as well of the difference between the skin and what might be beneath when "the beggar pulled off and flung aside his rags and skin, and became another Lyhhrt in a brushed silver casing" (19). Skin becomes nothing more than clothing for a Lyhhrt, something to conceal it rather than to make it stand out, as the ostentatious metal suits do.

A benign explanation for this change in practice is offered by one Lyhhrt: "We chose to look like common people now because other species are so frightened and suspicious of us" (43). Given the propensity for some GalFed species to judge based on surfaces, this is not necessarily an unwise policy. However, the Lyhhrt disguised as an O'e is using the false skin as a strategy to engage in spying, so there are sinister possibilities as well as benign ones linked with the practice. These sinister possibilities are reflected in the behavior of the renegade Lyhhrt who chooses to inhabit fleshly bodies directly. Lyhhrt in the bodies of others in the previous two books so place themselves or are so placed as a matter of necessity, for their salvation. In *Mindworlds*, however, the renegade Lyhhrt no longer see a human body as hellish, as was the case in *Flesh and Gold*, but as a path to power: one reports that living in a flesh body is useful because "fleshers have more power and influence than we do in clumsy metal workshells that only frighten and repel others" (189). Here the motive is not simply to avoid frightening others but to assume the power associated with the flesh. The renegade Lyhhrt who has made this choice is contrasted with the Lyhhrt saved by being implanted in Spartakos.

Though Hasso still thinks of this Lyhhrt as Baby, he has grown to maturity since the previous novel. However, his odd origins mean he has no place among his own people:

> I was conceived on this strange world and carried in the metal body of a robot to another one. That fellow Ned Gattes who guarded me sent me home safely, but by then it was I who had become too strange for us/my others, and they would not let me be One. I made my un/one self a gold and silver body and marched about like a bejeweled fool, but no matter how hard I worked for Galactic Federation I was no one and had no true being [54–55].

His grammar shows his confusion; he uses both the first person singular and the singular/plural combined forms, suggesting that he allies himself with the Lyhhrt conception of oneness on the one hand but also has a sense of individual identity. His own people agree, a fact which itself demonstrates that the Lyhhrt are indeed not the "one" they think they are. Another of the novel's Lyhhrt comments on this when he explains why he opted not to fission after the renegade Lyhhrt killed his companion: "I could have done that myself when he murdered my Other, but that one would not be *other*, and though we might like to believe that we are all the same person, there are differences, there are identities, and we need them" (179). The Lyhhrt on their homeworld insisting on their belief in their oneness, the novel suggests, need to adapt to a more complex reality than that. However, the renegade Lyhhrt's solution, of re-enacting the enslavement his people suffered by claiming the bodies of other intelligent beings, merely perpetuates the cycle of colonizing the bodies of others for one's own use. In the climactic conflict, when the renegade Lyhhrt tries to tempt another to follow in his path and place himself within the skin of another, the answer he receives is this: "*I longed to have an Other like you, but I cannot make myself live in the mind and body of another person*" (225).

Some medial position between stagnation and complete transmutation is essential. The Lyhhrt need to consider "the states of individuality, kinds of individuality we can allow among us, what we can afford to accept, and what we must refuse" (44). Individuality is essential *and* dangerous, and the novel leaves the Lyhhrt with the difficult task of negotiating between these conflicting realities, of finding a liminal space that does not marginalize but instead balances between the extremes of the absence of identity and the absence of a larger social world in which one can find a place and belong. In effect, they need to find a way forward, a way to become.

The Khagodi, by contrast, need to find an anchor for themselves by answering the question of where they came from. This aspect of the novel is less effectively worked out, though we are clearly invited to associate the Khagodis' problems with the Lyhhrts'. For instance, the Lyhhrt who turns to Hasso for help does so because he sees in Hasso a kindred spirit, another creature lonely because of how he is cut off from his society; Hasso, as we have noted, is marginalized in Khagodi culture because he is unlikely to be able to breed, just as the Lyhhrt rescued in *Violent Stars* is marginalized by Lyhhrt culture. Indeed, the danger of how Khagodi culture prioritizes reproduction manifests itself in another iteration of slavery, in the plot thread following Gorodek, a politically powerful Khagodi who has in effect purchased a bride, Ekket. She is not much better off than Koboi, despite being a full citizen, because of the laws in her district governing the disposition of women by their families. Koboi is woman as property in *Flesh and Gold*, Verona is in *Violent Stars*, and Ekket is in *Mindworlds*, but whereas the first two are victims of a criminal organization, Ekket is the victim of a misguided law. Just as Zamos marks its property with the star symbol, infertile female Khagodi must also wear symbols denoting their ineligibility as spouses. One such law, regarding the disposition of the brains of ESPs, has been changed, but there is work to be done.

The Khagodi fertility problem is a function of their disconnection from their planet. Not being native to it, they have a difficult time adapting to it, yet the answer to the question of their origins provides little satisfaction. The ship that crashed millennia ago was indeed a sort of ark, carrying specimens gathered by a powerful energy being (not a Qumedon, the novel makes clear). It, too, is an isolated being, lacking any others of its kind, so it serves as a sort of personification (insofar as a formless energy being can be a personification) of the series' existential crises. Unlike all the other beings in the series, this one really is alone and looking to find others. Unlike the Qumedon or Zamos, though, it has no desire for godlike power, only companionship. It has gathered creatures from different worlds not to create its own subjects but simply to find a place where it could "see if they were like me" (233). We learn, therefore, that the origins of the Khagodi are just as mysterious after their arrival on Khagodis is explained as they were before; when the alien Ark came to the planet, they managed to get out of the ship before it was trapped beneath the earth. Where they came from originally remains a mystery, though; delving into the past solves nothing, nor does finding the equivalent of the burning god who brought their eggs to the planet. There is no secret, nor is there any easy path.

Spartakos took as his mission freeing the O'e. In the camp where soldiers for the assault on Khagodis are supposedly being trained but are in fact simply being gathered as cannon fodder to be slaughtered, he sacrifices himself to save the lives of the O'e and the other mercenaries gathered there. But he can't lead them to freedom. Like the original Spartacus, he fails. As the O'e Azzah realizes, "Spartakos said he wanted to lead us freely into the world ... but, in the end we are the only ones who can lead ourselves" (248). Individuals might be able to help individuals and even influence the fate of a people, but the Lyhhrt can't be saved by Zamos or GalFed, and the Khagodi can't be saved by knowledge of their past. Self-determination is the only viable option. But for there to be self-determination, there must be a workable model of the self.

Seven

Science Fiction and Phyllis Gotlieb's Poetry

As discussed earlier, Gotlieb's self-definition as a Canadian poet and American SF writer creates the idea of a split between her literary accomplishments. Gotlieb herself initially evidently conceived of her work as a poet and a fiction writer as distinct, as superficially they would appear to be. She began writing science fiction, after all, because writer's block had silenced her poetry, and SF provided her with a way back into writing. However, the bifurcation faded as time passed. In her interview with David Mathew, Gotlieb notes that the chasm began to close in the 1970s, and eventually she "stopped being a productive poet simply from a lack of poem-shaped ideas. Now my aliens write poems, and I produce them very occasionally. I miss them, but if I tried to force them I'd produce only empty stuff" ("All the Blue Apes"). In an interview with *Challenging Destiny* in 1999, Gotlieb reiterated, "I don't write much poetry now. Maybe one or two poems a year, as they strike me. Gradually, my poetry began drawing from children's rhymes, comic strips, and all kinds of various popular genre elements—and SF. Then my aliens started to write poetry, so I thought, 'That takes care of that.' I like to make up songs, and throw them in. It just got subsumed, or absorbed" ("Interview").[1] That is, her poetry and SF merged; one of the final poems she published (and the final one printed in her last poetry collection), "Geffen and Ravna" (1994), is an explicit SF narrative, set in the GalFed universe. Late in her career, Goltieb wrote an editorial, "What Makes a Good Fantasy Poem?" in which she states,

> There are endless numbers of ways good poems can be written (to say nothing of the bad) but they all must be organic wholes sustained by the poet's ability to envi-

sion this whole before putting down the first line and making every word contribute to it. The only difference between a fantasy poem and any other is that it begins with a vision of otherworldliness [3].

Her perspective here differs from that of her early career, when she saw a clear delineation between the genres. However, even her earliest novel, *Sunburst*, has poetic elements, and the first serious scholarly critique of Gotlieb, Douglas Barbour's "Phyllis Gotlieb's Children of the Future: *Sunburst* and *Ordinary, Moving*," reads that novel though the lens of her poetry.

Some of Gotlieb's poetry is explicitly SF (or fantastical), and SF tropes and motifs recur in her non–SF poetry. Though often praised for her playfulness—"she sees life as a show, a more or less absurd circus or carnival," according to Tom Marshall (116), while Douglas Barbour notes her invocation of "counting-rhymes, game songs, riddles, jokes and traditional verses" ("Phyllis Gotlieb's Children of the Future" 72), for instance—the lightness and apparent simplicity of much of her poetry serves her interest in "family relationships, historical roots, and the cultural implications of biological or technological possibilities" (Lane 476). Especially interesting are Gotlieb's long poems, though the strong tradition of commentary on the long poem in Canada has had little to say about Gotlieb. D. M. R. Bentley has associated the long poem in Canada with the space between the epic and the lyric, the imperial and the personal, as a form that "is the record or chronicle of a cultural unit that exists in or beside a civilization and provides its constituents with a comforting sense of their identity and difference" (9); unsurprisingly, a poetic genre defined in such terms of difference or liminality is seen by many to "[arrive] at an unmappable form" (Kramer 102). Smaro Kamboureli, for instance, argues that the long poem "makes itself felt through its discontinuities, its absences, and its deferrals" (xiv). Reinhold Kramer, however, has challenged such readings, arguing that "if we look at recent long poems we discover mappable cultural forms and authorities" (102).

Gotlieb's verse comes at such topics from an unusual direction. It is perhaps unsurprising that applying SF conventions to poetry provides a different lens through which to view problems such as liminality, discontinuity, alienation, and absence. Nancy Johnston has noted Gotlieb's interest in mapping in her comments about Gotlieb's SF poem "Seeing Eye" (1974) and its protagonist Mercator, a poem in which "the lines lie on the page like a Mercator map" (Johnston 72), though she finds that Gotlieb's work "provide[s] a challenge to the concepts of the self by troubling and making permeable the boundaries between ourselves and alienated others" (72). Gotlieb employs SF tropes to address the problems of identity mapping; the cognitive estrangement inherent in much SF serves her well in this regard, but there is always a form to be found in her work. Though Gotlieb does, as Marshall suggests, raise the possibility of meaninglessness and absurdity rendering life unmappable, she is more inclined to find identity in structures, often in scientific or science-fictional terms. For instance, the short late poem "The Robot's Daughter" (2002) economically contrasts the speaker's desire to manifest biologically in heart and brain (albeit in terms that downplay the specificity of the body by associating the heart with the center and the brain with a cloud—before the concept of cloud computing, or the metaphor would be more complex) but instead manifests by growing parts that shift from ambiguously biological— "hook lens antenna"—to explicitly mechanical parts (a "ticking meter" and a spring coil), thereby problematizing the speaker's sense of identity. The poem ends with "her" (one assumes, given the title) lamenting that she does not know what song she can sing (*Red Blood Black Ink White Paper* 108).

More extensively explored is the creature cobbled together in "ms & mr frankenstein" (1978) by a man named Scarpino from (in part):

> smashed headlights ashtrays burnt bulbs
> popcan-rings empty ballpoints cereal-boxes
> crochet-hooks pacifiers cigarette-holders
> last year's calendars candle-stubs speedometers [*The Works* 242].

and other detritus. This construct is, despite its frail, ephemeral components, an "EMISSARY TO THE UNIVERSE!!!!" (*The Works* 244). This poem deals in comic but complex terms with the creation of a twenty-five-foot "junkman" built from a delightful array of kipple and likened to Godzilla, King Kong, the Easter Island statues, and the Matterhorn, among other things, including, as the title of the poem suggests, Frankenstein's monster. He blasts off into space almost as soon as he's created, with the words "cosmos i come" (243).[2] The poem focuses on the creators rather than on the creature, however. Indeed, it does so at one remove, by making the nameless female narrator the observer (largely) of Scarpino's construction. Scarpino's paternal urge is directed away from his wife and toward a transmogrification of junk as art. In his abstracted relationship with "ms frankenstein"—when he kisses her she says, "could have / got more juice out of a Rodin marble" (241)[3]—Scarpino is a rather light version of the more formidable and ambivalent male creator as exemplified by Edvard Dahlgren in *O Master Caliban!*, whose procreative and experimental urges come together, as it were. His juicelessness, however, suggests his failure as a father; the actual granter of life to the creature is the woman, who "christens" him with a bottle of champagne she breaks over his head, after which he jerks to life and blasts off into the universe. Unlike Lela in "A Grain of Manhood," Mrs. Scarpino does not need alien intervention to reproduce.

In various poems, especially her SF–oriented ones, Gotlieb explores the complexities of a coherent identity. A particularly good example of Gotlieb's practice can be found in one of her best-known poems, "Was/Man" (1978), which is about a werewolf. One might argue that, strictly speaking, the werewolf is not a creature of SF, but Gotlieb includes the poem in *Son of the Morning*, one of her collections of SF short stories, so she invites readers to see the poem as a piece with her SF work, and certainly it is of a piece with her consistent interest in questions of identify and in the blurring of the line between human and animal. She does occasionally blur SF and fantasy in other contexts, as for instance in the mythopoeic elements of "A Grain of Manhood" or the blending of religious fantasy and SF in the short story "Sunday's Child." She is also fond, as we have seen, of playing with the notion of the human/animal interface, which this poem does in a different way. It inverts the werewolf myth, in part through some linguistic play, to re-present this familiar hybrid creature of horror not as a man who must become a wolf when the moon is full but rather as a wolf which must become a man when the moon disappears. Even the title plays upon and blurs the distinction between man and animal. On one level, the title "Was/Man" plays on noun and verb forms: was/were man/wolf. The title compresses the relationship: the werewolf was man. However, it does more. Though the etymology of the word "werewolf" is doubtful, the usual speculation is that "werewolf" combines the Anglo-Saxon "wer," or "man," with "wolf." I should note that though the OED reports this proposed etymology, it expresses doubt about it based on the variant spellings of the word in the oldest texts. However, the OED offers no alternative etymological proposal, so the possible link to "wer" cannot be discounted (and indeed seems to be on the whole more likely than not). In any event, regardless of the word's etymology, the range of associations allowed by assuming a link to the Anglo-Saxon "wer" adds irresistible depth and texture to the poem. A werewolf is therefore literally a manwolf, as the alternative term for werewolf, wolfman, suggests. As the expression "fuzzy wuzzy" suggests (the nursery rhyme "Fuzzy Wuzzy Was a Bear"[4] is a good example; Gotlieb's verse, as noted above, is strongly influenced by nursery rhymes), Gotlieb may also be punning on the homonymic association between "was" and "wuz": "was/man" is "wuzman" is furry man, or wolfman. Even the poem's title, therefore, compresses much into its designation of the poem's character, a character who inverts and subverts the conventional associations of the werewolf or wolfman.

Conventionally in stories of such a creature, the aberrant and therefore abhorrent creature is the werewolf, but here, the human rather than the animal is presented as strange, alien, lacking. The conversion from wolf to man is presented in predominantly negative terms. Though "at first he found all that / grown flesh of his luxurious, new senses nipping him / every minute" (*The Works* 245), becoming a man is predominantly a process of loss; he "lost quite a lot of hair, his fangs pulled in about half an inch," and he loses his claws and tail (245). What he grows instead is bulk and a "crazy complex inefficient / nose" (245). Human flesh becomes a prison: "he wanted to gnaw on himself, drag off the excrescence / caught himself thinking of barred places, jail, cage, zoo / got scared he'd be trapped in this strange meat, man till he died" (245). A trapped animal can gnaw off a paw, but if the trap is the body itself, how does one gnaw oneself free? Becoming a man is not a release from negative bestiality to a positive, civilized, human world, as we might imagine, but rather an entrapment. If turning into an animal is something horrible, as it is consistently portrayed in werewolf stories, then surely turning back to a human would be good. Not from the wolf's perspective, Gotlieb suggests. When he becomes wolf again, he "dashed water in his thickening fur to douse the rank / civil insidious urge of the secret man" (246). Gotlieb puns on the meanings of "rank" as "status" and "bad smell"; human rank is rank. Being human stinks. The ritual of purification here involves the washing away of the human, the "civil insidious urge" that can be contrasted with the animal nature humans tend to think they need to suppress. Indeed, imaging civility as "insidious" and an "urge" undercuts its common associations. Civil behavior is public and valorized, not secretive and dangerous—not insidious—we think. And urges are what civil behavior normally suppresses or conceals. The wolf, however, must conceal the urge to civility, an insidious desire hidden within him, as the human must conceal the insidious urge to bestiality. The poem, however, valorizes the animal urge rather than the human one by allying its perspective with that of the wolf rather than with that of the human.

More complex and challenging are long poems such as "Ordinary, Moving" (1969) or "Geffen and Ravna." "Ordinary, Moving" is also a good example of the blurring of lines between SF and "mainstream" in Gotlieb's poetry; while it is probably not accurate to call this an SF poem, it certainly has SF elements and is thematically consistent with Gotlieb's key SF concerns. In it, Gotlieb explores through the use of collage, juxtaposition, concretism, and other manifestations of apparent discontinuity—especially vocal discontinuity, in the invocation not only of dialects but also of languages other than English—the emergence of a coherent identity, despite its multivocality.

"ORDINARY, MOVING / is the name of the game," the poem begins, with the title also functioning as the first line (*The Works* 104). It then describes the game as one combining the bouncing of a ball off a wall with physical gestures and recitations. Ian Lancashire's annotated edition of the poem cites a story by Gwendolyn MacEwen, "Tennis at Midnight," that invokes the game:

> The girls at noon bounced hard rubber balls under their knees or flung them rhythmically at the school wall, chanting in girl language: *ordinary, moving, left foot, right foot, curtsies, salutsies, turnsies*. The boys watched them, fascinated and bewildered and afraid. *Apples, peaches, pears and plums!* the girls screamed as they flung themselves in great suicidal leaps into the whirling maw of their skipping ropes. *Tell me when your birthday comes!* And dancing in the frenzied centre they called out the names of the months of the year—this year, any year: "JANuary, FEBruary..." until the schoolyard was a whirling circling planet of tastes and smells and colours and sounds erupting into chaos like the first dream of his life in which the sky broke up into a jigsaw of faces and figures and mythical animals and then it all fell down [cited by Lancashire].

MacEwen's description invokes some of the elements of how the poem charts the macrocosm in the microcosm. Gotlieb too likens the trajectories of girl and ball with the cosmic; the game goes:

> ononon
>
> TILL YOU GET TO *BIG MOVING !!!*
>
> particle, atom, molecule, world
> solar system, galaxy, supergalaxy, cosmos
>
> but start with the small, the ball on the wall
> that's how it went, and begin again [106].

The passage contrasts the ordinary moving of the title—and of children playing their game—with the big moving of the universe, suggesting a parallel and overlap between the two—mapping, in effect, the former on the latter in a reiterative and circling pattern. The capital letters, the italics, and the multiple explanation marks in the second line help stress the movement from the microcosm to the macrocosm.

It is tempting to speculate that Gotlieb's source for the title of the poem is the statistical concept of the ordinary moving average, which is a way of converting temporal data into spatial data and of creating a discrete line from disparate observations via smoothing. Moving averages function by combining smaller sets of observations in overlapping sequences (e.g., 1 2 3, 2 3 4, 3 4 5, etc.), averaging each of those smaller sets, and converting the points generated into a line. An ordinary moving average weights each set equally, rather than weighting more recent observations more heavily. This represents one of many examples of Gotlieb's interest in complex patterns, which recur in her fiction and poetry; *O Master Caliban!*, as discussed in Chapter Three, invokes a chess game, while *Emperor, Swords, Pentacles* invokes patterns derived from the tarot. Her first published work of poetry was *Who Knows One* (1961),[5] the title poem of which is a numbered sequence, including a climactic and complex counting sequence from one to thirteen and back again, and mathematical concepts and formulae recur in her poetry. Indeed, earlier in *Ordinary, Moving*, Gotlieb cites the Fibonacci sequence, another mathematical concept involving combined figures. In the Fibonacci sequence, each number is the sum of the preceding two numbers (i.e., 1, 1, 2, 3, 5, 8)—a kind of moving average in itself.[6] That is, Gotlieb's poem is constructed to invite readers to recognize the simultaneity of discrete points as well as the overlapping territory to create a map in which multiple voices and characters nevertheless coalesce into a united "we."

The first instance in which the poem invokes interrelated sets of counting is a good example of Gotlieb's technique in action. The underlying structural principle is a child's counting game, as the overarching metaphor for the poem would suggest, but language and page layout invites, indeed requires, these simple phrases to be complexly interwoven:

                              une, une, c'est la lune
                              deux, deux, c'est le jeu
     seven, eight   trois, trois—c'est à toi!
     nine, a-laura
     ten a-Laura   echod, shtaim
     Secord   hamelich bashomayim
                                  echod, shtaim, sholosh, ar-ba... [105].

The French passage in the central column translates as "one, one, it's the moon, two, two, it's the game, three, three, it's your turn" (Lancashire), and the Hebrew below it as "one, two, the king in heaven, one, two, three four."

From one perspective, how to read the sequence is clear; each vertical column is a unit. However, only the second unit has a consistent beginning point on the line (the French passage begins with the fourth line of that unit; each preceding line begins three spaces earlier), unit two overlaps with the end of unit one and the beginning of unit three, and unit three's lines do line up with the beginnings of lines in the French unit; only the two lines of blank space between the last line of unit one and the first of unit three serve as a clear visual delineation between them. The partial sharing of lines and the vertical alignment of lines in different units creates visual connections as well as visual disjunctions. Furthermore, each passage is in a different language, the two official languages of Canada first, albeit with French preceding English and occupying more lines, but the third in Hebrew. Most Canadians can probably read both the French and English passages (at least the portion of the French cited here) fairly easily, and given the common semantic ground—both passages are fragments of counting rhymes—many readers would probably assume that the Hebrew passage has similar semantic content. However, unless one is in fact at least competent in Hebrew, even this conclusion is inferential, based on assumptions about the similarities in pattern. That is, "reading" the third unit is possible, but only to a limited extent, and only based on its associations with the first two units, for the non–Hebrew reader, albeit in a provisional and very limited way.

Furthermore, the overlapping of the units invites the reader to read horizontally rather than vertically, though doing so makes no semantic sense. It does, however, make at least some rhythmic sense and invites further linkage between the sections via some homophonic resonances: "ten a-Laura echod, shtaim / Secord hamelich bashomayim / echod, shtaim, sholosh, ar-ba" is almost perfectly regular trochaic tetrameter ("echod" would be stressed on its second syllable in Hebrew, though the non–Hebrew reader might well read it trochaically, following the larger pattern), not the meter of either unit one or two admittedly, though various metrical patterns recur throughout the poem, another of the ways in which it maps sonic patterns beneath semantic differences. Its first two lines rhyme with each other, and the third line rhymes with the last line of the French passage. Admittedly, "seven, eight, trois, trois— c'est à toi" isn't trochaic, except for its first syllable, but it is scannable as tetrameter, rendering the four lines an imbedded quatrain moving quickly from very choppy and disordered to highly regular—from order to chaos metrically, if not semantically. One sort of pattern is thereby mapped on to another.

There are further ways this sequence links the disparate linguistic units. The French passage moves from a female form of one to a male form of two, whereas by contrast the Hebrew passage moves from the male form for one to the female form for two, repeating the semantic content but reversing the gender content. The French "jeu" means "game," which connects it with the poem's controlling metaphor, but it also puns on "Jew," anticipating the shift to Hebrew and providing homophonically the poem's first reference to Judaism, a motif woven throughout and given powerful impact when the recurrent device of invoking number games runs up against the line "I am Belsen number 7829" (123)—three of the numbers of the English sequence cited above, with the 2-Jew number inserted. I doubt it's an accident that Gotlieb converts the conventional version of the children's counting rhyme invoked in the English passage so that its refrain is a-laura rather than O'Leary, leading to the conclusion being "ten a-Laura Secord" rather than "ten O'Leary children." While the Laura Secord reference probably has other resonances,[7] its most evident one is the close echo between Secord and echod, which both imprints English on Hebrew and spins the count back from ten to echod, or one. It is perhaps worth noting in this regard that echod, like the English word one, suggests not merely singularity but unity. This short sequence of lines, therefore, creates numerous interlinkages on a visual, rhythmical, and sonic level and even more connections for those conversant with all three languages, and it does so in a sequence in which the actual semantic content of the words has little to do with the overall effect or with the passage's invocation of unity in diversity. And while the analogy to an ordinary moving average may not be exact, the passage's visual overlaps and reiterative uses of numbers, some repeated and others not, strongly suggests the creation of a coherent unity out of disparate components as by an ordinary moving average.

The visual, linguistic, and rhythmical elements in this passage recur throughout the poem in various ways. Here's another example. It looks like this, as printed on the page:

> we
> started
> something
> like a slug
> and grew without
> a thought or wish to
> something like a fish a
> frog a bird a pig a golly-
> wog and ultimately red and
> born a blueblack head or
> peppercorn or bald or
> blind or idiot or
> multiheaded
> ,poly-
> glot
> [107]

Arranged in a diamond shape on the page—spreading out and contracting—the passage read aloud is regular iambic tetrameter, albeit with a slightly odd rhyme scheme:

> we started something like a slug
> and grew without a thought or wish
> to something like a fish a frog
> a bird a pig a gollywog

> and ultimately red and born
> a blueblack head or peppercorn
> or bald or blind or idiot
> or multiheaded, polyglot

The process described here is simultaneously the process of evolution and gestation, a human and animal, and vegetal process—the associations between which also emerge as a motif in the poem. The associations of Jews with swine emerges later, for instance, and the term gollywog invoked here plays on the poem's play with anti-black as well as with anti-semitic racism. But the primary point about this passage is how its visual layout and its content collaborate to encompass unity and multiplicity. "We" become "a" thing, which is many things, climactically a "multiheaded polyglot." The poem's multiple languages and multiple speakers become thereby all part of a single body.

Furthermore, as the grammatical sense with which the passage must be read indicates, with the consistent enjambment and accelerated pace suggested by the lengthening lines, the two-dimensional diamond shape that appears on paper might be fleshed out imaginatively as an outward spiral then reversing and cycling back to its beginning point. The shape suggests, that is, a spherical spiral. A spherical spiral is the line described by movement from one pole of a sphere to the other on a consistent angle (other than 0 or 90, either of which would simply describe a straight line). The passage, therefore, is an image of the ball—the microcosm—with which the poem begins and the world—the macrocosm—which the poem describes, building it out of the multifold life forms and languages (the polyglot, rather than the polliwog) that inhabit the world. Place and identity are one.

The link between place and identity is also thematically central to the explicit SF poem "Geffen and Ravna." "Geffen and Ravna" was first published in *Torus* and then in *TransVersions 5* before being collected in *Red Blood Black Ink White Paper*, Gotlieb's collection of new and selected poems published in 2002, and a title that itself suggests simultaneously distinct categories that bleed together into a single identity. This poem is a narrative consisting of four sestinas, though Gotlieb does not observe strictly the rules governing the form. In the poem Gotlieb uses a few standard SF tropes to metaphorize the problematics of identity, especially in relation to issues of the self, sex, and the other, while using the sestina form and variations on it to underscore the interpenetrations and divergences of identity in the poem. If "ms & mr frankenstein" recasts SF's originary myth as a woman's narrative of the bizarre nativity of a junk robot and "Was/Man" redefines the werewolf's identity from the perspective of the wolf rather than the wer—as it were—then "Geffen and

Ravna" pushes the question of identity by collapsing the difference between human and alien.

The poem is set on a distant planet—"that last outpost world" (*Red Blood* 130)—with a human population living in Terra Station and an alien population in Farroes Colony; neither species, apparently, is indigenous to the icy, snowbound planet, which is an inimical environment to both. The poem tells the story of Geffen, a human Wardman, or prison keeper, in Terra Station. One of the Farroes, a female named Ravna, is captured as a spy and placed in his custody. Unsurprisingly, perhaps, the ensuing narrative is a love story of sorts between Geffen and Ravna; though one might expect such a love story to explore the bridging of cultural differences, however, Gotlieb has a more complex and less optimistic agenda in mind. Rather than providing a narrative of cultural rapprochement and growth to acceptance of the other, Gotlieb provides a poem in which movement outward is simultaneously movement inward (like the spherical spiral, perhaps) and the result is not a comforting bromide about loving the alien but instead an interrogative meditation about the alien self. Even the collision in the work between narrative and poetic form underscores its interest in the anxiety of identity.

The narrative is given form by the conventions of the sestina, as they are observed and subverted, in the same way that the characters and identities of Geffen and Ravna are formed only to be subsumed within the poem. The traditional sestina consists of six stanzas of six lines, followed by a tercet. The end word of each line in the first stanza recurs as an end line in each subsequent stanza, and the six words repeat, two per line, in the tercet. A conventional sestina follows a rigid pattern determining which word ends which line in each stanza, and which order they occur in the tercet. If we number the terminal words of the first line as 1 through 6 and then track their recurrence across the stanza and in the tercet, the conventional pattern is this:

stanza one:	1 2 3 4 5 6
stanza two:	6 1 5 2 4 3
stanza three:	3 6 4 1 2 5
stanza four:	5 3 2 6 1 4
stanza five:	4 5 1 3 6 2
stanza six:	2 4 6 5 3 1
(stanza one:	1 2 3 4 5 6)
tercet line one:	1 2
tercet line two:	3 4
tercet line three:	5 6

While this may appear on the face of it to be a bit of a jumble—the word ending line six on one stanza begins line one in the next but there is no other obvious sequence if you scan left to right—if you look closely, you'll note that in fact, each terminal word occupies the position occupied by the word it replaces as the pattern cycles through. The line six terminal word becomes the line one terminal word, and the line one word becomes the line two word; then the word that ended line six ends the second line, and the word originally ending line one moves to line four; then the original sixth word assumes the line four position while the original line one word moves to line five; then six becomes five and one becomes six; then six becomes six again as the original pattern is restored in the tercet (though to be fair, tercets are not consistently quite so fixed). And the same pattern inheres for each other word; as the the vertical grid above shows, in fact, that each number always has the same number above and below it in the pattern, which reflects the underlying consistency behind the apparent randomness. The name for this pattern is the retrograde cross, or, for those who prefer fancy Latin terminology, *retrogradio cruciata*. Another way to chart the pattern graphically is to see the pattern of terminal words as a spiral, which is more evident if one charts the line pattern vertically:

1		6	3	5	4	2
2		1	6	3	5	4
3	*	5	4	2	1	6
4		2	1	6	3	5
5		4	2	1	6	3
6		3	5	4	2	1

Use the asterisk as a beginning point for tracking, and assign it to any one of the numbers. In each case, the movement alternates regularly outward, one down, then one up, in a pattern corresponding to the order in stanza one. For instance, track 3 in column 1. Draw a spiral out from its position, beginning at the asterisk, downward (to line 4) then circling up (to line 2), then down (to line 5) then up (to line 1) and then down (to line 6):

The same pattern works for each terminal word. Despite the apparent randomness, therefore, the underlying pattern is in fact highly fixed—indeed, mathematically precise—and therefore highly predictable to anyone familiar with the form. The spiral pattern of the retrograde cross suggests the circular patterning we've seen Gotlieb use elsewhere, though one of the complexities in this point is her deliberate violation of that submerged structural precision.

The pattern controlling the positional shift for terminal words is the crucial structuring device. Sestina does not use rhyme, as it would be almost impossible to do so in conjunction with the constant shift in terminal word positions, for instance. Furthermore, no rule dictates line length or meter, though iambic pentameter tends to be popular in English examples. Gotlieb,

STANZA I		... new order ...	STANZA II	III	IV	V	VI
end-word 1		2nd	6	3	5	4	2
2		4th	1	6	3	5	4
3		6th	5	4	2	1	6
4		5th	2	1	6	3	5
5		3rd	4	2	1	6	3
6		1st	3	5	4	2	1

Diagram of sestina system, showing the spiral pattern. Created by Peter Wink.

however, not only violates the rule governing the order of repetition of end words but also is highly irregular metrically. Consequently, she turns the form against itself in multiple ways, violating its predictable pattern, disturbing the smooth surface to suggest the tensions beneath. This effect is enhanced by the metrical irregularity and the syntactical convolution Gotlieb frequently employs in the poem.

The most evident instance of Gotlieb's manipulation of the terminal position is in the third poem in the sequence, in which the central twist of the narrative is revealed: Geffen also is Farroes, having been surgically modified and apparently brainwashed to believe himself truly human in order to infiltrate Terra Station. Two of the terminal words in this poem are "mine" and "you," but rather than cycling through one appearance at the end of each line, "mine" ends two first lines and two final lines, while "you" also has two first-line positions and two final line positions. Every stanza ends either its first or its last line with one of these words, and two of them begin with one and end with the other (mine/you for stanza one, and you/mine for stanza three). The mere choice of these two words foregrounds the importance of the relationship between the two in the poem, but the additional stress placed on the two words by virtue of their heavy weighting at the beginning and/or ending of stanzas stresses the dichotomy of woman versus man, of human versus Farroes, but not in terms of straight opposition. It's not indicative and indicative or possessive and possessive: Ravna is "you" to Geffen, but Geffen is "mine" to Ravna. "You" suggests mutuality, whereas "mine" suggests hierarchy. Ravna is claiming Geffen and in doing so forcing him to reconsider his identity.

Is he who/what he thinks he is? Thinking he was human, he nevertheless felt alienated from his species; "the Wardman had never been known to need a woman" (130), we are told in the first poem, and in the third, he states, "If I am of Earth / I cannot love a woman of my people" (133). These words conclude one stanza but not a sentence; he continues at the beginning of the next stanza, "and if I am Farroes, I'm outlandish. You say, *mine*, / *mine!* But I want firesides, meat and drink, my people / Aren't Farroes" (133; italics in original). Here, the division between stanzas stresses the division within Geffen's self-perception; he is literally split between human and Farroes by the structure of the poem. Regardless of which he is, he is alienated from his sense of identity.

The dichotomy between human and Farroes, "your" and "mine," contrasts with the larger implication of another of the terminal words in this stanza, "people," a word that bridges the distance the characters find impassable. Its implications, in fact, resonate not only in the poem but in Gotlieb's work generally. Gotlieb has consistently chosen in her work to define any sentient creatures, regardless of species, as men and women—as people, in effect, rather than as alien and other. This point is clear in the poem from its beginning, when the "angular alien" (130) Ravna, with her patterned skin and back "spined like a lizard" (130), is also repeatedly defined as a woman—"barely a woman" (130), according to her captors, and as likely to be hunted as an animal as to be taken sexually as a woman, but nevertheless ineluctably linked to the human by this choice of noun, with both her and Geffen's physical selves are further stressed through the choice of words such as "body," "bones," "breath," and "eyes" as line-ending words, in addition to those already mentioned, throughout the four sestinas, especially as the terms do not apply exclusively to either one or the other of them. The problem Gotlieb explores, once again, is the tendency to see difference rather than kinship, and the SF tropes here clarify the point by rendering Geffen neither fish nor fowl, neither human nor Farroes, by virtue of his biomodifications, which metaphorize the contingency and liminality of identity.

Gotlieb's linguistic play, especially as underscored by the resonances of other of the repeated words, furthers the point. "If I am of Earth," Geffen says, on one level a statement of species alignment—being of Earth meaning being human—but on another a literal statement of physical reality, the latter meaning being true regardless of species but the former being true only of one species, in a punning interrelation that undercuts the reliability of such an assertion of identity. And if he's not, he's outlandish—both literally foreign and also bizarre, weird, but a word with a similar root in physical reality: land.

One mines land, and Ravna's repeated "mining" of Geffen plumbs his depths, just as the literal levels of Terra Station (levels is one of the tag words in the first poem) resonate with metaphorical levels, or depths, in people; "always other levels / Of meaning rose in her words" (130), we are told of Ravna. By contrast,

> Of *spying*, skirmish, *levels, Station, Geffen*
> lifelong an unquestioner of levels
> cared nothing; he looked and wanted Ravna, a woman
> no matter how stark the tips of her spines
> [130; italics added; these are four of the six tag words of this poem].

Here the syntactic convolution, which one might superficially think merely bows to the exigencies of the sestina form, in fact forces the reader to re-evaluate the sentence's meaning not only line by line but almost word by word, in a grammatical manifestation of the poem's peeling away of one appearance, one surface, to reveal something else beneath. Or, perhaps more accurately, to reveal the ephemerality of the constructed identity. The first line on its own appears to include Geffen among a list of nouns associated with Terra Station (including the word "station" itself) or, in the case of "skirmish," a noun linked to the human conflict with the Farroes; he appears to be one with that group. The second line, however, presents only the terminal noun of the previous line, Geffen, as modified by the phrase "lifelong an unquestioner of levels," thereby hinting that he is to be differentiated from the previous nouns in the group. The third line clarifies the actual opposition despite the apparent congruity in its own verbal structure; the first word, the verb "cared," is then negated by the following modifier. What appears to be an assertion that Geffen cared about these things (which would be consistent with his lifelong unquestioning) is instead an assertion of the opposite. The line itself is split, turning from what Geffen does not care for to what he does care for, the "woman" Ravna, a woman despite her alien nature—"no matter how stark the tips of her spines" (130).

The poem ends by abandoning the physical which has so weighted its earlier stanzas while also abandoning the possibility of narrative resolution and the cohesiveness of identity, by converting Geffen, stripped of Ravna, into rumor, dream, and claim, a character whose fate becomes multiple, not fixed:

> The rumor that he was Farroes faded away.
> Some dream he went hunting and was tusked. Some remember,
> or claim, he hung about tavern kitchens complaining of cold,
> gnawing stale crusts with his wine. Or, that snow
> claimed him, to die unfound.

> Or: there was no Ravna,
> no Geffen, only the baffled and weary drifting away
> from a cold world where there are none left to remember [135].

After their deaths, they are denied even existence; if identity is really only memory—and Geffen's amnesia about his Farroes origins is a key point in the poem—then did they ever exist? Well ... no ... they are only characters in a poem, after all, and a SF poem at that, one set on a non-existent planet in a time that has not yet come to pass. These latter facts especially foreclose on our ability to imagine they *might have* existed, as we might do in a realist context. But more profoundly, if Geffen's human identity is a construction—and much more literally than any human identity is a construction, if we accept the constructivist view of identity formation—then he does not really exist, either. Even his body is a construction, with his identity, his character, encoded from without rather than within to create the illusion of humanity. And Ravna is also a construction, in both the general and the particular. She is seen through human eyes, and then through the eyes of an invented human, so she is only ever seen from the outside in the poem. She can be known by her body, and known by her words, but neither is her essence, which is unknown, unknowable, and perhaps unreal; her "mine" is unmineable.

Gotlieb takes a poetic form heavily reliant on highly ordered patterns of construction and repetition and subverts its constructional elements to turn them to her thematic purpose. As the human or Farroes body implies a specific structure and order, so does sestina form imply a specific order and structure. The breakdown—or subversion, perhaps—of the latter is a structural metaphor for the problematic of the former. Even more than in her fiction, Gotlieb here weaves together form and content.

The majority of Gotlieb's poetry is not SF or fantasy oriented, but nevertheless, her own (presumably tongue-in-cheek) differentiation between her career as a Canadian poet and a U.S. writer of SF is problematized somewhat by the interpenetration between the two outputs. SF-oriented poetry is relatively rare, and Gotlieb is one of the few writers to have made significant contributions to that small *oeuvre*. Though these poems can be read in isolation from Gotlieb's SF prose fiction (indeed, all have been published in Gotlieb's poetry collections, while she has included only two in her fiction collections), reading them in relation to her fiction helps clarify our understanding of both.

Eight
Final Fictions

There was a brief hiatus between "The Newest Profession" and Gotlieb's next short story, "Body English," in 1986. Including "Body English," Gotlieb published only five more short stories in the last several years of her career, plus a collaboration with Jean-Louis Trudel. Most of these are very short, almost sketches rather than fully developed narratives, with only two, "Among You" (1993) and "End City" (1997) of any substantial length. As a rule, these stories revisit earlier themes in very limited or focused bursts (two of them, "Body English" and "We Can't Go on Meeting Like This" [1992], can be seen as complementary pieces, exploring the same basic premise), much as the coda to Gotlieb's career, *Birthstones*, revisits ideas first raised in "Sunday's Child." This is not to suggest that Gotlieb was not continuing to do new things or that her later work lacks merit, but that work does consistently have a retrospective feel about it, as reminiscent of her earlier work even while providing new narratives. Gotlieb seems to be looking back with an eye to refining earlier ideas. "Body English" and "We Can't Go on Meeting Like This," for instance, both revisit the notion of colonizing the body of others that played such an important role in Gotlieb's trilogies, while "Among You" harkens back to the beginning of Gotlieb's career, with its focus on an alien species, the Thorb, that have an even more extreme plasticity of form than the Nevid on "A Grain of Manhood," and "End City" seems very much to be a response to *Sunburst* thirty years later.

"Body English" and "We Can't Go on Meeting Like This" are brief and comparatively minor pieces. The first is as much an experiment in dialogue as anything, as the entire story consists of direct speech, with the speakers differentiated by paragraphing rather than the use of quotation marks. Chuck and Jacko run a business in which a hazily suggested technology allows others temporarily to inhabit Chuck's body while his consciousness is temporarily displaced into their bodies. Gotlieb revisits her interest in the limitations of the body; Chuck and Jacko's clients are as a rule people suffering from some profound physical suffering or deformity from which Chuck's body temporarily releases them—while he temporarily suffers it for them. His second client is happy to be "losing this pain" (106) even temporarily by riding Charles's body, while he assumes her suffering; when she notes that Chuck does not look very good when she returns to her body, he points out, "I had to wait ... inside your body, you know" (106). Though Chuck and Jacko seem to be partners, the relationship is in fact clearly exploitative, with Jacko assuming none of the risk while enjoying the profits, while Chuck suffers psychological anguish, at the very least. As GalFed co-opts the brains of telepaths for their own ends and profit, Jacko (does his name hint at "jackal," while Chuck's hints either at "meat" or at beast to be preyed upon, such as "woodchuck") co-opts the body of his putative partner for *his* own profit. Though permanent usurpation of Chuck's body seems impossible, his short shelf-life is strongly suggested; he will burn out soon and have to be replaced by another meat puppet (to borrow a term from William Gibson).

"We Can't Go on Meeting Like This" humorously adopts the clichéd and empty promise illicit lovers sometimes make and applies it to a very different scenario from the usual clandestine encounter. As in "Body English," the displacement of one's consciousness into another body is possible here, but in this instance, people use the possibility to place themselves inside the bodies of animals. In a novel take on the problem of law not being able to keep up with technology, "If lovers come and couple as animals it is not yet a legal infraction of the marriage vows" (199); legally, having sex in an animal's body is not adultery. It is, however, morally problematic, as the story suggests by hinting that for such lovers this practice is "perhaps [...] their pornography" (199). Furthermore, it literalizes the conversion of the human to the bestial at which Gotlieb has gestured in various earlier stories, presented here as a "choice" (199), though, rather than as the result of an unfortunate mutation (as in *Sunburst*), or genetic experimentation leading to failed human experiments (as in *O Master Caliban!*) or the unveiling of the beast within via telepathy as happens to Quantz in *A Judgment of Dragons*, or in any of the other ways Gotlieb shows the beast in the human by putting the human in the beast. Here, most disturbingly and depressingly, maybe we simply *want* to be animals, and not even for good reasons. When the woman who has taken on the body of the lioness leaves, her lover thinks of her husband, "the old and possessive lion under the skin. He thinks of looking for another woman, another lioness"

(201). The appositive construction here blurs the distinction; are the woman and lioness separate here, or does he simply equate them? The final image in the story is of the lions themselves, empty of human consciousness and inscrutable, in their cage. The reader is left to wonder whether the genuine animal is a more dignified beast than its human occupants.

"Among You" is rather more substantial but still a fairly tightly focused narrative. That it is the lead story in *Blue Apes* suggests that it is also a significant story. The Thorb are shape-shifting aliens who, when their planet was besieged, "broadcast their children as seed out into the void" (16); these "seeds" came to Earth unaccompanied by adults, so they have grown to adulthood without any cultural guidance or signposts from their own kind. Utterly disconnected from their own culture, they become liminal figures, living on the edge of the human without really fitting into that world either. Their physiological plasticity allows them to change their shape and therefore imitate almost anyone they might wish, which provides them with job options that threaten to erase their own identities. Earth is for them an alien environment where their true forms—their true identities, therefore, given Gotlieb's tendency to link the physical and the psychological—cannot be adopted: "there is no way to live in that shape on this world" (7). Instead, Rain, the story's protagonist, makes his living doing "sym-therapy" (10), using his ability to change his form to simulate the bodies and identities of people with whom his clients want or need to be able to interact (e.g., a dead husband or a convenient escort for the evening). Staying in any one form too long carries with it the danger of becoming fixed in that form, but the marginalized Thorb seem to have few other options; the only other Thorb we see in the story is a vagrant. He is recognizeable to Rain (and to passersby) as a Thorb because he literally can't hold himself together; his body shimmers and mutates, stressing his lack of fixity.

In short, the Thorb can be useful to humans as avatars of the departed or desired, allowing humans to fetishize what they have lost or to enact fantasies, but otherwise have no place as "a real culture among the multicultures of nations" (15). Living as a "man of a thousand faces" (17), Rain is in fact faceless: "which is he?" (17), he wonders, considering the ones he has adopted.[1] The plasticity of form that seemed so promising in "A Grain of Manhood," where it allowed for the creation of a child for Lela and James despite James's sterility, the Nevid germ plasm allowing Lela to will her child not merely into human form but into the image of her husband, shows a darker side here, where it becomes a metaphor for the absence of identity.[2] Again, body and consciousness are linked. The metaphor functions by suggesting that humans are perhaps not as individuated as we might think. In his trade, Rain has discovered that even though he assumes supposedly different identities by mimicking humans, what he really does is simply assume minor variations on a theme. His first assignment in the story is Albert, "another in the line" (8). At the end of the story he imagines his next client as another Albert. He is, in effect, lost among the aliens.

The climax of the story makes the point clearly. Walking home, Rain sees the vagrant Thorb, unable even to hold a coherent form; the vagrant's "body shifts and flows" (22) without control. This visible plasticity draws the attention of some louts, who beat and berate him. When Rain intervenes, he finds himself also morphing without clear design, becoming an animal-like predator: "his head and neck push thickly out of the collar, his shirt opens, the tie snaps and falls away, his arms reach out of his sleeves, they are fanged and furred, tawny, spotted and savage" (23)—a transformation reminiscent of the conventional human-to-werewolf metamorphosis of film, a transformation Gotlieb approaches from a different perspective in the poem "Was/Man" (see Chapter Seven).[3] Rain "does not even know what he has been trying to make of himself" (23–24), we are told. As this statement suggests, more is at issue than the immediate transformation; making something of oneself is a standard social idea. Rain's lack of identity or direction risks his loss of status as "human" in the GalFed sense of the term—which, unfortunately, does not seem to be available in the world of this story. "Among You" is a strong example of Gotlieb's later treatment of her recurring themes, even back to the beginning of her career. It shows her offering a more complex and sceptical take on the implications of such stories as "A Grain of Manhood" (which seems to be explicitly echoed, given the several parallels) as well as the bulk of her GalFed stories, in that transcendence and transmutation offer far less promise than they tend to in Gotlieb's earlier work. While even her first novel ends on a note of only cautions optimism, this story ends with almost inescapable pessimism. Becoming human or "human" is a possibility presented as on balance positive, if not desirable, for figures such as erg–Dahlgren, but for Rain, it offers only an endless parade of simulations.

However, Gotlieb's most significant late story is the uncollected "End City." "End City" contrasts with most of the GalFed books, harkening back to *Sunburst* in its skeptical view of ESP. However, in this story Gotlieb carries her exploration in a different direction, through her alternate to the "dull normal" human, Shandy Johnson, that novel's protagonist. Shandy Johnson is impervious to ESP, able neither to transmit nor receive thoughts. The protagonist of "End City," by contrast, is the similarly-named Sheleen Johns. Opposite to Shandy, Sheleen Johns has powerful telepathy and is unable to contain or control it, broadcasting her thoughts and emotions into the minds of others unintentionally. The similarity of the names—"Shandy" and "Sheleen" share an initial syllable and number of syllables and both have a Celtic air about them ("Shandy" is a Celtic name, while the "een" suffix is a Celtic diminutive form), while "Johnson" and "Johns" closely echo each other—suggests that Gotlieb is inviting a degree of comparison between the two protagonists. Like Shandy, as well, Sheleen has undergone a slower than normal physical maturation, looking only 14 at the age of 19, and like Shandy as well, she lacked a stable home life, being passed from surrogate parent to surrogate parent.

Furthermore, as in *Sunburst*, ESP in "End City" is not natural but caused explicitly by contamination of the human genome:

> Whatever had drifted into the City with air or dust all those years ago had brought a thousand subtle scourges, and some of the cures had been as fearsome as the diseases. Asher knew—she had never hidden it—that Higgs-Partree herself had been born with extra teats. The Social Engineers had made sure that surgery had removed both them and her reproductive capacity. She had worked most of her life to cut them out of the genome [50].

In *Sunburst*, the result is an evolutionary throwback; in "End City," the result is likened to disease, and the social order is attempting to eradicate such scourges. Like Sorrel Park, as well, End City is isolated, cut off from an Earth with which the populace has lost contact and further stratified into an above-world and literal underworld, in that it is subterranean, inhabited by those deemed socially acceptable and those deemed socially unacceptable respectively. Overside and Underside are analogous to the town of Sorrel Park and the Dump, the difference being that the underworld here is not so much a prison as a sort of place of escape from a repressive authority. The Dump has its Dumplings, Underside its trolls, as they are termed, the association with mythical monsters suggesting the extent to which they are marginalized. The Dumplings are often actually physically malformed, the trolls at least metaphorically so, by the conditions of life:

> The trolls have got twisted because there was no use for them. If we could find a use for them that would convince them that's what they want and need—then they'd calm down. No, we need somebody to pull us up. Everyone around here has been depressed so long they think it's how life is supposed to work. I think she [Sheleen] has something that could help give them hope [52].

However, a key distinction is in how ESP is imaged as problematic. ESP in *Sunburst* is dangerous primarily because of the "types that have it," as Shandy says (*Sunburst* 45). As discussed in Chapter Two, *Sunburst* associated psi powers with body type and with social class; those predisposed by physiology and background to be delinquent are also predisposed to develop psi. ESP is problematic because those most likely to develop it are also the most likely, for physiological and social reasons, to have underdeveloped moral senses and therefore the ones most likely to use it detrimentally. In "End City" by contrast, the problem is inherent in ESP itself; it's like a disease, rather than a genetic precondition, a widespread social ill (literally) detrimental to all. It need not be used consciously to be harmful, but is harmful simply by virtue of existing.

Furthermore, Sheleen and Shandy contrast as key figures in addressing the problematics of ESP. Shandy's value is that she is is not a telepath, and, even more so, is impervious to ESP: she cannot be read by others or receive telepathic communication from them. Sheleen, however, *is* telepathic, or partially so; though she cannot *receive* the thoughts of others, she is a powerful telepath and cannot control or block broadcasting her thoughts and feelings into the minds of others. She is, in effect, the opposite of Shandy; whereas Shandy is almost impossible to notice unless one looks right at her, Sheleen is impossible *not* to notice, unless her telepathic transmissions are blocked artificially. As in the GalFed books, there is technology here that allows for blocking ESP. When Sheleen first dons one of the blocking devices, "Suddenly there was a particular quietness that no one had ever felt before. As if her mind's workings had been in the background of everyone's consciousness for as long as they could remember" (49). Without the ability to block, she is dangerous to everyone; when she broadcasts in a negative state of mind, she can burn out the brains of others.

Even in less extreme circumstances, though, the projecting telepath is dangerous because she breaks through barriers of the regular citizens, making them too conscious of their isolation on this inhospitable world, causing panic. Too much unmediated insight into another's mind is dangerous because, rather than creating a sense of oneness or community—as telepathy is often idealized as doing—it exacerbates one's sense of aloneness. On a hostile planet cut off from communication with Earth, this is perhaps even more dangerous than it would be in a more amenable environment. However, if negative broadcasting can create bad social results, perhaps this power can be manipulated to beneficial social effect. This idea, however, renders the potential of ESP in this story even more threatening. It could be used to manipulate the populace into a cowed state, with the government using Sheleen's ability to create a sort of lotusland effect rather than a terror effect, by training her to project calming, distracting thoughts. The dystopian possibilities are stark. As Asher, one of the characters, notes, "She'll be dangerous to herself if she doesn't learn control. She could be killed, or maybe even kill if she got angry enough"; however, if she learns control from someone twisted and smart, "She'll really be dangerous" (52).

Consequently, ESP itself is inherently dangerous in this world. It must be eradicated, if possible. All children born are tested at the Psych Works, and children showing signs of ESP or other genetic drift are taken by the State— hence, no doubt, one reason for some folk to flee to Underside, to escape a *de facto* totalitarian regime, however well-intentioned its actions might be. The woman running the hospital herself, Dr. Higgs-Partree, suffered a non–ESP mutation, as a result of which she was sterilized. One of the agendas of the government is to breed such mutations back out of the humans, as they are perceived as a threat. ESP is especially dangerous because it is potentially too traumatic—or, on the flip side, too seductive. Sheleen's former lover attempts to take her back from the hospital by force, because when she broadcast positive feelings, the effect on him was euphoric and addictive. Asher later recalls what Sheleen's positive projection felt like, after feeling it in the hospital:

> He couldn't move, just crouched there with his skin prickling. After a lifetime of waiting for something to happen, everything had. It was like being drunk and stoned and high and his mind skimming all over the universe. He had never felt so alive. The Sheleen Effect. Some fear underneath that too. He recalled coming down off whatever forms of ecstasy he had been able to scour out in his teens, too familiar with the sickly letdown, hollow under the breastbone, that threatened him now that the gold mist had faded [52].

Positive or negative, therefore, uncontrolled ESP is a threat to social order. Consequently, it must be controlled, caged. Sheleen's training to suppress her projection is described in terms that suggest the repressive undercurrents: "the engines of the city fix her teeth, brighten her hair, cage her, mask her, tame her" (56).

At the beginning of her career, Gotlieb challenged the notion of ESP as a boon to humanity by associating it with the primitive and the animalistic, as a remnant of an earlier phase of human evolution that should have been left behind. Late in her career, she returned to the idea of ESP as problematic from a different perspective. It is something that contaminates rather than advances humanity; it is not something natural that we should have evolved beyond but a literal aberration that the state wants to eradicate. Although it could have uses, the dangers it represents are greater than the benefits. Even in the story's final image, which holds out some hope of union between Asher and Sheleen, the hand she offers him is both attractive and potentially dangerous:

"for a moment he thinks she's about to give him the finger but at the last, the very last second she grins again, opens it like a branch of roses and he takes it gingerly, for fear of thorns" (60).

The final short story published with Gotlieb's name on it as author was her collaboration with Jean-Luis Trudel, "Waiting Till the Stars Scream," published in *TransVersions* 8/9, in 1998. It is not really a Gotlieb story but nevertheless again touches, near the end of her career, on her recurring themes. Gotlieb provided a brief outline for a *TransVersions* contest. The writer who came up with the best story derived from Gotlieb's idea got the story published in the magazine, listed as co-written with Phyllis Gotlieb. Her input, therefore, is relatively minor. Trudel's story makes use of the Gotlieb stand-by device of telepathy but explains it not as a genuine ability to read minds but rather as an ability to shift between realities. As one character reports, "our scientists think so-called telepaths do not actually read minds; instead, they affect quantum probabilities" (113). That is, they select a reality in which what they think someone is thinking *is* what that someone is thinking, which then becomes the reality occupied by the characters. Such a view of the nature of physical reality is atypical of Gotlieb.

Though subjectivity features frequently in her work, it is always clear (eventually, anyway) that there is only one objective reality: either the character is hallucinating or otherwise misperceiving, or the character's perception is more accurate than that of others, as in the case of Han Li in *Heart of Red Iron*, who is the only one—initially—who can perceive Prima's messages. She is neither delusional (though many think so early in the story) nor creating or accessing an alternate reality but merely perceiving something real that most cannot, because it lies outside the range of their organs of perception, just as some sounds or colors lie outside the range of the perception of some people or animals. The closest Gotlieb comes to the sort of multiverse idea suggested by Trudel is in "The Other Eye" (1992). In this story, the protagonist, Mem—whether she is an alien or some sort of mutated human being is not clear—goes blind in one eye, which then becomes capable of perceiving a different world from the one she inhabits. The people of this world differ from those of Mem's; they are "figures, with pink and brown skins, not fur" (55) (it is possible that they are multi-racial humans, but that cannot be determined with certainty from the story). Mem's community, and Mem herself, wonders whether "this is some brain injury or I have gone mad" (55), so the story does not foreclose on the possibility that Mem's perceptions are false, but it also allows the possibility that Mem in fact has access to some other/higher world; indeed, it seems on balance to suggest that she does. This minor story seems to offer a variation on the trope of the blind seer, but it is far too brief and elliptical to yield certainty.

Just as "End City," Gotlieb's final sole-author short story, revisits from a different perspective key aspects of her first novel, her final novel focuses more directly than any of her other work on the theme of reproduction. Her first published story, "A Grain of Manhood," and her final one, *Birthstones*, reflect her abiding interest in motherhood and the maternal, bringing her career full circle, in a way. In *Birthstones*, however, the issue (as it were) assumes central importance, as the focus of the novel is the plight of the alien Shar, a people who due to genetic contamination have suffered a horrific and deleterious gender-specific mutation. Shar females increasingly are born as "limbless" creatures "with no intelligence and stunted senses" (24); they are, in effect, good only for use as breeding machines, maintained to reproduce the genetically and intellectually sound males of the species but otherwise hidden away as grotesque monstrosities. On the face of it, the novel would therefore seem to be of a piece with the pervasive alienation (literally) of mothering in SF even today. Jane Donawerth has found, for instance, that mothers are "dead, lost or hostile" ("Feminist Dystopia of the 1990s" 51) even in recent feminist SF, while Susan Kornfeld has noted that "recent works predominantly suppress or demonize mothers, and at times completely transform or displace maternal function" (65); motherhood, specifically the biological reality of reproduction, is under erasure in SF. However, despite Gotlieb's apparent invocation of the monstrous maternal, *Birthstones* in fact challenges and problematizes the suppression of the maternal. The novel focuses on conflict between those who wish to preserve the status quo, in which the female is reduced merely to biological essentialism, and those who by contrast wish to reverse the genetic contamination that led to the problem and to reclaim and restore the maternal.

The debilitating mutation is explicitly linked to environmental degradation, and this degradation is explicitly linked to capitalist commercial enterprises, specifically enterprises whose exploitation of Shar bears more than a passing resemblance to colonialist exploitation:

> Eventually [Shar] was discovered by aliens, some of whom were Earthers. But they and all the others came only to dig in the world's soil and rock, and empty out the deep lodes of minerals, gems and fuels. The breakdown of the environment increased exponentially, and one day a Shar woman bore a limbless daughter with no intelligence and stunted senses. And then another bore the same, and one more yet [24].

In effect, the rape of the world denatures it, though significantly without sterilizing it.[4] The Shar can still breed, but only with these mindless lumps of fertile flesh, which can bear relatively normal, healthy males but only replications of themselves as mindless wombs in female form. And breeding under these circumstances is itself horrific: "only the ones with the fiercest passion for children would go into the dark halls where the monsters waited" (138). Though these halls are intended as care/maintenance facilities—hospitals, in effect, for the terminally vegetative—as the grammar here suggests, Shar women have become, for Shar men, manifestations of the monstrous. They have been placed out of sight, hidden, and therefore fetishized as the abject other; one might see the female Shar as manifestation of Kristeva's "radically excluded" (2), the "non-assimilable alien, a monster" (11), and/or as Barbara Creed's monstrous feminine, "woman as monstrous womb" (1).

The initial Shar response to the mutation is a dualized shaming: "the Shar, horrified, stored them away and shamed the mothers. Some mothers killed themselves after bearing these mutants" (24)—and, as the novel suggests, in some instances, these monster offspring have themselves been slain. Shame here is something external, projected onto the other; Shar women are in effect blamed for what they are becoming. The shame is internalized as well, though; the Shar project shame onto the mutant women, but they also do not seek help from the outside because they "were ashamed to call for help" (25). "Shame" is a wonderfully flexible word, as is demonstrated here. It can refer to something imposed societally on individuals, bringing disgrace or discredit on them in the eyes of society. It can *also* refer to one's own subjective feeling of having done something wrong. Furthermore, it has a specifically sexual (and sexist) valence in relation to female sexuality; sexual sin is specifically female sin, as the ascription of "shame" to women who transgress sexually attests. Indeed, the "shame" in this context is literalized as illegitimate offspring, as definition 3c of "shame" in the Oxford English Dictionary makes clear, defining it as "violation of a woman's honour, loss of chastity" and as "a child born out of wedlock." "Shame" becomes manifest as the child born of a sinful woman. As these connotations for "shame" suggest, Gotlieb is playing with complex ideas here, having to do with sexual politics and identity politics, but also in the broader picture having to do with politics, pure and simple.

Politically, as I've noted, the mutation of Shar women is explicitly linked to capitalist colonialism. While it cannot reasonably be argued that the exploitation of the planet was designed deliberately to compromise the native population, the novel makes clear that the economic interests of the resource exploiters are served by the inhibitions on Shar breeding. As the Emperor, Aesh, notes, "The more time we take caring for females who ought to be able to care for themselves—and our children—the less trouble we cause the 'benefactors.' All of this government is a sham" (127). Needless to say, a small and desperate native population is much easier for outside exploiters to control than a thriving and self-sufficient one would be. The companies exploiting Shar see both the alien world and the aliens themselves as product. And this too is sexualized.

The plot of the novel focuses on the problem of the Shar mutation and how to reverse it. The companies who have profited from Shar reluctantly help fund the search for a cure, but it is clear in the novel that they do not see actually finding such a cure as in their best interests. They are involved in plotting to subvert the research, as reflected in the assassination attempts directed at Aesh and at Delius, the primary human figure in the novel, which are carried out by Shar but which are also obviously instigated by the corporations. The clearest manifestation of the corporatist exploitation of Shar comes in the figure of Vanbrennan, founder of Xanthotrek, one of the companies profiting from the planet Shar. He is presented as a figure sexually attracted to Shar women, a man who kidnapped such a woman years ago and smuggled her to his home, hoping to breed with her (again, in a reversal of the Shar/human relations in "Sunday's Child"). His attempt to sabotage the experiments to reverse the Shars' problem is coupled (no pun intended) with his desire to acquire a new Shar woman, Ruah, since his former sex slave has died, without issue. This is the most obvious instance of treating the people themselves as "toys for aliens" (86) in a specifically sexual way, but the novel underscores the point, preventing it from appearing as the aberrant desire of one crazy human, by employing repeated sexual metaphors in relation to the companies themselves.

When we encounter the orbiting stations in which the companies are located, for instance, we are told that "the orbiting storehouses and offices [are] shaped like titanic eggs" (158), an image which recurs. Instead of nurturing its natives, Shar has become the inseminator of these alien eggs, providing them with sustenance in the form of profits. The biological metaphor is reiterated in the recurring image of the companies suckling. The first reference to the space stations calls them "the orbiting community that sucks on the world" (103), and shortly afterward, the Shar Givor refers to "the aliens who do nothing but suck our world's wealth and despise us" (109); the idea of the "aliens" eating the Shar is a leitmotif in the novel, one that underscores the symbolic implications of the breeding problems of the Shar as a people; we might recall, as well, here the Ix who wanted to feed on the Lyhhrt in the Lyhhrt trilogy. But in *Birthstones* it is an eating imaged specifically in terms of the maternal; the planet is like a giant breast being suckled by the corporations.

However, Gotlieb does not settle for a simple us/them dichotomy, in which the Shar are merely passive victims of exploitative offworlders, as the Lyhhrt are, to a considerable extent, of Zamos and of the Ix. She also suggests that the mutation of the women reflects more immediate and internalized Shar characteristics—home truths, as it were. Though the mutation affects the women, for instance, the *cause* of the mutation is located within the males, rather than the females. To correct the problem, it will be necessary "to rectify the DNA of the Shar males" (25). This location of the reduction of the women to abjection within the DNA codes of the men reflects the symbolic encoding of women as other and abject by men. The Emperor's quotation, above, about the inability of Shar women to care for themselves *and their children* (and his use of the words "ought to be able to care for themselves" to express the idea suggests how engrained is the notion of feminine maternal responsibility) expresses the general Shar antipathy to the female. Even absent a mind-erasing mutation, the novel suggests, Shar culture is predisposed to a sexist reduction of the female. Its own governance is a sham(e).

The Emperor's comment, however, is a relatively mild instance this antifeminist Shar sensibility. There are more egregious examples. If the alien exploiters wish to keep the Shar from breeding and to use them as products, many of the Shar themselves are happy in an all-male society, free from female presence. All Shar males must for at least a brief period assume caretaker duties for the "unwomen," as they are called, but few see in the duty anything but duty, a burden. Many Shar, in fact, *like* life without women. Some fill the lack by donning symbolic woman costumes or by engaging in homosexual relationships, but culturally, the Shar have ambivalent feelings (at best) about women. There are those who believe, for instance, that their deity "Angry-God destroyed woman because she was foul and evil!" (109). In some regions, the sacrifice of young females to the god is still practiced, and even in the supposedly more civilized population centers, the duty of care is a dubious one at best. At one point, the discarded body of an "unwoman"[5] is spotted in the rubbish by a character, and we learn as well that actually caring personally and privately for such women is a crime. In effect, a woman cannot be a family member but must become a ward of the state. Institutionalized neglect and even destruction of women has deep roots on Shar.

For some, therefore, the reduction of women to mere wombs, mindless breeding material, is a good thing. The Shar themselves can be likened to their alien exploiters in this regard—and they are. As one character notes, "I know there are many Shar who don't want whole women. And I'm sure there are exploiters among the aliens in orbit who are happy to see the Shar with a low birth rate" (102). An other who is equal and autonomous is a threat; better to deny it any status. Restoration of whole women would bring (or return) into play an entirely different social dynamic than the homosocial one that governs Shar. Restoring women will require not only successful scientific correction of genetic defects but also social re-engineering. The Shar Makkow notes that the process will require teaching Shar how "to live with true women," and the human Delius thinks but does not say, "To say nothing of loving them" (31). The one whole Shar woman who is a major character in the novel, Ruah, serves primarily as the novel's commentary on the problem of viewing the other as animal or monstrous. Vanbrennan views her as a possession, a sex toy to meet his desires and needs without regard to hers, but he is by no means unique in viewing that which does not seem obviously to be like him as inherently inferior. As we are told, "her body did not fit anyone else's idea of a human being" (118), since Shar look to human eyes more like odd doglike creatures than fellow sentient creatures. Consequently, Ruah is viewed consistently as a mere animal, by various humans, not just the children who torment her but also by Vanbrennan's agents. Indeed, the exploiters of the planet express the by-now familiar idea that the Shar are "just animals that ought to be in cages" (206); as the Shar see their woman as bestial things to be hidden away, so do the corporate profiteers see the Shar as abject others, dirty and nauseating.

As female alien, in effect, Ruah serves as the novel's symbolic representation of the female under attack, metaphorized as the alien under attack by virtue of its alienness. However, if the novel erases the female and elides the maternal, it does not do so in order to present a womanless world as a viable alternative. Instead, it does so precisely to challenge the idea that, even were it biologically possible, a world without women would be a worthwhile one. The defeminizing of Shar is linked with capitalist exploitation and with a gene-deep misogyny. The forces that elide the maternal, the novel suggests, are antithetical to cultural survival. The artistic ideal repeatedly referred to in the novel is the frieze representing the lost past on Shar, when women were in fact part of the social fabric. It shows "women with bablies suckling them, and children dancing, playing games or riding the backs of their fathers. All colored in red, blue and yellow with dyes—their grains were visible—made from the soil and rocks of the land" (20): both sexes and children, rendered literally from the soil of their planet, an artistic image of natural harmony. The image also clearly shows both female *and* male Shar involved in childcare; in contrast to the Emperor's remark about women caring for children, this artistic ideal shows both genders working in concert to care for children. The hope the novel holds out is that this artistic depiction is not merely the fantasy of the artist but a recoverable reality.

Admittedly, it holds this hope out in the form of a plausibility-stretching *deus ex machina*, late in the novel. One of the GalFed explorers discovers "a newborn female in an area of Shar that hadn't been much explored" (195), who proves to be a "'lusus naturae,' that whole or almost whole female who was so rare as to be a freak" (205). The irony that the "lusus naturae" (literally, "freak of nature") is normal rather than monstrous suggests the extent to which the normal has been marginalized on Shar. Nor does this find represent, really, a miracle fix. Even assuming that such females can continue to be found and bred true, thereby possibly simplifying and accelerating the process of regeneration, Gotlieb makes quite clear that full recovery, if it occurs at all, will require ongoing work and the passing of several generations. Her final novel, like her first, ends with cautious optimism coupled with a clear sense of the hard work still ahead.

Conclusion

Gotlieb's SF career began with a grain of manhood and ended with a birthstone, opening as it closed, with a focus on seeds and beginnings. This optimism is qualified, however, by a clear sense of the challenges faced by the newly born, and by those attempting to raise them. Gotlieb's works rarely end with cheery promise but instead with a sense that while much might have been accomplished, much remains to do. David Ketterer's suggestion that Canadian SF occupies a place between the optimism of American SF and the pessimism of British SF finds applies well to Gotlieb, especially if we accept the assertion made by him and others that Gotlieb was and remains the pre-eminent Canadian SF author. It is perhaps an over-simplification to suggest that all Canadian SF occupies, or should occupy, the sort of medial space Ketterer carves out for it. Certainly, Robert J. Sawyer, the best-known and most successful Canadian SF writer currently working, takes a highly optimistic view of the future,[1] while Peter Watts, less well-known but a daring and original writer himself, makes British pessimism seem almost quaint—nor are they the only figures who do not fit easily into Ketterer's construction.

Perhaps this uneasy balance between positive and negative possibility is itself a factor in the relative neglect Gotlieb's work has suffered. She is ambiguous. Will Shandy succeed in finding a way to integrate the Dumplings into the larger human world? Will the ergs achieve their quest for recognition as part of the community of rational creatures? What will the achievement of their gestalt mean for the Ungrukh? Will the Lyhhrt successfully negotiate the tension between their desire for oneness and their need for individuality? Will Shar women be restored? Readers seeking closure in relation to such questions and others may find her novels frustrating. Indeed, some of her stories seem intent on frustrating easy interpretation, "Sunday's Child" perhaps being the most significant example, while none of them really invite it. Her work requires work from the reader.

Such ambiguity, and such readerly effort, is an expectation of literary fiction, but much less so of SF. And despite the literary elements of her work, Gotlieb has defined herself, as we have seen, as a SF writer. She can be contrasted on this front with Margaret Atwood, another renowned Canadian poet and novelist. Unlike Gotlieb, despite writing several clearly SF novels, Atwood has consistently denied that these works are SF, insisting, for instance, that her work is Speculative Fiction, not Science Fiction: "Science fiction has monsters and spaceships; speculative fiction could really happen," she has stated, in one of her numerous denials of genre affiliation (Potts).[2] As literary texts, rather than genre texts, books such as *The Handmaid's Tale* (1985) can better get away with ambiguity—what is Offred's fate?—than can ones avowedly written within genre parameters. Literary Canadian fictions can be ambiguous; Gotlieb's ambiguity is arguably a detriment to her widespread popularity.

Furthermore, Gotlieb does not depict a comfortable world. For Gotlieb, the universe is not benevolent but rather more inclined to hostility; it is a backdrop for complex tapestries of human interaction, in which the mind matters, but it is also a material space against which her characters must struggle to survive, in keeping with Atwood's identification of survival as a key Canadian literary theme. Gotlieb's characters must struggle with their own biology, with each other, and with the material conditions in which they find themselves, most overtly demonstrated, perhaps, in the figure of *Heart of Red Iron*'s Prima, in whom consciousness and the combination of material elements are ineluctably linked. Transmuting those elements is deeply problematic and not always possible. Everything has a cost. But life finds a way, even in the most inimical circumstances. The native hominids who turn up late in *Heart of Red Iron* seem like an odd excrescence, not required by the plot (and indeed, they have no real impact on events and disappear as quickly as they arrive), nor consistent with the prevalent view, held by all the characters and even seemingly endorsed by the narrative voice, that Barrazan V is hostile to life. They might seem to offend against narrative logic and economy. However, they speak to one of Gotlieb's key themes: fecundity.

Gotlieb returns almost obsessively to the womb. Survival may be a prevalent Canadian literary theme, but Gotlieb answers the obstacles placed in the way of survival by the universe with prolific fecundity. Reproduction has a major role in all of her novels and many of her short stories; it is perhaps a coincidence that her first and final SF publications focus so strongly on pregnancy and birth, but as coincidences go, it is not only a highly likely one but also one that is perfectly apropos. She thematizes reproduction as a biological imperative, a psychological need, even as an imitative act engaged in by rational creatures to try to come to terms with the universe. In this respect, Gotlieb does tend to lean in the direction of those skeptical about scientific advances, often making her imitator/creators deeply problematic characters, whether ultimately redeemable like Dahlgren or ultimately despicable like Zamos. The "mad scientist" trope is of more than passing significance in her work. However, she does not descend to cliché in her depiction of such figures but rather presents a wide array of them, refusing to settle for simple equations.

Even when the equations might seem simple, they don't add up that way. *Sunburst* does not offer the simplistic assertion that delinquency is class- and physiologically based, even though it invokes those concepts as part of its exploration. *Birthstones* presents the most literal version imaginable of the monstrous-feminine, but it does so to subvert rather than to endorse the abjection of women. Everything in between is comparably tendentious and complex, requiring careful reading and consideration. The extent of her achievements becomes clear only when one looks across her career rather than simply at her best-known and most accessible work. This is especially clear when one recognizes variations rung on her themes across her canon. This book does little more than scratch at the surface of Gotlieb's fiction and poetry, barely penetrating the skin. Gotlieb consistently leaves her characters with much left to do; her readers are in the same condition.

Chapter Notes

Introduction

1. An additional novel, the SF thriller "Fifth of Gemini," was completed in the 1970s but never published. The manuscript is available at the Merril Collection of Science Fiction, Speculation and Fantasy at the Toronto Public Library branch on College Street. A thriller with a contemporary setting and dealing with genetic manipulation, the novel is anomalous among the rest of Gotlieb's output; had it been published, Gotlieb's reputation today might be somewhat different. However, as it is unpublished, I will have little more to say about it here. Her mainstream novel, *Why Should I Have All the Grief?* (1969), does not acknowledge her SF.
2. The Governor General is the Queen of England's representative, or vice-regent, in Canada, with numerous powers, including the power to prorogue or dissolve parliament and to name the Prime Minister, though in practice, the Governor General follows the will of the electorate or of the sitting government in such matters. The Governor General is perhaps most visible to the Canadian populace as the sponsor of the Governor General's Awards. These were established in 1937 by Canadian Governor General Lord Tweedsmuir, better known as John Buchan, author of novels such as *The Thirty-Nine Steps* (1915), and they are given annually in various literary and other categories.
3. Sawyer has also called Gotlieb an inspiration ("Phyllis Gotlieb Honoured Today in Canada's Federal Parliament"), and his Robert J. Sawyer Books, an SF imprint of Red Deer Press, published Gotlieb's final novel, *Birthstones* (2007). Sawyer personally selects books to be published by the imprint, and he is quoted on the back cover of the book, calling her "the grand dame of Canadian SF."
4. However, see John Clute, "Fables of Transcendence: The Challenge of Science Fiction," in which he argues for the essential Canadianness of van Vogt's SF.
5. These novels are usually referred to as the Starcats trilogy or series, much to Gotlieb's distaste. She refers to them as the "Ungrukh Chronicles" (284) in the Author's Note at the end of *The Kingdom of the Cats*. She was a guest at the SFRA conference in Guelph, Ontario, in 2003, at which time she confirmed to me, in conversation, her dislike for the "Starcats" designation and her preference for the term "Ungrukh chronicles." That, therefore, is the term I will use when referring to this series.

Chapter One

1. The following 1960s stories are not reprinted in either of Gotlieb's story collections: "No End of Time" (*Fantastic Science Fiction Stories*, June 1960; reprinted in *Thrilling Science Fiction*, April 1973), "A Bone to Pick" (*Fantastic*, October 1960); "Valedictory" (*Amazing Stories*, August

1964), "Planetoid Idiot" (*The Magazine of Fantasy and Science Fiction*, May 1967; reprinted in Robert Silverberg's *To the Stars: Eight Stories of Science Fiction*, 1971, and translated into the Spanish for *Antologia de Ficcao Cientifica* 2, 1970); and "The Dirty Old Men of Maxsec" (*Galaxy*, November 1969). Other stories that remain uncollected are "SCORE/SCORE" (Stephen Clarkson's anthology *Visions 2020*, 1970; reprinted in Jack David and Michael Park's anthology *Playback: Canadian Selections*, 1978); "End City" (*Science Fiction Age*, March 1997); and "Waiting Till the Scars Scream" (coauthored by Jean-Louis Trudel, *TransVersions* 8/9, 1998).

2. Quest narratives can certainly be more complex than the basic structure suggests, and a quest narrative in which the main action is antecedent to and framed by the narrative present without precedent. *The Odyssey*, for instance, also employs a framing narrative with much of the action actually having occurred temporally prior to the first appearance of Odysseus in the text, when he narrates the bulk of the antecedent action. Nevertheless, it is a relatively unusual approach to such a narrative, especially in such a short and economical version.

3. There are of course exceptions. The music of Pan in Kenneth Grahame's *The Wind in the Willows*, for instance, is beneficent, singing a song of a salvific nature that nurtures and protects life; significantly in relation to Gotlieb, the specific context involves the protection of a lost child by Pan. Frances Hodgson Burnett invokes music similarly, albeit via allusion rather than through the literal invocation of the seducing music of the supernatural: the first time we meet Dickon (a name Gotlieb uses for a character in "Gingerbread Boy," albeit with any connection to Burnett's character unlikely), the wild boy of the moors with a preternatural ability to nurture flora and fauna, he is playing a pipe and surrounded by animals he has rescued. Nevertheless, the predominant motif is of music as dangerously seductive, leading the auditor into danger and perhaps to death. An interesting inversion of the pattern, in which music played by a human being in the living world can summon a spirit from the otherworld, is John Mead Falkner's *The Lost Stradivarius*, but inverting the direction of the call does not make the outcome any more positive. Falkner underscores the point by setting part of his narrative on the islands associated with the Sirens.

4. Gotlieb was Jewish, so one ought to be careful about assuming too much about how the New Testament might have influenced her work. However, this very story references Virgin birth, and the "salt of the earth" passage is one of the Bible's most famous. It seems reasonable to assume that Golieb would have been aware of this symbolic association and willing to use it. Her fiction rarely draws explicit attention to Judaic as opposed to Christian tradition, though it does at times, as shall be addressed later. It does also at times explicitly invoke Christianity.

5. Roughly translates as, "In the place where such riches rot, pleasant spices must spread; white, blue and red blooms shine brightly in the sun. Flowers and fruit cannot wither where it fell down into the earth, for all grass must grow from dead grains; no wheat could be brought home otherwise." Again, this is a Christian poem derived primarily from New Testament traditions rather than from Jewish ones. However, Gotlieb not only studied English literature but also demonstrates elsewhere in her work a familiarity with medieval literature (sections of *The Kingdom of the Cats* make use of elements of York cycle of medieval mystery plays, and some of her poetry shows similar influences). It is therefore not unreasonable to assume her familiarity with such associations.

6. Though the focus of this chapter is Gotlieb's early short fiction, the following discussion will range occasionally further ahead, as dealing fully with the basics of GalFed now will be more efficient than dealing with its development piecemeal in later chapters.

7. First published in 1575 but probably performed a decade or more earlier, the play *Gammer Gurton's Needle* is one of the earliest surviving examples of secular English comedy. Dickon sets neighbors at each others' throats by lying about who stole the eponymous needle, thereby bringing to the surface hidden tensions and antagonisms. All ends well when the needle is found, but the potential for a community crisis drives the comedy.

8. Pope provides the title for one of the Ungrukh stories, "The King's Dogs," in *A Judgment of Dragons*. The Ungrukh stories are especially concerned with how humans can come to an accommodation with the alien—and vice versa.

9. Gotlieb's mainstream novel *Why Should I Have All the Grief?* focuses on the impact of Auschwitz on the lives of its protagonists and of post-war Jewish life generally. Her poetry also occasionally addresses the Holocaust. Such references are rare in her SF, though the possibility of genocide is a recurring theme, as is genetic experimentation, and the Jewish experience does inform stories such as "Tauf Alef," "Son of the Morning" and "Nebuchadnezzar" (the latter two of which

comprise part of *A Judgment of Dragons*), and Gotlieb's final novel, *Birthstones*. She also wrote an article on Hasidic elements in the poetry of A. M. Klein.

10. A note attached to the manuscript of the story reads, "Originally THE MONKEY WRENCH—because of Gordon Dickson's MONKEY WRENCH renamed ROGUE'S GAMBIT by Frederik Pohl, forgetting Alan Caillou's novel of same name." Gotlieb restored her original title when the story was collected in *Blue Apes*. "Rogue's Gambit" is an appropriate enough title, though, given the importance of game-playing in the story.

11. This idea recurs, notably in *O Master Caliban!* as will be discussed in greater detail in Chapter Three. This story prefigures that one in another way, in that both involve a battle of wits between a man and a machine, manifesting itself in the playing of a game, *Go* in "Monkey Wrench," chess in *O Master Caliban!* Machine minds also crop up as key figures in "Tauf Aleph" and Gotlieb's final trilogy, though in less psychologically problematic ways.

12. The closest Gotlieb came subsequently to an SF thriller (though spies and thrilleresque skulduggery do have roles in some of the GalFed novels) is the unpublished novel "Fifth of Gemini." "The Dirty Old Men of Maxsec" is also one of Gotlieb's few genuinely dystopian tales.

13. Gotlieb's literary proclivities were clearly evident from the beginning of her career. A note in Gotlieb's hand attached to the manuscript reads, "'arty & hifalutin' said agent."

14. Both stories do share a wry nod to Ray Bradbury's "A Sound of Thunder" (1952), one of the most famous time-travel stories. "No End of Time" tells us that the first time he used the Chronotome, Krisomer managed to bring a dinosaur corpse into the future, and after that disaster brought only minerals for a decade "before he timidly tried out a few butterflies" (106), and the story makes clear that the past can't be tinkered with; even though Socrates has died in the future, a simulacrum of him is created and sent back to the past to satisfy "the perquisites of the monster Time" (125). In "Valedictory," Rogan makes a joke about the mud on shoes that so far is all that has been brought back to the future, not changing "the fabric of time much" and continues, "So you don't have to worry about stepping on butterflies" (47).

Chapter Two

1. Bakka Books is possibly Canada's premiere SF bookstore. In 2000, the store decided to introduce a series reprinting classics of Canadian SF. The first volume was James de Mille's *Strange Manuscript Found in a Copper Cylinder* (1888). *Sunburst* was the second volume. Frederick Phillip Grove's *Consider Her Ways* (1947) followed, but it was the final volume in this unfortunately aborted series.

2. Darko Suvin notes the generally useful application to SF of the bildungsroman structure, "with its initially naive protagonist who by degrees arrives at some understanding of the novum for her/himself and for the readers" (79). Shandy functions much as Suvin suggests here, as does Jommy Cross in *Slan*.

3. The cover copy of the original edition stresses the nuclear monster, telling us on the front that "a fiendish race of demonic children is spawned in the genetic chaos of a runaway reactor explosion"; the back cover tells us of "the worst of the human garbage ... a breed of terrible children, possessed of terrifying supernormal powers. They were a new race of monster...." Not only is the description of the novel misleading, the use of the term "supernormal" is at odds with its actual use in the book. The Berkley edition of *Slan*, by contrast, stresses human cruelty and "the mystery of the slans' strange existence and superiority" (back cover).

4. Fredericks traces the trend from H. G. Wells (whose *Men Like Gods* [1923] has provided a handy title for chapters on the subject in books such as Fredericks' and Donald A. Wollheim's *The Universe Makers*) through Olaf Stapledon, Philip Wylie, Stanley G. Weinbaum, van Vogt, and Theodore Sturgeon. One might without much difficulty expand the list to include Henry Kuttner's *Mutant* (1953) and Wilmar Shiras's *Children of the Atom* (1953; a banner year, also introducing Jerome Bixby's "It's a *Good* Life," one of the most famous stories of the superhuman child the genre has produced, and Sturgeon's *More than Human*, a classic of the superhuman genre "in which the first evolutionary breakthrough since the dawn of individual consciousness is achieved by a group of telepathically-linked outcasts and freaks" [McGuirk 145], as well as Arthur C. Clarke's *Childhood's End* and Alfred Bester's *The Demolished Man*, less directly relevant to the superhuman child

theme but both concerned with the implications of the evolution of the mind and its concomitant development of "super" powers); Shiras's book especially has more than a slight similarity to *Sunburst*. Nor has the theme vanished in recent years, as books such as John Brunner's *Children of the Thunder* (1989), George Turner's *Brain Child* (1991), or Robert J. Sawyer's *Factoring Humanity* (1993) or *Triggers* (2012) demonstrate—though Sawyer offers a considerably more optimistic view of the implications of psi than is the norm.

    5. A sly inversion, perhaps, of the common SF designation ESPer for a telepathic; it served as title for the 1958 edition of James Blish's *Jack of Eagles*, and the term has been frequently used elsewhere. An imper would be the opposite. Since Shandy's behavior might also be described in some ways as impish, there is perhaps a pun hidden in the term as well.

    6. Mead was prolific, and I have been unable to track down the source for this quotation, despite going through several of her books and essays, and inquiring of her biographers, and even of her daughter, about whether they recognized it. The consensus was that this sounded like something Mead would say, though not like something she would have written in one of her earlier anthropological studies but perhaps said in a public talk or an essay later in her career, when she was that rarity, an academic celebrity. It would make sense for the quotation to have come from something Mead would have said relatively close to when the book was written, but it is also worth noting that her earlier anthropological studies were readily available in popular paperback editions in the late 1950s, so Gotlieb could have found this phrase in almost anything Mead had produced prior to 1964—or, she could have simply made it up as a Mead-like idea, though that seems unlikely to me.

    7. The reference is to Ariel's song in Act 1, Scene 2, leading Ferdinand to Miranda:
> Full fathom five thy father lies;
> Of his bones are coral made;
> Those are pearls that were his eyes:
> Nothing of him that doth fade
> But doth suffer a sea-change
> Into something rich and strange [461–66].

Ferdinand at this point believes his father to have drowned; the song describes the transformation of his corpse beneath the sea. Though this might seem ominous, nobody is really dead, and the play instead deals with ultimately promising transformations and self-discoveries. *The Tempest* plays a larger role in Gotlieb's next SF novel, as we shall see in the next chapter.

    8. Sheldon defines the three basic categories of endomorph, mesomorph, and ectomorph, as well as numerous variations depending on which traits predominate, in *Varieties of Delinquent Youth*. In brief, endomorphs are inclined to roundness of fattiness in bodily form, mesomorphs are inclined to muscularity, and ectomorphs to thinness; one might think in terms of round, triangular (broad shoulders, narrow waist) and straight as defining the basic body types. Sheldon's study concluded that "as a generalization, then, the 200 delinquent youths [studied by Sheldon] are decidedly mesomorphic" (729).

    9. Consider for instance the Gluecks' assertion that their research "does not lead us to the pessimistic conclusion that persistent delinquency springs largely from the germ plasm and is inevitable. We repeat what we previously have said: *In delinquency we are dealing not with predestination but with destination*. We believe that imaginative and intensive experimentation with prophylactic and therapeutic measures, providing it is timely and thorough, should produce evidence that the destination of children toward delinquency is capable of change in a substantial proportion of instances" (*Physique and Delinquency* 265).

    10. Indeed, Wells explicitly invokes evolution as a motif in the novel, imagining his Martians as creatures that have evolved from creatures very like humans into horrifying monsters. On the one hand, they are imaged as creatures almost of pure mind, "minds that are to our minds as ours are to those of the beasts that perish, intelligences vast and cool and unsympathetic" (ch. 1), but on the other they are given physical traits such as tentacles and dietary habits such as the consumption of blood that associate them not merely with the animal but with the horrifying and monstrous. However, Wells also explicitly problematizes a simple equation of the Martians with the alien other by suggesting that they evolved from creatures similar to humans and by repeatedly comparing their depredations to European colonialism and to how humans treat animals generally. This comparison is implicit even in the above passage, which identifies human minds, in comparison to

Martian ones, as akin to those of animal ones in comparison to human ones. We might note here that *Odd John* does very similar things with the relationship between its superhuman and humans (even using, albeit metaphorically, animal references similar to Wells's to suggest the monstrosity of the superhumans).

11. The term "supernormal" is used by Gotlieb in the novel, and it explicitly excludes the psis. Urquhart responds to Shandy's theory that psis are subnormal by asking, "Psi is definitely not the attribute of the supernormal?" (151); Shandy concurs.

Chapter Three

1. *Sunburst* remains Gotlieb's only book to have appeared in multiple editions from different publishers; most of her fiction is out of print, though copies are relatively easy to find. One hopes that the recent e-book reissue of *O Master Caliban!* will be only the first of numerous such reissues.

2. Gotlieb does explicitly invoke Frankenstein in the poem "ms & mr frankenstein" (see Chapter Seven), as well as in her unpublished novel, "Fifth of Gemini," in which Dr. Burin, who has conducted experiments with quintuplets, frets, "If I work in secrecy with these men who look all alike, people think perhaps I am a Frankenstein" (6).

3. TVTropes.org has an entry for this term as applying to a non-human, often an artificial being, desiring to be human. However, the term has also been used to refer to symptoms of gelotophobia, or the wooden expression sometimes manifested in people suffering from social anxiety, especially the fear of being mocked (see Titze e.g.); it can also be used to refer to the behavior of those who repeatedly and deliberately choose to lie (see Miller e.g.). Pinocchio is of course the wooden puppet who wanted to be a boy, and whose nose grows when he lies, first introduced in Carlo Collodi's novel *The Adventures of Pinocchio* (1883).

4. Zabus points out, "Although Erg-Queen [*sic*; Gotlieb never capitalizes "erg" in this context] is a five-armed, insectiform, silver machine crowned with antennas, she suggests Sycorax in the impression she gives of 'a pampered hive queen' (p. 36) and in her rival expertise with robotics, which evokes the blue-eyed hag's black magic" (197). While this is certainly true, erg–Queen is not merely a Sycorax figure but more a kind of literalization of the link between Prospero and Sycorax in the play; the numerous parallels between them—they are both figures of magic, both are banished to the island, both have a single child (of opposite sex), both have a twelve-year period associated with them, and both keep the island spirits as slaves—invites us to see them as linked. *O Master Caliban!* strengthens the link by making erg–Queen herself a sort of offspring/reflection of aspects of Dahlgren, rather than an objectively entirely distinct figure, as Sycorax is.

5. Despite their common source in Shakespeare's play and broad similarities (e.g., the isolated scientist on a distant, threatening planet, the arrival of a spaceship), there is little to suggest a direct influence of *Forbidden Planet* on *O Master Caliban!* Though Robbie the robot synthesizes whiskey for the cook, as erg–Dahlgren does for Dahlgren, and though Robbie's genderless status is akin to the ergs' (Robbie even makes clothes, making him perhaps the source of Clothier, the erg responsible for making clothing for the humans on Barazzan V, a minor but interesting and amusing figure), there are no substantial similarities between the two works. One might, however, argue that on some level the ergs are reminiscent of *Forbidden Planet*'s monsters from the Id, externalized manifestations of the unconscious fears and desires of Dahlgren and the other scientists responsible for their creation. In a way, they are creations that become the downfall of their creator, as the Krell brain machine is the downfall of its creators in the movie. Even so, this similarity is sufficiently general to make an argument for influence difficult. For a discussion of the relationship between *The Tempest* and *Forbidden Planet*, especially in terms of Freudian psychology, see Tim Youngs's "Cruising against the Id." For more of an argument for parallels between the film and Gotlieb's novel, see Zabus 194–97.

6. Indeed, oceanic metaphors, especially ones strongly reminiscent of drowning, the fate apparently suffered by the passengers and crew of the ship in *The Tempest*, recur throughout the book, as subtle ongoing reminders of the link between the two works. At the end of the first chapter, for instance, when Ardagh begins to drift off to sleep, we are told, "sleep began to wash over her in an uneasy ebb and flow; in the troughs of its waves she saw first Dahlgren's face, and

then Sven's" (22). An example of the metaphor in drowning terms is used later when Shirvanian emerges from his telepathic link to the erg-Queen: "He came up briefly out of that ocean of electricity where he felt he was drowning" (212). Such recurring metaphors weave something of a Shakespearean sea-change into the development of the characters over the course of the book.

    7. ESP "speech" is represented in this novel by italics preceded and followed by a period. Direct linguistic but non-verbal communication between machines is represented by italics unaccompanied by quotation marks. These distinguishing practices are preserved in the quotations included here.

    8. This novel postdates the Ungrukh Chronicles, so some of the following discussion will anticipate points that first assumed central importance in those books.

    9. Entities consisting only or primarily of brains are popular in Gotlieb; they would include, in addition to Prima, the Encid, the Lyhhrt, and the Qsaprinli, not to mention the decanted brains living in bottles we encounter in the Ungrukh Chronicles.

    10. Gotlieb uses the "mod" designation occasionally in other contexts, most amusingly in the author bio that appears in the collection *Visions 2020*, containing her short story "SCORE/SCORE" (also about machine intelligence). The biography reads,

> Ecosystems mammal class gotlieb mod phyllis number 1 designated and manufactured in toronto from multinational components; coprogenitor with mod calvin number 1 of subsequent generation 3 models; programs poems *within the zodiac* and *ordinary, moving*; novels *sunburst* and *why should i have all the grief*? Continues operation.

This is immediately humorous in context, since the story is about identity confusion between human and machine, but considered more broadly in the context of Gotlieb's work it is actually of a piece with her problematizing of the idea of identity.

    11. The cover copy of the novel includes in this respect an odd error. The inside front cover flap's brief plot summary describes mod-Dahlgren as Sven's "mechanical twin," which misrepresents his actual status as the mechanical twin of Sven's *father*. It is nevertheless a telling conflation. Peter Havergal is, however, presented as an almost twinlike image of Sven (albeit with two fewer arms!).

    12. See the subsequent chapter for a far more detailed discussion of golems.

Chapter Four

    1. All but one of these stories are collected in Gotlieb's *Blue Apes*. "The Military Hospital" was first published in the anthology *Fourteen Stories High* in 1970 and then reprinted in *The Magazine of Science Fiction and Fantasy* in 1974; "Mother Lode," first published in *The Magazine of Fantasy and Science Fiction* in 1973, has been translated into Italian for inclusion in the anthology *Aliene, Amazzoni, Astronaute* (1990) and also appears in *Northern Stars: The Anthology of Canadian Science Fiction* (1994); "Sunday's Child" was first published in *Cosmos* in 1977 and anthologized in *Fall and Rise* (2007); "Tauf Aleph," perhaps Gotlieb's most highly regarded short story, first appeared in Jack Dann's second anthology of Jewish-themed SF, *More Wandering Stars* (1981), and has been anthologized in *Tesseracts* (the first volume of the ongoing anthology series of Canadian SF and Fantasy) in 1985 (Gotlieb co-edited the second volume with Douglas Barbour) and in *The Norton Anthology of Science Fiction* (1999); and "The Newest Profession" first appeared in the collection *Speculations* (edited by Isaac Asimov and Alice Laurance) in 1982 and was reprinted in *Ark of Ice: Canadian Futurefiction* (1992). The one uncollected work from this period is the 1970 story "SCORE/SCORE," which first appeared in *Visions 2020* and was reprinted in the 1978 anthology *Playback: Canadian Selections*. Two of the stories which make up the first volume of the Ungrukh Chronicles were also published separately during the 1970s, "Son of the Morning" in *The Magazine of Fantasy and Science Fiction* in 1971, and "The King's Dogs" in the Robert Silverberg-edited anthology *The Edge of Space: Three Original Novellas of Science Fiction* in 1979. These last, however, will be discussed in the context of their appearance in *A Judgment of Dragons*.

    2. This is actually a very odd claim. Neither "Aesh" nor "Shar" mean anything in English, the language being spoken (presumably) by Nadja, Mandros and Stella. They are in fact Hebrew words, as Gotlieb explains in the author's note to *Birthstones*: "When I first created the species 'Shar' I kept unconsciously giving them Hebrew nouns for names. As I realized this I decided that

the names seemed to fit, so I kept on doing it whenever the Shar turned up in my work" (217). She notes that "shar" means "gate" and "aesh" means "fire," both of which might be relevant in the context of this story. Why, however, characters would identify these as words in "your" language to non–Hebrew-speakers is unclear, except insofar as their incomprehensibility in "our" language might suggest either the profusion of different languages—and therefore of the inability to communicate—associated with the Tower of Babel, or more specifically the real communication gap between the humans and the Shar: even when they think they are speaking the humans' language, the Shar remain incomprehensible.

    3. It's a logical enough inference, insofar as any such idea has logic behind it. After all, if Christ is the human child of God conceived in the Virgin Mary, it would not seem unreasonable to conclude that the Anti-Christ would be Satan's child conceived on a human woman.

    4. See, for instance, Catherine A. Cory, 56ff.

    5. The "they" referred to here would be men, whose perspective on the mother is shared here; mother as mere womb casing, lacking agency or any markings of humanity, represents a male construction (presumably a desirable one, for men, anyway) of the maternal. This notion of the maternal assumes far greater significance in *Birthstones*, which gives the Shar females—and the male reaction to them—far more focused attention, though, as noted above, the Shar in this story and that novel are not really entirely congruent.

    6. Gotlieb's story was published in 1972, Irigiray's *Speculum of the Other Woman* in 1974 in French, and not in English until 1985, so I am not suggesting that Gotlieb was influenced by Irigiray here, but rather that Irigiray's ideas about constructions of the maternal help clarify theoretically what Gotlieb is exploring artistically.

    7. One might consider the term "antagonist" as similar. There is a tendency to conflate the concept of the antagonist and the villain, given that "antagonist" is the term used to describe the character in fiction who stands in opposition to the protagonist. However, there is no moral connotation attached to the term or this relationship, however much the majority of specific instances might correspond to the hero/villain dichotomy. However, a protagonist may be a villain, even a moral monster, and the forces antagonistic to him or her on the side that would conventionally be termed "good." Shakespeare's Richard III or Macbeth might be good examples of protagonists who are nevertheless villainous, the antagonists of whom represent good.

    8. There are several such instances. The 1976 TV-movie sequel to *Rosemary's Baby*, for instance, features Rosemary's grown son trying to resist his demonic heritage. Neil Gaiman and Terry Pratchett's 1990 novel *Good Omens* deals humorously with attempts to prevent the Anti-Christ from choosing evil. An interesting recent example is the season five episode of the television series *Supernatural*, "I Believe the Children Are Our Future" (broadcast date October 15, 2009), in which the child Jesse, son of a human mother and demon father, has to choose between accepting or rejecting his role as Anti-Christ (fortunately for all concerned, he rejects the role).

    9. One might note in this regard that the story of Jonah can be seen as a metaphorical re-enactment of birth. See, for instance, Claudia D. Bergmann's "Jonah 2:1–11: Expressing a Personal Crisis through the Birth Metaphor." A further Jonah connection the story makes, at its conclusion, is to associate Cortez with the name "Jonah" in its metaphorical meaning as "jinx," since Jonah was thrown overboard by the ship's crew while he sailed to Tarshish, as they blamed him for the foul weather threatening their ship; they saw him as cursed and threw him into the sea to propitiate God (see the Book of Jonah chapter one). Ironically in this instance, it is the metaphorical whale that is trying to eject the Jonah figure for trying to lead the crew out of its belly.

    10. One need not look far to find constructions of Quebec, even recently, as Canada's spoiled child in English Canadian media. *Toronto Sun*, 2011: "Like the Spoiled Child, Quebec is forever wanting" ("Hey Quebec"); David Walburg, 2012: "Quebec is often perceived as the petulant, spoiled child of Canada"; Charles Owen, 2012: "Having Quebec within our confederation is like living with a spoiled child" (qtd in Russell); etc.

    11. The name may be a pun, suggesting both Lazarus and lazar, or leper, associating DeLazzari with raising the dead and with a disease that disintegrates the body. We might contrast this name with that of Lazarus Emmanuel Kappstein in "A Bone to Pick."

    12. The name "Og" is scriptural, naming an Amorite king. The name means "giant," therefore applying to O/G. Ironically, the scriptural Og was killed at the battle of Edrei by the Israelites, rather than being in any way the savior of the chosen people.

Chapter Five

1. With the permission of the University of Ottawa Press, portions of this chapter, significantly revised, come from "Mind Matters: Intellect and Identity in the Works of Phyllis Gotlieb," *Worlds of Wonder: Readings in Canadian Science Fiction and Fantasy*, Reappraisals: Canadian Writers 26, ed. Jean-François Leroux and Camille R. La Bossière (Ottawa: University of Ottawa Press, 2004), 105-17.

2. The Qumedni are entities that exist as "a pulsing vortex of energy" (*Judgment* 41). They come from an alternate plane of existence referred to as a continuum in *The Kingdom of the Cats* (13) (in contrast to the planetary home they have in "Phantom Foot"), and have such prodigious powers to alter time, space, and perception that there is little to differentiate them from gods. The parallels between the Qumedni and Q of *Star Trek: The Next Generation* are numerous and might lead one to speculate about Q's origins, since *ST:TNG* premiered two years after the last Ungrukh novel was published. Consider the following:

  i. The name Qumedni is in its first syllable the name of Q.
  ii. Qumedni have no individual names; Q is merely a convenient label, applied to Q and to all others of his kind.
  iii. The Qumedni live in a continuum, as do Q and his kind.
  iv. The Qumedni have no corporeal existence but assume the bodies of those with whom they wish to interact; Q is a being of pure energy who assumes human form to interact with Picard and company.
  v. The Qumedni are beings with almost godlike power, even over time; Q is a being of almost godlike power, even over time.
  vi. The Qumedni do not generally interact with humans but occasionally cause mischief; those from the Q continuum rarely interact with humans, except the mischievous Q.
  vi. The Qumedon known as Kriku (the name he assumes when in Ungrukh form) is something of a rebel and innovator among his people, especially in his intense interest in lesser life forms such as the Ungrukh; Q is something of a rebel among his people, especially in his interest in lesser life forms such as humans.

These similarities may be mere coincidence, and there are also differences between Q and the Qumedni; the Ungrukh were created by Kriku, for instance, and I am not aware of Q engaging in such an act of creation, nor is Q generally used with the religious overtones applied to the Qumedni. However, the similarities are numerous enough to make one wonder what books were lying around when *ST:TNG* was in the planning stages.

3. Élisabeth Vonarburg has pointed out that woman SF writers are fond of characters "with extra-sensory powers, especially telepathy" (181), but Gotlieb seems especially fond of it as a device, though she is at times skeptical about its benefits. She uses it in all ten of her SF novels and many of her short stories, ascribing it to numerous species, including the human one.

4. Fortunately, GalFed is not static. We learn in *Flesh and Gold* that this procedure has come to be seen as the use of "a misguided technology" and that "the practice had long been stopped" (142). Whether the subsequent practice among the Khagodi of keeping these brains alive and in storage, without using them but also without killing them, represents much of a mercy is perhaps worthy of some debate.

5. In this regard, the Ungrukh Chronicles contrast interestingly with the valorization of the mind abstracted from the body in cyberpunk, which emerged as a major SF movement during the years in which the Ungrukh Chronicles were published; they spanned 1980-1985, while William Gibson first referenced cyberspace in the 1982 story "Burning Chrome" and published the seminal cyberpunk novel, *Neuromancer*, in 1984, a book in which the protagonist Case feels trapped in "the prison of the flesh" (6).

6. Expressions such as "the brains of the operation" or insults such as "birdbrain" demonstrate the conflation of brains and mind in the popular consciousness.

7. In chapter two, I discussed the importance of Olaf Stapledon's *Odd John* to Gotlieb's ideas in *Sunburst*. As we saw there, head size is important in *Odd John*. Gotlieb may have taken some hints for the Ungrukh from another Stapledon novel, *Sirius*, in which a scientist breeds a new kind of superdog. Stapledon pays close attention to the physiological changes necessary to breed a dog with human-like intelligence—including the necessity of increasing brain capacity. Sirius also has

problems as a result of not having hands but paws lacking opposable thumbs, a limitation confronted by the Ungrukh as well: "they had finger prostheses but not fingers, hand substitutes but not hands. They could not do delicate operations" (*Kingdom* 75).

   8. The criticism began almost immediately. Alexei Panshin's review of the book in *The Magazine of Fantasy and Science Fiction*, for instance, avers that the Gethenian ambisexuals "seem purely male, partly because [Le Guin] chooses always to call them 'he'" (51), and Joanna Russ, while blaming the problem primarily on the deficiencies of English as a language lacking a gender-neutral pronoun (though also critiquing Le Guin for other failures to address female experience), nevertheless regretted that "these people must be called 'he' throughout" (90).

   9. Many SF stories deal with this chilling idea of literal bodily possession by aliens. It is perhaps the SF version of demonic possession and is almost invariably presented in SF as a bad thing. Robert A. Heinlein's *The Puppet Masters* (1951) is a particularly well-known example. Lyhhrt possession of the body of another being becomes a point of considerably more contention in the Lyhhrt trilogy.

   10. See Heidegger's discussion in *What Is Called Thinking*, in which he asserts that because animals lack hands, thereby literally being unable to gather (a debatable claim, as anyone who has ever watched squirrels or chipmunks can attest), they lack the ability to know or question their being.

   11. This is a genuine medical condition, though Thorndecker is not a typical case (for instance, it usually involves cretinism). See the entry on Kocher-Debré-Sémelaigne syndrome in Pryse-Philips for a brief definition of the actual syndrome.

   12. Interestingly, Robert Zelazny's 1982 novel *Eye of Cat* likens a catlike alien to the last of the Navajos, thereby "reinforc[ing] a colonialist history of seeing native peoples, like animals, as insufficiently possessing the land which then justifies its appropriation and also their treatment as less-than-fully-human subjects" (Vint 11). I do not know whether Gotlieb had read this book, or, even if she had, whether it influenced the explicit association between the Ungrukh and First Nations peoples. Her creation of the Ungrukh predates Zelazny's novel, but *Kingdom of the Cats* was published three years after *Eye of Cat* appeared.

Chapter Six

   1. Note the equation of brothels and zoos, by the way. This reference to a bizarre law is not only an amusing satirical dig at bureaucratic classification but also a subtle reminder of the thematic commodification of "animals" in Gotlieb's work. See the short story "We Can't Go on Meeting Like This" (discussed in Chapter Eight) for a more direct exploration of the sexual commodification of animals.

   2. We might here recall the short story "The Newest Profession," which does not explicitly reference GalFed but is about the breeding of humans genetically modified for various environments, including the sea, and the Frogs from the Ungrukh Chronicles. We might infer that the Frogs represent the initial versions, bred hundreds of years ago, here resurrected as slaves.

   3. When characters "speak" telepathically in these books, Gotlieb's convention to so indicate is to use italics, framed by colons that take the place of quotation marks.

   4. Here we see Gotlieb picking up a plot point from an earlier work and reusing it. The Ix bear more than a passing resemblance to the Shar as they appear in "Sunday's Child," even down to using the bodies of aliens as vessels in which to grow their young, though in the case of "Sunday's Child" the offspring is a Shar/human hybrid, rather than a Shar that has simply consumed its "mother," as the Ix young would evidently do.

   5. Even the titles hint at opposed states or concepts, if not the actual border points. *Flesh and Gold* contrasts the organic and inorganic, the biological and the metallic, in its title, though the association between bodies and gold acquires other significances. *Violent Stars* contrasts the immediate viscerality of violence with the cold distance of space. *Mindworlds* directly contrasts internal and external spaces, drawing attention to the association between the mind and its context.

   6. The novel was retitled *Harry Potter and the Sorcerer's Stone* in the American edition, a title change that unfortunately blurs the alchemical connection, though the idea of what the

philosopher's stone does, if not the correct term for it, is clear enough in the Americanized version.

7. See Principe *passim* for an up-to-date and readable detailed history of alchemy.

8. Well-known examples of tales of alchemical chicanery would include Chaucer's "Canon's Yeoman's Tale" from *The Canterbury Tales* (ca. 1387–1400) or Ben Jonson's play *The Alchemist* (1610). In such works, greedy patrons are duped out of their money by charlatans promising to transmute base elements into gold for them. Zamos, by contrast, has found a way really to do it for himself.

9. Sometimes "tethumekh" is italicized, sometimes not. This may be the result of editorial inconsistency, as I can discern no pattern to the shifts. When quoting, I have retained italics when they appear in the novel.

10. Rowling did not invent Flamel. He was a historical figure. After his death, the legend of his alchemical accomplishments grew: "His legend involves meeting a Spanish *converso* [...] around 1380, obtaining a copy of the *Book of Abraham the Jew*, and allegedly solving the riddle of the Philosopher's Stone in time to bring his wife, Pernelle, back from the dead and gain immortality for himself" (74).

11. Gotlieb revisits the idea that a powerful telepath might have addictive appeal to others in "End City."

Chapter Seven

1. The folding of poetry into the landscape of Gotlieb's aliens becomes evident in her later novels. For instance, Skerow, a Khagodi who first appears in *Flesh and Gold*, is a poet who produces examples of the "*seh* written by Khagodi in the Northern Spine Confederacy," three lines of one, three and five syllables in any order. It is not the only form of poetry produced in the Spines, but certainly the one considered by critics in equatorial lands to be the most dry and frigid" (42). One sample should suffice to give a sense of whether the critical perspective reported in the novel seems accurate, or whether Gotlieb is having some fun at the expense of critics:

> *o*
> *this desert*
> *I drown in moonlight*
> [42; there is no terminal punctuation]

2. Given Gotlieb's recurrent interest in reproduction as a theme, and given the occasional hints at sexuality in this poem, there may be a sexual pun in this verb choice.

3. One of Auguste Rodin's (1840–1917) best-known sculptures is *The Kiss*, which depicts Francesca da Rimini about to kiss Paolo Malatesta, the brother of her husband Giovanni. For this adulterous transgression, they are murdered by Giovanni. Their story is recounted in Dante's *Inferno*. Rodin's work was consistently naturalistic and grounded in accurate depictions of the flesh, which rendered his work controversial; this sculpture especially was controversial for its frank eroticism. As a work of art, it demonstrates quite aptly that one can get plenty of "juice" into the act of artistic creation, in contrast to the apparently sterile relationship between the dry creator Scarpino and his rather more earthy wife.

4. Fuzzy Wuzzy was a bear.
Fuzzy Wuzzy had no hair.
Fuzzy Wuzzy wasn't fuzzy, was he?

5. These poems were originally published by John Robert Colombo on a single large sheet, though the publication tends to be described as a pamphlet in bibliographies of Gotlieb's work.

6. Dan Brown's invocation of the Fibonacci sequence in *The Da Vinci Code* as part of how Robert Langdon solves that book's mysteries has perhaps given this mathematical principle far greater cultural currency than it has ever had. The television show *Touch* also invoked the Fibonacci sequence as part of its attempts to rationalize its central gimmick: certain savants can see patterns in numbers that can help change the course of events. The link of the Fibonacci sequence to the "golden ratio" and to patterns recurring in nature—for instance, in the spiral pattern of a shell or in the patterns of how the components of flowers or pine cones interrelate—ties in with Gotlieb's invocation of complex circling/spiraling patterns here and elsewhere, as we shall see.

7. "Perhaps the most celebrated heroine in Canadian history" (Forster 226), Laura Secord aided in the War of 1812 by warning British troops at Beaver Dams, in the Niagara peninsula, of an impending American attack, thereby ensuring a British victory. She subsequently suffered decades of penury before finally being recognized, in her eighties, by the Prince of Wales, and given a substantial reward, as well as overdue public recognition. Today, however, she is perhaps better known as the namesake of a popular confectionery company, the maker of Laura Secord chocolates.

Chapter Eight

1. The "man of a thousand faces" was the silent film actor Lon Chaney, famous for his ability to use makeup to disguise himself thoroughly in his roles. This reference underscores subtly the performative nature of Rain's "identity."
2. "A Grain of Manhood" begins with Lela lying "formless" under the bedsheets (148), "Among You" with Rain waking in the morning "in semiform" (7), his body's plasticity rendering it slowly shapeless during slumber. But whereas Lela's narrative is a full quest, in which her visit to the otherworld is followed by a return and a reclamation of identity, and ending—significantly—with a birth, there seems no such possibility for Rain.
3. The most famous movie werewolf (indeed, he is arguably the most famous werewolf in any medium) is Larry Talbot, played by none other than Lon Chaney, Jr., son of the man of a thousand faces, in several Universal films.
4. Recall the clearly different explanation for the state of Shar females in 'Sunday's Child." In that story, the Shar's own actions caused their fertility problems, which then led them to seek out other worlds to claim and subjugate in order to find a path back to fertility. In this story, that premise is largely reversed, as the Shar now become the victims of a metaphorical rape of their world.
5. "Unwoman" as a verb meaning "to deprive of the qualities or traits of a woman; to remove from the category of women" (OED) has a long provenance, dating back at least until the seventeenth century. Its provenance as a noun is much more recent (indeed, it does not appear as a noun in the OED or in any other dictionary I checked), deriving from the fiction of another female Canadian SF writer/poet's work: Margaret Atwood's *The Handmaid's Tale*, published in 1985.

Conclusion

1. Admittedly, Sawyer has dual Canadian/U.S. citizenship.
2. To be fair, Atwood expresses no antipathy for the genre as such, merely rejecting the categorization of what she does in novels such as *The Handmaid's Tale* or the MaddAddam Trilogy (*Oryx and Crake* [2003], *The Year of the Flood* [2009], and *MaddAddam* [2013]) as SF. She has authored not one but two studies of the fantastical in literature, *Strange Things: The Malevolent North in Canadian Literature* (1995), and the science fiction-specific *In Other Worlds: SF and the Human Imagination* (2011). She was guest of honor at the 2003 Academic Conference on Canadian Science Fiction and Fantasy, at which she professed to be "very honoured" to have been invited (11), adding, "needless to say, I wouldn't be here if I had a disrespectful attitude towards the genre"("*Handmaid's* Tale" 12). Nevertheless, she did also repeat her notorious and often-cited identification of SF with "the talking squids of Saturn" (12).

Works Cited

Adams, Alice E. *Reproducing the Womb: Images of Childbirth in Science, Feminist Theory, and Literature*. Ithaca: Cornell University Press, 1994. Print.
Adso of Montier-en-Der. "Letter on the Origin and Time of Antichrist." ca. 950. Trans. Bernard McGinn. 1979. Web.
Amazing Stories 38.3 (1964). Print.
Armitt, Lucie, ed. *Where No Man Has Gone Before: Women and Science Fiction*. London: Routledge, 1991. Print.
Atwood, Margaret. "*The Handmaid's Tale* and *Oryx and Crake* in Context." *Further Perspectives on the Canadian Fantastic: Proceedings of the 2003 Academic Conference on Canadian Science Fiction and Fantasy*. Ed. Allan Weiss. Toronto: ACCSFF, 2005. 11–18. Print.
———. *In Other Worlds: SF and the Human Imagination*. Toronto: McClelland, 2011. Print.
———. *Strange Things: The Malevolent North in Canadian Literature*. Oxford: Clarendon, 1995. Print.
———. *Survival: A Thematic Guide to Canadian Literature*. 1972. Toronto: Anansi, 2012. Print.
Axtell, James. *The European and the Indian: Essays in the Ethnohistory of North America*. Oxford: Oxford University Press, 1981. Web.
Baert, Barbara. "Caliban as a Wild-Man: An Iconographical Approach." *Constellation Caliban: Figurations of a Character*. Ed. Nadia Lie and Theo D'haen. Amsterdam: Rodopi, 1997. 43–59. Print.
Barbour, Douglas. "Phyllis Gotlieb." *Canadian Fantasy and Science-Fiction Writers. Dictionary of Literary Biography* vol. 251. Ed. Douglas Ivison. Detroit: Gale, 2002. 108–20. Print.
———. "Phyllis Gotlieb's Children of the Future: *Sunburst* and *Ordinary, Moving*." *Journal of Canadian Fiction* 3.2 (1974): 72–76. Print.
Barnosky, Jason. "The Violent Years: Responses to Juvenile Crime in the 1950s." *Polity* 38.3 (2006): 314–44. Print.
Barr, Marleen S. *Feminist Fabulations: Space/Postmodernist Fiction*. Iowa: University of Iowa Press, 1992. Print
———. *Lost in Space: Probing Feminist Science Fiction and Beyond*. Chapel Hill: University of North Carolina Press, 1993. Print.
Bell, John. *The Far North and Beyond: An Index to Canadian Science Fiction and Fantasy in English-Language Genre Magazines and Other Selected Periodicals of the Pulp Era, 1896–1955*. Halifax: Dalhousie University School of Library and Information Studies, 1998. Print.
Bentley, D. M. R. "Colonial Colonizing: An Introductory Survey of the Canadian Long Poem." *Bolder Flights: Essays on the Canadian Long Poem*. Ed. Frank M. Tierney and Angela Robbeson. Reappraisals: Canadian Writers 21. Ottawa: University of Ottawa Press, 1998. 7–29. Print.
Bergmann, Claudia D. "Jonah 2:1–11: Expressing a Personal Crisis through the Birth Metaphor." *Seminary Ridge Review* 7.1 (2004): 5–15. Print.
Bliss, Jane. *Naming and Namelessness in Medieval Romance*. Woodbridge: D. S. Brewer, 2008. Print.

Bloch, Chayim. *The Golem: Legends of the Prague Ghetto*. [1919]. Trans. Harry Schneiderman. New York: Rudolf Steiner, 1972. Print.
Bloom, Harold. Introduction. *Caliban*. Ed. Bloom. New York: Chelsea House, 1992. 1–4. Print.
Briscoe, Susan. "Not Lost in Space: Phyllis Gotlieb." *Books in Canada*. Web.
Browning, Robert. "Caliban upon Setebos; or, Natural Theology in the Island." *Robert Browning: The Poems* vol. 1. Ed. John Pettigrew and Thomas J. Collins. New Haven: Yale University Press, 1981. 805–12. Print.
Brunet, Michel. "Quand un historien se mêle de lire dans la boule di cristal." *Visions 2020*. Ed. Stephen Clarkson. Edmonton: Hurtig, 1970. 123–27.
Brydon, Diana. "Re-writing *The Tempest*." *World Literature Written in English* 23.1 (1984): 75–88. Web.
Chanady, Amaryll. "Representations of the Native and the New World Subject." *Canada and Its Americas: Transnational Navigations*. Ed. Winfried Siemerling and Sarah Phillips Casteel. Montreal: McGill-Queen's University Press, 2010. 85–101. Print.
Clute, John. "Fables of Transcendence: The Challenge of Canadian Science Fiction." *Paradis* 20–27. Print.
_____. *Science Fiction: The Illustrated Encyclopedia*. New York: Dorling Kindersley, 1995. Print.
Colombo, John Robert. "Four Hundred Years of Fantastic Literature in Canada." *Out of This World: Canadian Science Fiction and Fantasy*. Comp. Andrea Paradis. Quarry Press/National Library of Canada, 1995. 28–40. Print.
Cornell, Christine. "The Interpretive Journey in Ursula k. Le Guin's *The Left Hand of Darkness*." *Extrapolation* 42.4 (2001): 317–27. Print.
Cory, Catherine A. *The Book of Revelation*. Collegeville: Liturgical Press, 2006. Print.
Creed, Barbara. *The Monstrous-Feminine: Film Feminism, Psychoanalysis*. New York: Routledge, 1993. Print.
Davis, Michael, ed. *Samson Agonistes*. By John Milton. London: Macmillan, 1968. Print.
Deery, June. "The Biopolitics of Cyberspace: Piercy Hacks Gibson." *Future Females, the Next Generation: New Voices and Velocities in Feminist Science Fiction Criticism*. Ed. Marleens. Barr. Lanham: Rowman & Littlefield, 2000. 87–108. Print.
Delabastita, Dirk. "Caliban's Afterlife." *Constellation Caliban: Figurations of a Character*. Ed. Nadia Lie and Theo D'haen. Amsterdam: Rodopi, 1997. 1–22. Print.
Donawerth, Jane. "The Feminist Dystopia of the 1990s: Record of Failure, Midwife of Hope." *Future Females, the Next Generation: New Voices and Velocities in Feminist Science Ficion Criticism*. Ed. Marleen S. Barr. New York: Rowman and Littlefield, 2000. 49–66. Print.
_____. *Frankenstein's Daughters: Women Writing Science Fiction*. Syracuse: Syracuse University Press, 1997. Print.
_____, and Carol A. Kolmerten, eds. *Utopian and Science Fiction by Women: Worlds of Difference*. Syracuse: Syracuse University Press, 1994. Print.
Dorsinville, Max. *Shakespeare Without Prospero: Essay on Quebec and Black Literature*. Erin: Press Porcepic, 1974. Print.
Drache, Daniel, and Roberto Perin. "Introduction." *Negotiating with a Sovereign Quebec*. Ed. Daniel Drache and Roberto Perin. Toronto: Lorimer, 1992. 1–10. Print.
DuPree, Don Keck. "Nicholas Flamel: The Alchemist Who Lived." *Harry Potter and History*. Ed. Nancy R. Reagin. Hoboken: Wiley, 2011. 73–90. Web.
Elliott, Dyan. *Fallen Bodies: Pollution, Sexuality, and Demonology in the Middle Ages*. Philadelphia: University of Pennsylvania Press, 1999. Print.
Empson, William. "A Defense of Delilah." *The Sewanee Review* 68.2 (1960): 240–55. Print.
Esmonde, Margaret P. "From Little Buddy to Big Brother: the Icon of the Robot in Children's Science Fiction." *The Mechanical God: Machines in Science Fiction*. Ed. Thomas P. Dunn and Richard D. Ehrlich. Westport: Greenwood, 1982. 85–98. Print.
Forster, Merna. *100 Canadian Heroines: Famous and Forgotten Faces*. Toronto: Dundurn, 2004. Web.
Fredericks, Casey. *The Future of Eternity: Mythologies of Science Fiction and Fantasy*. Bloomington: Indiana University Press, 1982. Print.
Gibson, William. *Neuromancer*. New York: Ace, 1984.
Glueck, Sheldon, and Eleanor Glueck. *Delinquents in the Making, Paths to Prevention*. New York: Harper, 1952. Print.

———. *Physique and Delinquency*. 1956. New York: Kraus, 1970. Print.
Goldsmith, Arnold L. *The Golem Remembered, 1909–1980: Variations of a Jewish Legend*. Detroit: Wayne State University Press, 1981. Print.
Gotlieb, Phyllis. "The Alien at the Feast: The Publishers of and the Audience for Fantastic Literature in Canada." *Out of This World: Canadian Science Fiction and Fantasy Literature*. Comp. Andrea Paradis. Quarry Press/National Library of Canada, 1995. 197–203. Print.
———. "All the Blue Apes: An Interview with Phyllis Gotlieb by David Mathew." *Infinity Plus*. 2000. Web.
———. "Among You." *Blue Apes*. Edmonton: Tesseract, 1995. 7–25. Print.
———. *Birthstones*. Calgary: Robert J. Sawyer Books, 2007. Print.
———. "Blue Apes." *Blue Apes*. Edmonton: Tesseract, 1995. 226–71. Print.
———. "Body English." *Blue Apes*. Edmonton: Tesseract, 1995. 105–09. Print.
———. "A Bone to Pick." *Fantastic, Stories of Imagination* 9.10 (October 1960): 48–71. Print.
———. "The Dirty Old Men of Maxsec." *Galaxy* 27.4 (November 1969): 53–95. Print.
———. *Emperor, Swords, Pentacles*. New York: Ace, 1982. Print.
———. "End City." *Science Fiction Age* 5.3 (March 1997): 45–60. Print.
———. "Entrevue: Phyllis Gotlieb." *Solaris* 69 (1986): 16–17. Print.
———. *Fifth of Gemini*. ts. Merril Collection, Toronto Public Library, College St., Toronto, Ontario.
———. *Flesh and Gold*. New York: Tor, 1998. Print.
———. "Gingerbread Boy." *Son of the Morning and Other Stories*. New York: Ace, 1983. 80–94. Print.
———. "A Grain of Manhood." *Son of the Morning and Other Stories*. New York: Ace, 1983. 148–59. Print.
———. "A Grain of Manhood." ts. Merril Collection, Toronto Public Library, College St., Toronto, Ontario.
———. "Hasidic Influences in the Work of A. M. Klein." *The A. M. Klein Symposium*. Ed. Seymour Mayne. Ottawa: University of Ottawa Press, 1975. Print.
———. *Heart of Red Iron*. New York: St. Martin's, 1989. Print.
———. "Interview with Phyllis Gotlieb." *Challenging Destiny*. 1999. April 24, 2005. Web.
———. *A Judgment of Dragons*. New York: Berkley, 1980. Print.
———. *The Kingdom of the Cats*. New York: Ace, 1985. Print.
———. "The Military Hospital." *Blue Apes*. Edmonton: Tesseract, 1995. 86–104. Print.
———. *Mindworlds*. New York: Tor, 2002. Print.
———. "The Monkey Wrench." ts. Merril Collection, Toronto Public Library, College St., Toronto, Ontario.
———. "Monkey Wrench." *Blue Apes*. Edmonton: Tesseract, 1995. 110–144. Print.
———. "Mother Lode." *Blue Apes*. Edmonton: Tesseract, 1995. 59–85. Print.
———. "The Newest Profession." *Blue Apes*. Edmonton: Tesseract, 1995. 202–225. Print.
———. "No End of Time." ts. Merril Collection, Toronto Public Library, College St., Toronto, Ontario.
———. "No End of Time." *Fantastic Science Fiction Stories* 9.6 (June 1960): 105–26. Print.
———. *O Master Caliban!* ts. Fair copy with cuts. 1976. Merril Collection, Toronto Public Library, College St., Toronto, Ontario.
———. *O Master Caliban!* 1976. Toronto: Seal, 1979. Print.
———. "The Other Eye." *Blue Apes*. Edmonton: Tesseract, 1995. 53–58. Print.
———. "Phantom Foot." ts. Merril Collection, Toronto Public Library, College St., Toronto, Ontario.
———. "Phantom Foot." *Son of the Morning and Other Stories*. New York: Ace, 1983. 131–47. Print.
———. "Planetoid Idiot." *The Magazine of Fantasy and Science Fiction* 32.5 (May 1967): 4–75. Print.
———. *Red Blood Black Ink White Paper: New and Selected Poems 1961–2001*. Toronto: Exile, 2002. Print.
———. "SCORE/SCORE." *Visions 2020*. Ed. Stephen Clarkson. Edmonton: M. G. Hurtig, 1970. 211–21. Print.
———. *Sunburst*. Greenwich: Fawcett, 1964. Print.
———. "Sunday's Child." *Blue Apes*. Edmonton: Tesseract, 1995. 145–97. Print.

———. "Tauf Aleph." *Blue Apes*. Edmonton: Tesseract, 1995. 26–52. Print.
———. "Valedictory." *Amazing Stories* 38.8 (1964): 46–52. Print.
———. *Violent Stars*. New York: Tor, 1999. Print.
———. "We Can't Go on Meeting Like This." *Blue Apes*. Edmonton: Tesseract, 1995. 198–201. Print.
———. "What Makes a Good Fantasy Poem?" *TransVersions* 1.2 (1995): 3. Print.
———. *The Works: Collected Poems*. Toronto: Calliope Press, 1978. Print.
———, and Jean-Louis Trudel. "Waiting Till the Stars Scream." *TransVersions* 8/9 (1998): 109–17. Print.
Grace, Dominick. "Mind Matters: Intellect and Identity in the Works of Phyllis Gotlieb." *Worlds of Wonder: Readings in Canadian Science Fiction and Fantasy*. Reappraisals: Canadian Writers 26. Ed. Jean-François Leroux and Camille R. La Bossière. Ottawa: U of Ottawa P, 2004. 105–17.
Haresnape, Geoffrey. "No Fish, but an Islander: An Early Portrayal of Caliban as a First Nation Beothuk of Newfoundland." *Shakespeare in Southern Africa* 11 (1998): 1–13. Web.
Hazleton, Lesley. *Mary: A Flesh-and-Blood Biography of the Virgin Mother*. New York: Bloomsbury, 2004. Web.
Heidegger, Martin. *What Is Called Thinking?* 1954. Trans. J. Glenn Grey. 1968. New York: Harper Perennial, 1976. Print.
"Hey Quebec, Enough Already." *Toronto Sun*, March 29 2011. Web.
Idel, Moshe. *Golem: Jewish Magical and Mystical Traditions on the Artificial Anthropoid*. Albany: State University of New York Press, 1990. Print.
Irigiray, Luce. *Speculum of the Other Woman*. 1974. Trans. Gillian C. Gill. Ithaca: Cornell University Press, 1985. Print.
Jerome. *Jerome's Commentary on Daniel*. 406. Trans. Gleason L. Archer, Jr. Grand Rapids: Baker, 1958. Web.
Johnston, Nancy. "'and nobody knows where we are going from here': Phyllis Gotlieb's Speculative Poetry." *Perspectives on the Canadian Fantastic: Proceedings of the 1997 Conference on Canadian Science Fiction and Fantasy*. Ed. Allan Weiss. Toronto: ACCSFF, 1998. 69–74. Print.
Kakoudaki, Despina. "Pinup and Cyborg: Exaggerated Gender and Artificial Intelligence." *Future Females, the Next Generation: New Voices and Velocities in Feminist Science Fiction Criticism*. Ed. Marleen S. Barr. Lanham: Rowman & Littlefield, 2000. 165–95. Print.
Kambourelli, Smaro. *On the Edge of Genre: The Contemporary Canadian Long Poem*. Toronto: University of Toronto Press, 1991. Print.
Kang, Minsoo. "Building the Sex Machine: The Subversive Potential of the Female Robot." *Intertexts* 9. (Spring 2005): 5–22. Web.
Ketterer, David. *Canadian Science Fiction and Fantasy*. Bloomington: Indiana University Press, 1992. Print.
King, Andrew. "Sidney and Spenser." *A Companion to Medieval Romance: From Classical to Contemporary*. Ed. Corinne Saunders. Malden: Blackwell, 2004. 140–59. Web.
Kinnaird, John. *Olaf Stapledon*. Mercer Island: Starmont, 1986. Print.
Kornfeld, Susan. "Suppression and Transformation of the Maternal in Contemporary Women's Science Fiction." *Extrapolation* 45.1 (Spring 2004): 65–75. Print.
Kramer, Reinhold. "The Contemporary Canadian Long Poem as System: Freisen, Atwood, Kroetsch, Arnason, McFadden." *Bolder Flights: Essays on the Canadian Long Poem*. Ed. Frank M. Tierney and Angela Robbeson. Reappraisals: Canadian Writers 21. Ottawa: University of Ottawa Press, 1998. 101–14. Print.
Kristeva, Julia. *Powers of Horror: An Essay on Abjection*. 1980. Trans. Leon S. Roudiez. New York: Columbia University Press, 1982. Print.
Kulyk, Christine L. "Consider Her Ways: Canadian Science Fiction and Fantasy by Women." *Out of This World: Canadian Science Fiction and Fantasy Literature*. Comp. Andrea Paradis. Quarry Press/National Library of Canada, 159–69. Print.
Lancashire, Ian, ed. "Ordinary, Moving." By Phyllis Gotlieb. *Representative Poetry Online*. Web.
Lane, M. Travis. "Gotlieb Phyllis." *The Oxford Companion to Canadian Literature*. 2d ed. Eds. Eugene Benson and William Toye. Don Mills: Oxford University Press, 1997. 476–77. Print.
Lefanu, Sarah. *Feminism and Science Fiction*. Bloomington: Indiana University Press, 1989. Print.
Le Guin, Ursula K. "Is Gender Necessary?" *The Language of the Night: Essays on Fantasy and Science Fiction*. New York: Putnam, 1979. 161–69. Print.

———. "Is Gender Necessary? Redux." *Dancing at the Edge of the World: Thoughts on Words, Women, Places*. New York: Harper, 1989. 7–16. Print.
———. *The Left Hand of Darkness*. New York: Ace, 1969. Print.
Letson, Russell. "Portraits of Machine Consciousness." *The Mechanical God: Machines in Science Fiction*. Eds. Thomas P. Dunn and Richard D. Erlich. Contributions to the Study of Science Fiction and Fantasy 1. Westport: Greenwood Press, 1982. 101–08. Print.
Lie, Nadia, and Theo D'haen, eds. *Constellation Caliban: Figurations of a Character*. Amsterdam: Rodopi, 1997. Print.
Lutts, Ralph H. "The Wild Animal Story: Animals and Ideas." *The Wild Animal Story*. Ed. Ralph H. Lutts. Philadelphia: Temple University Press, 1998. 1–21. Print.
Lynn, Elizabeth A. "Introduction." *Sunburst*. By Phyllis Gotlieb. Boston: Gregg, 1978. v–xv. Print.
Malamud, Randy. *Poetic Animals and Animal Souls*. New York: Palgrave, 2003. Print.
Marshall, Tom. *Harsh and Lovely Land: The Major Canadian Poets and the Making of a Canadian Tradition*. Vancouver: University of Vancouver Press, 1979. Print.
Mazis, Glen A. *Humans, Animals, Machines: Blurring Boundaries*. Albany: SUNY Press, 2008. Print.
McGuirk, Carol. "NoWhere Man: Towards a Poetics of Post-Utopian Characterization." *Science-Fiction Studies* 21.2 (1994): 141–54. Print.
Mead, Margaret. *People and Places: A Resource Book*. Cleveland: World Publishing, 1959. Print.
Meyer-Baer, Kathy. *Music of the Spheres and the Dance of Death: Studies in Musical Iconology*. Princeton: Princeton University Press, 1970. Print.
Miller, Mark J. "The Pinocchio Syndrome: Lying and Its Impact on the Counseling Process." *Counseling and Values* 37.1 (1992). Web.
Milton, John. *Samson Agonistes*. Ed. Michael Davis. London: Macmillan, 1968. Print.
Moss, Rachel E. *Fatherhood and Its Representation sin Middle English Texts*. Cambridge: D. S. Brewer, 2013. Web.
"Nephilim." *Encyclopaedia Judaica*. 2d ed. Ed. Michael Berenbaum and Fred Skolnik. Detroit: Macmillan Reference, 2007. Web.
Newell, Dianne, and Victoria Lamont. "Rugged Domesticity: Frontier Mythology in Post-Armageddon Fiction by Women." *Science Fiction Studies* 32.3 (2005): 423–41. Print.
Nicholls, Peter, and John Clute, eds. *The Encyclopedia of Science Fiction*. Gollancz, 2011. Web.
Origen. *The Writings of Origen. Volume II: Origen Contra Celsum*. Trans. Frederick Crombie. Edinburgh: T. & T. Clark, 1872. Web.
Panshin, Alexei. "Books." Rev. of *The Left Hand of Darkness*, by Ursula Le Guin. *The Magazine of Fantasy & Science Fiction*, 37.5 (1969): 50–51. Print.
Paradis, Andrea, comp. *Out of This World: Canadian Science Fiction and Fantasy Literature*. [np]: Quarry Press/National Library of Canada, 1995. Print.
Pearl. Ed. Sarah Stanbury. Kalamazoo: Medieval Institute Publications, 2001. Print.
Pearson, Wendy Gay. "Postcolonialism/s, Gender/s, Sexuality/ies and the Legacy of *The Left Hand of Darkness*: Gwyneth Jones's Aleutians Talk Back." *The Yearbook of English Studies* 37.2 (2007): 182–96. Web.
Phips, Spencer. "A Proclamation. Whereas the Whereas the Tribe of *Penobscot* Indians...." 1755. *Archive of Americana*. Web.
Potts, Robert. "Light in the Wilderness." *The Guardian* 26 April 2003. Web.
Principe, Lawrence M. *The Secrets of Alchemy*. Chicago: University of Chicago Press, 2012. Print.
Pryse-Philips, William. *Companion to Clinical Neurology*. 3rd ed. Oxford: Oxford University Press, 2009. Print.
Rabkin, Eric S. "The Composite Fiction of Olaf Stapledon." *Science-Fiction Studies* 9.3 (1982): 238–48. Print.
Ransom, Amy J. *Science Fiction from Québec: A Postcolonial Study*. Jefferson: McFarland, 2009.
Rose, Mark. *Alien Encounters: Anatomy of Science Fiction*. Cambridge: Harvard University Press, 1981. Print.
Rosen, Susan A. C. "Littoral Women Writing from the Margins." *Women Writing Nature: A Feminist View*. Ed. Barbara J. Cook. Lanham: Lexington Books, 2008. 21–31. Print.
Rosinsky, Natalie M. *Feminist Futures: Contemporary Women's Science Fiction*. Studies in Speculative Fiction No. 1. Ann Arbor: UMI Research Press, 1984. Print.

Runté, Robert, and Christine Kulyk. "The Northern Cosmos: Distinctive Themes in Canadian SF." *Out of This World: Canadian Science Fiction and Fantasy Literature*. Comp. Andrea Paradis. Quarry Press/National Library of Canada, 1995. 41–50. Print.
Russ, Joanna. "The Images of Women in Science Fiction." *Images of Women in Fiction: Feminist Perspectives*. Ed. Susan Koppelman Cornillon. Bowling Green: Bowling Green University Popular Press, 1972. 79–94. Print.
Russell, Paul. "Today's Letters: Majority Say It's Time for Quebec to Go." *National Post*, May 14, 2012. Web.
Sales, Ian. "*Sunburst*, Phyllis Gotlieb." *SF Mistressworks*. Web.
Sanders, Arnold. "Sir Gareth and the 'Unfair Unknown': Malory's Use of the Gawain Romances." *Arthuriana* 16.1 (2006): 34–46. Web.
Sanders, Joe. "Tools/Mirrors: The Humanization of Machines." *The Mechanical God: Machines in Science Fiction*. Eds. Thomas P. Dunn and Richard D. Erlich. Contributions to the Study of Science Fiction and Fantasy 1. Westport: Greenwood Press, 1982. 167–76. Print.
Saunders, Corinne J. *Magic and the Supernatural in Medieval English Romance*. Cambridge: D. S. Brewer, 2010. Print.
Sawyer, Robert J. "Phyllis Gotlieb and Kelly Gotlieb." SFWriter.com. July 17 2009. Web.
———. "Phyllis Gotlieb Honoured Today in Canada's Federal Parliament." SFWriter.com. November 27, 2009. Web.
Scholem, Gershom G. *On the Kabbalah and Its Symbolism*. 1960. Trans. Ralph Manheim. New York: Schocken, 1965. Print.
Scholtmeijer, Marian. *Animal Victims in Modern Fiction: From Sanctity to Sacrifice*. Toronto: University of Toronto Press, 1993. Print.
Shakespeare, William. *The Tempest*. Ed. Stephen Orgel. Oxford: Oxford University Press, 1987. Print.
Shaw, Debra Bonita. *Women, Science and Fiction: The* Frankenstein *Inheritance*. Houndmills: Palgrave, 2000. Print.
Shawcross, John T. *The Uncertain World of* Samson Agonistes. Woodbridge: D. S. Brewer, 2001. Print.
Sheldon, William H. *Varieties of Delinquent Youth: An Introduction to Constitutional Psychology*. New York: Harper, 1949. Print.
Sherwin, Byron L. *The Golem Legend: Origins and Implications*. Lanham: University Press of America, 1985. Print.
Shinn, Thelma J. *Worlds Within Women: Myth and Mythmaking in Fantastic Literature by Women*. Contributions to the Study of Science Fiction and Fantasy, Number 22. New York: Greenwood, 1986. Print.
Spinoza, Benedict de. *The Ethics and On the Improvement of Understanding*. Trans R. H. M. Elwes. Stillwell: Digireads.com, 2008. Web.
Stapledon, Olaf. *Odd John and Sirius*. New York: Dover, 1972. Print.
Stephens, Walter. *Demon Lovers: Witchcraft, Sex, and the Crisis of Belief*. Chicago: University of Chicago Press, 2002.
Stone-Blackburn, Susan. "Consciousness Evolution and Early Telepathic Tales." *Science-Fiction Studies* 20.2 (1993): 241–50.
Suvin, Darko. *Metamorphoses of Science Fiction: On the Poetics and History of a Literary Genre*. New Haven: Yale University Press, 1979. Print.
Swanson, Roy Arthur. "The Spiritual Factor in *Odd John* and *Sirius*." *Science-Fiction Studies* 9.3 (1982): 284–93. Print.
Taylor, Neil. "Ferdinand and Miranda at Chess." *Shakespeare Survey* 35 (1982): 113–18. Print.
Tilley, Carol. "Seducing the Innocent: Fredric Wertham and the Falsifications That Helped Condemn Comics." *Information and Culture: A Journal of History* 47.4 (2012): 383–413. Web.
Titze ,Michael. "Gelotophobia: The Fear of Being Laughed At." *International Journal of Humor Research* 22.1–2 (2009): 27–48. Web.
"Unjustly Neglected Works of Science Fiction: A Survey." *Science-Fiction Studies* 20.3 (1993): 422–32. Print.
Van Vogt, A. E. *Slan*. Rev. ed. 1968. New York: Berkley, 1975. Print.
Vaughan, Alden T., and Virginia Mason Vaughan. *Shakespeare's Caliban: A Cultural History*. Cambridge: Cambridge University Press, 1991. Print.

Vint, Sherryl. *Animal Alterity: Science Fiction and the Question of the Animal.* Liverpool: Liverpool University Press, 2010.
Vogel, Howard J. "Healing the Trauma of America's Past: Restorative Justice, Honest Patriotism, and the Legacy of Ethnic Cleansing." *Buffalo Law Review* 55.3 (2007): 981–1046. Web.
Vonarburg, Élisabeth. "Women and Science Fiction." *Out of This World: Canadian Science Fiction and Fantasy Literature.* Comp. Andrea Paradis. Quarry Press/National Library of Canada, 1995. 177–87. Print.
Walburg, David. "My Canada Includes Quebec." *Yorkton News.* August 24, 2012. Web.
Weiss, Allan. "Beyond Human: Fading Boundaries Between Human and Machine in Canadian Science Fiction." *Foundation* 81 (2001): 68–75.
_____, ed. *Further Perspectives on the Canadian Fantastic: Proceedings of the 2003 Conference on Canadian Science Fiction and Fantasy.* Toronto: ACCSFF, 2005.
_____, ed. *Perspectives on the Canadian Fantastic: Proceedings of the 1997 Conference on Canadian Science Fiction and Fantasy.* Toronto: ACCSFF, 1998.
Wells, H. G. *The War of the Worlds.* 1898. *Project Gutenberg.* Web.
Wolfe, Gary K. *The Known and the Unknown: The Iconography of Science Fiction.* Kent: Kent State University Press, 1979. Print.
Wollheim, Donald A. *The Universe Makers: Science Fiction Today.* New York: Harper and Row, 1971. Print.
Wolmark, Jenny. *Aliens and Others: Science Fiction, Feminism, and Postmodernism.* New York: Harvester, 1994. Print.
Wordsworth, William. "My Heart Leaps Up When I Behold." 1802. *William Wordsworth: Complete Poetical Works.* Bartleby.com. Web.
Yaszek, Lisa. *Galactic Suburbia: Recovering Women's Science Fiction.* Columbus: Ohio State University Press, 2008. Print.
Youngs, Tim. "Cruising Against the Id: The Transformation of Caliban in *Forbidden Planet*." *Constellation Caliban: Figurations of a Character.* Eds. Nadia Lie and Theo D'haen. 211–29. Print.
Zabus, Chantal. "A Calibanic Tempest in Anglophone & Francophone New World Writing." *Canadian Literature* 104 (1985): 35–50. Web.
_____. *Tempests After Shakespeare.* Houndmills: Palgrave, 2002. Print.

Index

Adam (Biblical character) 95, 96, 120, 121, 122
Adams, Alice E. 105
Adso 103, 105
Alchemy 157–158, 159, 160, 213–214n6, 214n7, 214n8, 214n10
"Among you" 187, 189–190, 215n2
Amsu 109–111, 164
Androids 23–24, 33, 65, 72, 94, 107–108, 120; see also Mod-Dahlgren; O'e
Animals 7, 24, 33–34, 35, 44–45, 48–50, 56–61, 65, 66, 67, 70–71, 73, 76, 78, 80, 81, 83–84, 85, 89–90, 93, 94, 96–98, 110–113, 127–128, 134–139, 141–143, 151, 154, 159, 161, 162, 165, 174–175, 184, 188–189, 190, 193, 194, 199, 206n3, 208–209n10, 213n10, 213n12, 213ch6n1
Anthropocentrism 7, 8, 57, 69, 124, 126, 135–139, 141–142, 149, 199
Anti-Christ 103–107, 109, 211n3, 211n8
Armitt, Lucie 3
Artificial beings 6, 120, 125–126, 209n3; see also Androids; Clones; Golem; Robots
Asimov, Isaac 115, 210n1
Atwood, Margaret 2, 4, 64, 202, 215n5, 215ch8n2
Axtell, James 144

Babbage, Charles 95
Baert, Barbara 85
Banks, Iain 8
Barbour, Douglas 2, 5, 8, 42, 56, 70, 74, 172, 210ch4n1
Barnosky, Jason 54
Baron, Neil 2
Barr, Marleen S. 2, 65
Bell, John 1
Bentley, D. M. R. 172

Bester, Alfred 120, 207n4
The Bible 12, 15–17, 20, 95, 102, 103, 105, 106, 109, 119–120, 121, 133, 142–143, 163, 165, 206n4, 211n9, 211n12
Birthstones 4, 5, 6, 10, 12, 100, 187, 195–200, 203, 205n3, 207n9, 210n2, 211n5
Bliss, Jane 52
Bloch, Chayim 121
Bloom, Harold 77, 78
Blue Apes 10, 189, 207n10
"Blue Apes" 29, 31, 109, 111–113
"Body English" 126, 187–189
"A Bone to Pick" 24, 27, 28–29, 31, 33, 205ch1n1, 211n11
Brackett, Leigh 3
Bradbury, Ray 207n14
Brin, David 120, 127
Briscoe, Susan 3
Browning, Robert 63, 75, 78–81, 82, 83, 84, 86
Brunet, Michel 114–115
Brydon, Diana 74, 80, 85
Burwell, Jennifer 1

Caesarius of Heisterbach 108
Caliban 74–76, 77–82, 83–86
"Caliban upon Setebos" see Browning, Robert
Canadian Science Fiction 1, 2, 4, 5, 8, 9, 29, 33, 42, 64, 65, 98, 115, 138, 148, 149, 201, 202, 205n3, 207n1, 210n1
Capitalism 27, 30–31, 32, 195–197, 199
Chandy, Amaryll 97
Chaucer, Geoffrey 104, 214n8
Christ 15–16, 18, 103, 106–107, 164, 211n3
Christianity 14, 16, 18, 103–104, 164–165, 206n4, 206n5
Clarke, Arthur C. 104, 207n4

Clones 67–68, 81, 85, 87, 90, 93, 94–95, 112, 142, 150, 151–152, 154, 156, 159, 162, 163–164, 166, 169
Clute, John 1, 2, 8, 205n4
Cnidori 120, 122–125
Colombo, John Robert 2, 8–9, 32, 214n5
Colonialism 9, 26–27, 30–32, 64, 74, 86–87, 88, 91, 96–98, 100, 101, 109–113, 119, 125, 143–46, 147, 150, 155, 159, 168, 181, 187, 195–97, 208n10, 213n12
Computers 30, 37, 39, 72, 83, 95, 114–116, 120, 207n11, 209n5, 210n10
Cornell, Christine 136
Creator Matrix One *see* Erg-Queen
Creed, Barbara 196
Cyborgs 72, 120, 156, 162

Dahlgren, Edvard 2, 31, 32, 64–73, 75, 76, 77, 78–79, 80–84, 85–86, 87–88, 90, 91, 93, 95, 96, 98, 102, 121, 128, 131, 135, 142, 143, 145, 160, 162, 173, 203, 209–210n6
Dahlgren, Sven 32, 65–66, 67, 69, 70, 73, 75–77, 80–81, 85, 87, 90, 91–92, 93, 97–98, 160, 209–210n6, 210n11
Davidson, Avram 120
Davis, Michael 15, 17
Deery, June 98
Delabastita, Dirk 77
Delinquency, juvenile 50–51, 54–55, 60, 61, 76–77, 192, 203, 208n8, 208n9
Del Rey, Lester 116
Demon *see* Devil
Descartes, René 130
Devil 23, 103–106, 108, 133, 141, 207n3, 211n8, 213n9; *see also* Satan
Dickson, Gordon R. 4, 8, 207n10
"The Dirty Old Men of Maxsec" 33, 36–39, 112, 206n1, 207n12
Donawerth, Jane 3, 32, 72, 73, 195
Dorsinville, Max 74
Drache, Daniel 115
Dystopia 33, 36–39, 101, 192, 207n12

Elliott, Dyan 108
Ellison, Harlan 36
Emperor, Swords, Pentacles 7, 10, 27, 127, 129, 131, 134, 137, 138, 139–140, 142, 145–147, 177
Empson, William 15
Encid 129–131, 133–134, 135, 210n9
"End City" 187, 190–194, 195, 206n1, 214n11
Erg-Dahlgren *see* Mod Dahlgren
Erg-Queen 6, 64, 67, 68, 69, 71–73, 75, 78, 79, 80–81, 82–83, 84, 85, 88, 94, 95, 97, 98, 115, 116, 119, 155, 209n4, 210n6
Ergs *see* Robots

Esmonde, Margaret P. 116
ESP *see* Psi powers

Fair unknown 52–53, 104–105
Fairy tales *see* Folk tales
Feminism 1, 2–3, 65, 195–198
Fibonacci sequence 177, 214n6
"Fifth of Gemini" 205n1, 207n12, 209n2
First Nations peoples 74, 96–97, 100, 143–145, 149, 213n12
Flamel, Nicholas 160, 214n10
Fleming, Ian 37
Flesh and Gold 10, 126, 150, 152, 153–154, 155–160, 161, 163, 165, 166, 167, 169, 212n4, 213n5, 214n1
Folk Tales 13–14, 15, 23, 35, 111–112
Forbidden Planet 6, 79, 209n5
Frankenstein 6, 43, 64–66, 68, 69, 72, 73, 120, 173, 209n2
Fredericks, Casey 42, 43, 207n4

Galactic Empire 7–9, 24–25, 32–33, 40, 98, 148–149
Galactic Federation *see* GalFed
GalFed 2, 5, 7, 8–9, 11–12, 24–33, 36, 39–40, 63–64, 66, 67, 76, 85, 86, 91, 92, 93, 96–98, 100, 108–111, 113, 128, 130, 132, 135, 138, 140–141, 148, 153, 155, 159–160, 163, 166–167, 168, 170, 171, 188, 190, 192, 200, 206n6, 207n2, 212n4, 213n2
"Geffen and Ravna" 171, 175, 180–186
Genetic engineering 6, 23–24, 31, 33, 65–67, 70–71, 73, 90, 112–113, 127, 139–140, 151, 156, 159–160, 161, 188, 199, 205n1, 206n9, 213n2
Ghyrrm 27–29, 33
Gibson, William 188, 212n5
"Gingerbread Boy" 23–24, 102, 206n3
Glueck, Eleanor 54–55, 208n9
Glueck, Sheldon 54–55, 208n9
Godzilla 173
Goldsmith, Arnold L. 120
Golem 69, 96, 109, 120–126, 210n12
Gotlieb, Calvin (Kelly) 4, 5, 210n10
"A Grain of Manhood" 6, 12–22, 23, 28, 39, 63, 98, 105, 109, 111, 174, 187, 189, 190, 195, 206, 215n2
Green, Terence M. 42

Harrison, Harry 63–64
Harry Potter series 52, 157–158, 160, 213–214n6, 214n10
Hazleton, Lesley 16
Heart of Red Iron 6, 10, 27, 32, 63, 64, 86–98, 100, 115, 118, 128, 134, 151, 194, 202, 210

Heidegger, Martin 142, 213n10
Heinlein, Robert 24, 36, 42, 213n9
The Holocaust 5, 206n9
Hopkinson, Nalo 4
Hypnoforming 133, 137, 142, 143, 154, 164

Idel, Moshe 122
Identity 4, 12–13, 19–21, 39–40, 52, 63, 89, 91, 98, 114–116, 120, 121, 124, 129, 133, 139–140, 143, 146–148, 150, 154, 157, 166–168, 172–175, 180–181, 183–186, 189–190, 196, 210n10, 215ch8n1, 215ch8n2
Indian *see* First Nations peoples
Irigiray, Luce 105–106, 211n6
Ivison, Douglas J. 1, 2
Ix 150, 154–157, 162–163, 164–165, 197, 198, 213n4

Jerome, St. 103
Jewishness 5, 6, 9, 29, 96, 103, 119–125, 130, 178, 180, 206n4, 206n5, 206–207n9, 210n1, 210–211n2
Johnson, Samuel 28
Johnson, Shandy 42–53, 55–56, 58–61, 89, 104, 128, 190–192, 201, 207n2, 208n5, 209n11
Johnston, Nancy 1, 133, 172
"A Judgment of Dragons" *see* *A Judgment of Dragons*
A Judgment of Dragons 7, 10, 27, 33, 121, 127, 130–135, 137, 138, 139, 140–143, 147, 148, 150, 160, 188, 206n8, 206–207n9, 210n1, 212n2
Juvenile delinquency *see* Delinquency

Kakoudaki, Despina 72
Kamboureli, Smaro 172
Kang, Minsoo 72, 116
Kay, Guy Gavriel 4
Keats, John 112
Ketterer, David 1, 2, 4, 5, 7, 42, 138, 201
Khagodi 27, 141, 150–154, 158–160, 165–169, 212n4, 214n1
King, Andrew 52
King Kong 173
The Kingdom of the Cats 7, 10, 97, 100, 127, 135, 138, 143–145, 147–149, 205n5, 206n5, 212n2, 213n7, 213n12
"The King's Dogs" *see* *A Judgment of Dragons*
Kinnaird, John 44
Klein, A.M. 5, 121, 206–207n9
Kolmerten, Carol A. 3
Kornfeld, Susan 195
Kramer, Reinhold 172
Kristeva, Julia 196
Kulyk, Christine 2, 8

Lamont, Victoria 42, 60
Lancashire, Ian 176, 177
Lane, M. Travis 172
Lefanu, Sarah 2
Le Guin, Ursula K. 3, 135–136, 213n8
Letson, Russell 66
Levin, Ira 103, 211n8
Liminality 24, 47, 94, 112, 154, 168, 172, 184, 189
Lovecraft, H.P. 104
Lutts, Ralph H. 56
Lyhhrt 6, 10, 27, 33, 86, 97, 113, 140–141, 150, 152–153, 154–155, 156, 157, 161–170, 197–198, 201, 210n9, 213n9
Lynn, Elizabeth A. 42, 54

MacEwen, Gwendolyn 176
MacLennan, Hugh 114
Malamud, Randy 57
Marshall, Tom 172, 173
Mazis, Glen A. 110
Mead, Margaret 46–47, 53, 208n6
Merril Collection 205n1
Meshar 86, 88, 92, 100
Metamorphosis *see* Transmutation
Meyer-Baer, Kathy 14
"The Military Hospital" 9, 99, 116–119, 135, 210n1
Milton, John 12, 15–20, 21, 23, 63, 69
Mindworlds 10, 150, 152, 153, 161–162, 163, 164, 165–167, 169, 213n5
Mod-Dahlgren 6, 33, 67–69, 71, 72, 73, 75, 77, 80, 81, 82–84, 85–86, 87, 88, 90–91, 92–93, 94, 95–97, 98, 118, 119, 150, 155, 161, 190, 209n5, 210n11
Mod 777 *see* Erg-Queen
"Monday's Child" 102
"Monkey Wrench" 29–30, 31, 83, 89, 207n10, 207n11
Monsters 7, 17, 42–44, 49, 57–58, 65–69, 70–71, 73, 80–81, 97, 120, 121, 123, 173, 191, 196, 202, 207n14, 207ch2n3, 208–209ch2n10, 209n5, 211n7
Moore, C. L. 3
Moss, Rachel E. 52
"Mother Lode" 9, 100, 108–111, 130, 210n1
Mothering 6, 15–16, 33, 65–66, 68, 69, 70–74, 87, 91–92, 95, 98, 105–106, 107, 110–111, 115, 116–118, 165, 195–196, 197–198, 199–200, 211n5, 211n6, 211n8, 213n4; *see also* Procreation
"ms & mr frankenstein" 65, 173–174, 180, 209n2
Murray, Charles Augustus 74
Mutation 6, 24, 41, 43–44, 57–58, 60, 64–

67, 69–70, 77, 80, 87, 100, 145–146, 160, 188, 189, 193, 194, 195–197, 198
Mystery plays 145
Mythology 7, 14, 15, 16, 17, 104, 120–123, 174, 176, 191, 206n2, 206n3

"Nebuchadnezzar" *see A Judgment of Dragons*
Nephilim *see* Anti-Christ
Nevid 13, 14, 21–22, 187, 189
Newell, Dianne 42, 60
"The Newest Profession" 111, 113, 126, 139, 187, 210n1, 213n2
Nicholls, Peter 2
"No End of Time" 33–35, 36, 37, 38, 39, 205n1, 207n14
Norton, Andre 3
Nursery Rhymes 23, 102, 172, 174, 214n4

O Master Caliban! 3, 6, 8, 10, 11, 63–86, 87, 88, 90, 91, 92, 93, 135, 137, 139, 155, 173, 177, 188, 207n11, 209–210
The October Crisis 114–115
Odd John 41, 42–51, 53, 55–56, 60, 209n10, 212n7
O'e 154, 156–157, 159, 161, 162, 167, 169–170
O/G 6, 33, 119–120, 124–125, 150, 211n12
The Omen 103–104
Ordinary, Moving (book) 4, 172, 177, 210n10
"Ordinary, Moving" (poem) 175–180
Origen 103
Orwell, George 38
"The Other Eye" 194–195

Paradis, Andrea 1, 2
Parenting *see* Procreation
The Pearl 20–21, 206n5
Pearson, Wendy Gay 136
Perin, Roberto 115
"Phantom Foot" 6, 7, 24–27, 29, 127, 212n2
Phips, Spencer 144
Piercy, Marge 120
Pinocchio 69, 93, 122, 209n3
"Planetoid Idiot" 31–32, 100, 150, 206n1
Pope, Alexander 28, 206n8
Potts, Robert 202
Pregnancy 12–14, 16–17, 18–19, 21–22, 28, 39, 44, 87, 92, 105, 115, 124, 160, 163, 202
Principe, Lawrence M. 158, 160, 214n7
Procreation 6, 12–14, 16–17, 18–19, 20–22, 23–24, 33–35, 39–40, 48, 51–52, 61, 63, 64–65, 66, 67–69, 72–74, 75, 79–80, 85, 86, 87–88, 92–93, 94–95, 98, 99, 100, 101–102, 105, 110–111, 112, 113, 120, 123, 146–147, 150, 155, 158–161, 164–165, 169, 173–174, 191, 195–196, 198, 199–200, 202–203, 211n9, 214n2, 215n4; *see also* Mothering; Pregnancy
Procyons *see* Shar
Psi powers 7, 12, 25–26, 32, 43–44, 46, 47–51, 55–56, 58, 60–62, 77, 84, 85, 87, 109–110, 128–130, 132–133, 135, 138, 139, 141, 142, 146, 152, 153, 154–155, 158, 160, 164, 169, 188, 190–194, 207n4, 208n4, 208n5, 209n11, 210n6, 210n7, 212n3, 213n3, 214n11
Psychology 2, 12, 13, 28, 36, 45, 50, 53–55, 63, 77, 85, 92, 97, 106, 116–117, 133, 166–167, 188, 189, 203, 207n11, 209n5

Qsaprinli 27, 134, 137, 138, 145–147, 210n9
Quest narrative 13–14, 21, 35, 52–53, 77, 90, 201, 206n2, 215n2
Qumedni 7, 25–27, 127, 133–135, 145, 147, 162, 169, 212n2

Rabkin, Eric S. 42
Radiation, effects of 42, 51, 52, 65, 70, 207n3
Ransom, Amy J. 1
Red Blood, Black Ink, White Paper 3, 173, 180–181
Religion 5, 69, 77, 99, 100, 102–105, 109, 111, 113, 132, 166, 174, 198, 212n2
Robots 6, 64–73, 75–90, 93, 94–98, 99, 115–120, 143, 150, 155–156, 160, 161, 190, 201, 209n5; *see also* Erg-Dahlgren; Erg-Queen; O/G; Spartakos
"The Robot's Daughter" 173
Romance, Medieval 14, 52–53, 79, 104–105
Rose, Mark 43
Rosen, Susan A. C. 151
Rosinsky, Natalie M. 2
Runté, Robert 8
Russ, Joanna 1, 213n8

Sales, Ian 54
Samson Agonistes 12, 15–18, 19–20, 21
Sanders, Arnold 104
Sanders, Joe 71
Sargent, Pamela 3
Sasquatch 105
Satan 14, 103–107, 133, 211n3
Saunders, Corinne 13
Sawyer, Robert J. 4, 201, 203n3, 208n4, 215conc.n1
Scholem, Gershom G. 120, 121–122, 123
Scholtmeijer, Marian 57
Schroeder, Karl 4
"SCORE/SCORE" 99, 114–116, 206n1, 210n10, ch4n1
Secord, Laura 177, 178, 179, 215n7

"Seeing Eye" 172–173
Seguin, Pierre 74
Sestina 180, 181–186
Shakespeare, William 6, 51, 63, 74–78, 79, 82–83, 84, 85–86, 209*n*5, 210*n*6, 211*n*7
Shar 99–102, 104–106, 108, 195–200, 201, 210–211*n*2, 211*n*5, 213*n*4, 215*n*4
Shaw, Debra Bonita 3
Shawcross, John T. 15
Sheldon, William Herbert 53–54, 208*n*8
Shelley, Mary 64–65, 69
Sherwin, Byron L. 122, 124
Shinn, Thelma J. 3
Silverberg, Robert 36, 206*n*1, 210*n*1
Sir Gawain and the Green Knight 104
Skywalker, Luke 52
Slan 5, 42–43, 55, 207*n*2, 207*n*3
Slavery 15–16, 17, 32–33, 65, 75, 76, 77, 90, 97, 113, 115, 130, 140–141, 150–157, 159–164, 166, 167, 168–169, 197, 209*n*4, 213*n*2
Socrates 34–35, 207*n*14
Somatotypes 53–55, 89, 97, 208*n*8
Son of the Morning (book) 10, 12, 174
"Son of the Morning" (story) see *A Judgment of Dragons*
Spartakos 6, 33, 86, 126, 150, 155–157, 161, 162, 164, 165, 167, 169–170
Spinoza, Benedict de 130–131
Stapledon, Olaf 41, 42–43, 44–46, 47–51, 53, 55–56, 60, 207*n*4, 209*n*10, 212–213*n*7
Star Trek 8–9, 69, 212*n*2
Starcats see Ungrukh
Stephens, Walter 108
Stone-Blackburn, Susan 56
Sturgeon, Theodore 42, 207*n*4
Sunburst 2, 3, 5, 6, 8, 10, 11, 24, 40, 41–62, 63, 64, 70, 89, 97, 100, 128, 137, 172, 187, 188, 190–192, 203, 207*n*1, 208–209, 210*n*10, 212–213*n*7
Sunburst Award 42
"Sunday's Child" 22, 99–108, 109, 112, 113, 150, 174, 187, 197, 201, 210*n*1, 213*n*4, 215*n*4
Superhumans 24, 41, 42–53, 55–56, 60–62, 64, 137, 207–208*n*3, 208*n*4, 209*n*10, 209*n*11
Supernormal see Superhumans
Swanson, Roy Arthur 44
Swift, Jonathan 85, 87

"Tauf Aleph" 5, 6, 29, 31, 69, 86, 99, 109, 114, 119–126, 206*n*9, 207*n*11, 210*n*1
Taylor, Neil 83
Telepathy see Psi powers
The Tempest (Shakespeare) 6, 51, 74–76, 77–78, 79–80, 81–86, 208*n*7, 209*n*4, 209*n*5, 209*n*6

Tethumekh 158–159, 162, 214*n*9
Thorb 187, 189–190
Tilley, Carol 54
Time Travel 33, 34–36, 207*n*14
Transformation see Transmutation
Transmutation 13–15, 17–18, 21, 38, 44, 51–53, 61, 112–113, 136–138, 142–143, 151, 157–159, 161, 168, 190, 195, 202, 208*n*7, 214*n*8
Trudeau, Pierre Elliott 114
Trudel, Jean-Louis 187, 194, 206*n*1

Ungrukh 2, 7, 10, 27, 31, 32–33, 63, 70, 86, 88, 97, 113, 126, 127–149, 150, 153, 154, 201, 205*n*5, 206*n*8, 210*n*8, 210*n*9, 210*ch*4*n*1, 212–213

"Valedictory" 33, 35–36, 39, 205*n*1, 207*n*14
Van Vogt, A. E. 2, 4, 5, 8, 42–43, 205*n*4, 207*n*4
Vaughan, Alden T. and Virginia Mason 74
Vint, Sherryl 138, 139, 213*n*12
Violent Stars 6, 10, 150, 154, 156, 157, 158, 159, 160, 162–163, 164–166, 169, 213*n*5
Virgin Mary 14, 16, 106, 206*n*4, 211*n*3
Vogel, Howard J. 144
Vonarburg, Élisabeth 2, 212*n*3

"Waiting Till the Stars Scream" 194, 206*n*1
"Was/Man" 174–175, 180, 190
Watts, Peter 4, 201
"We Can't Go on Meting Like This" 187, 188–189, 213*n*1
Weiss, Allan 1, 65
Wells, H.G. 57, 207*n*4, 208–209*n*10
Wendigo 105
Werewolf 174–175, 180, 190, 215*n*3
Wertham, Fredric 54
Who Knows One 2, 177
Why Should I Have All the Grief? 5, 63, 121, 205*n*1, 206*n*9, 210*n*10
Wilson, Robert Charles 4
Wolfe, Gary K. 43, 57, 137
Wollheim, Donald A. 132, 207*n*4
Wolmark, Jenny 2
Women in SF 3–4
Wordsworth, William 112
The Works 173, 175, 176

Yaszek, Lisa 1
Yefni 31, 86, 88
Yrln 27

Zabus, Chantal 74, 76, 84, 85, 209*n*4, 209*n*5
Zamyatin, Yevgeny 37

www.ingramcontent.com/pod-product-compliance
Ingram Content Group UK Ltd.
Pitfield, Milton Keynes, MK11 3LW, UK
UKHW041947140426
5217IPUK00014B/690